1-12-16   5/2018   #2

MATTITUCK-LAUREL LIBRARY

Long Island's Lighthouses
Past and Present

DISCARDED

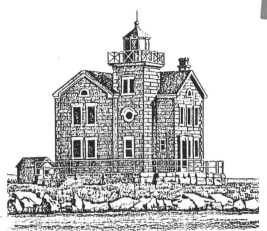

Robert G. Müller

D1295347

Long Island Chapter of the
US Lighthouse Society
Patchogue, New York
2004

Copyright © 2004
Long Island Chapter of the US Lighthouse Society
PO Box 744
Patchogue, NY 11772
All rights reserved

Cover
Shinnecock Bay Lighthouse
by Don Lubov

Inside Front Cover
Map of Long Island by Paul Bradley
showing light stations by chapter numbers

Inside Back Cover
Early 1900s Third Lighthouse District Chart

Back Cover
Plum Island Lighthouse
by Dianne J. Keating

LCCN: 2003-116957
ISBN: 0-9745347-0-6
Manufactured in the United States of America

Quality Book Production by
Heart of the Lakes Publishing
Interlaken, New York 14847

Dedication

My efforts in creating this work are dedicated

to

The members and supporters of the
Long Island Chapter of the US Lighthouse Society,

The many lighthouse keepers and families who created this
magnificent history, and continue to be a part of that history as
they strive to preserve it,

The Muller and Wagenhauser families, for whom I hope to
"keep a good light,"

and

A brighter future for the
Cedar Island and Plum Island lighthouses.

Contents

Acknowledgments

It may be a cliché to say that there are too many people to thank, but it is certainly true in this case. In the five years I have been actively researching and preparing this book, there have been hundreds of people who have made a difference. Trying to thank all of them would not only require another volume—it would also inevitably include some horrible oversight on my part and insult someone. I must, however, acknowledge the contributions of some, the quality and/or quantity of which have made a palpable difference in the final product. For all who helped, yet may not be listed below, I hope the great efforts I have made to portray the history contained herein are recognized as my sincerest form of thanks.

Al Williams; Kevin Brennan; Louis Anderson; Tom Rysedorph; Tony Tuliano; Gottfried and Marilyn Mahler; Frank Estler; Don Daly; Les Walter; Bill Scheuber; Dwight Porter; Bill Bright; Arnie Leiter; Bob and Warren Allen; Judy Carpenter; Cathy Robbins; Nelson Wetmore; Barbara Cairns; Violet Marquis; Trudy Brockett; Ruth Rowland; Nunzio Quartuccio, Jr.; Victor Quartuccio; Vivian Jensen Chapin; Art Bouder, Jr.; Charlie Burnham; Chuck and Carol Charnquist; Donna Pinchak; Ed Whitford; Nancy E. Gregg; Suzanne Hall; Ellen Fithian Halsey; Scott Schubert; Francis Hopkinson Smith III; Pam Prota; Jean Ruland; Bernard J. Roy; Andy Boisvert, Jr.; Irene Morris; Jack Fletcher; Rich Kenney; Sherry Lane; Pat Shapiro; John Parkhurst; George Martin; Joshua Ruff; Wayne Wheeler; Dave Snyder; Mike Seewald; Thomas A. Tag; Tom Taylor; Cliff Benfield; Van Field; Jim Crowley; BM2 Jeff Brown (USCG Station Shinnecock); Brian Parkerson (USCG Station Eaton's Neck); Gayle Haines; Bob LaRosa; Tony Poldino; Frank Knoll; Hank Bungart; Pam Setchell; Doug Shaw; Barbara Forde; Tricia Wood; Tom Ambrosio; Don Talmage; Hugh King; Natalie A. Naylor; Brunwyn Hannon; Deb Willet; Mitzi Caputo; Karen Martin; Sue Habib; Barb Kepple; Candace Clifford; Bob Mackreth; Bill Bleyer; Kathie Mancini; the Price family; Daron Malakian; Michael Schenker; Diamond Darrell; Malcolm and Angus Young; George Lynch; Zakk Wylde; Yngwie J. Malmsteen; Southold Historical Society; Montauk Historical Society; Fire Island Lighthouse Preservation Society; Huntington Lighthouse Preservation Society;

East End Seaport Museum and Marine Foundation; Long Island Maritime Museum; Oysterponds Historical Society; Patchogue-Medford Library; Port Washington Library; Long Island Studies Institute; East Hampton Library; Smithtown Library; Suffolk County Historical Society; East Islip Historical Society; Three Village Historical Society; John Jermain Library; The Merchant Marine Academy Library; The Emma S. Clark Memorial Library; The Sag Harbor Whaling Museum; Long Island Museum of Art, History, and Carriages; Fire Island National Seashore; Suffolk County Parks Department; Historical Museum of Southern Florida.

Thanks are also owed to the members of the Long Island Chapter of the U.S. Lighthouse Society, attendees at the many tours and cruises I have been fortunate enough to lead, the audiences at my lectures (especially those with tough questions), visitors to my web site, subscribers to my e-mail list, members of the Collectors' Forum (Hi Wackos!), and the readers of this book, for whom it was created.

Special thanks are owed to a three artists who are big supporters of our preservation and education work: North Fork artist Don Lubov created the image of the Shinnecock Bay Light especially for the cover of this book. Prints of his artwork (of Shinnecock and most other Long Island lights) can be ordered from him at Gifts by Lindon, 218 Main Street, Box 670, Greenport, New York 11944-0670, 631-477-0165. Noted lighthouse illustrator Paul Bradley, Jr., has done several projects for us, some specifically for this book. Copies of his work can be obtained from him at: Lighthouse Graphics, 2008 Northeast 49 Street, Fort Lauderdale, Florida 33308. 954-491-4479. South Shore artist Dianne J. Keating's Plum Island watercolor, on the back cover, is one of my favorite lighthouse paintings. Prints of this and other Long Island lighthouses can be obtained by contacting her at 631-563-0159.

Those family members, friends, and coworkers who have encouraged me (even if occasionally making fun of my obsession with this project) are appreciated. My mother has been a big supporter, as had my Aunt Jean and Uncle Ben until their loss in mid-2003. My father's many remembrances of "the good old days" probably had a great deal to do with my interest in history. My sister,

Judy, in addition to her letter folding and envelope stuffing duties, is probably my best publicity person.

The late Al Chiesa, who was President of the East Islip Historical Society (and involved in many other community activities), allowed me a great deal of latitude in my Vice President duties while I completed the book. His leadership, humor, honesty, and commitment to the community will be greatly missed.

Finally, but certainly not least, the efforts of several people as this book came to fruition in 2003 must be noted: Dick and Mary Ackerson, Brian Keena, Barbara Torre, and Rebecca Devaney handled many of my former chores with the Society, freeing me up to research and write. Jayme Breschard, Carol and Jim House, Jerry Leeds, John Voross, Fred and Stephen Fragano, Susan Russell, Rob Darby, Bob Scroope, Nancy Bahnsen, and Sean Pollock all made important contributions to the book. Walt Steesy guided us through the publication process. And without Diane Mancini, you would not be holding this book in your hands. Since the beginning, Diane has worked on research, photography, photo selection and placement, and, of course, the editing of my writing.

All of the people described above, and so many more, are responsible for whatever good comes from this book. The mistakes contained herein, as there must inevitably be some, are wholly mine.

Bob Müller

Preface

The book you are about to read is the culmination of over five years of research and study. When I started the project in 1998, I had no idea just how vast our local lighthouse heritage would be. Many of you, upon reading this book, will probably end up with similar sentiments.

The sources consulted in creating this work include local, regional and national sources, including the National Archives, U.S. Coast Guard Historian's Office, museums, historical societies, lighthouse societies, libraries, historians, preservationists, government officials, former lighthouse keepers and descendants thereof, and residents of communities where a light station has played an important role. Also sought were archival books, documents, photographs, and postcards, both originals and copies. These sources revealed a great amount of information, much of it conflicting with other sources. Nearly all of the research materials in this book are now part of the collection of the Long Island Chapter of the U.S. Lighthouse Society.

I have endeavored, as much as possible, to separate fact from folklore. There is much folklore surrounding lighthouses, from ghost stories to explanations for place names and tales of the adventures of keepers. As time progresses, these tales infiltrate the facts and threaten to change the history of what was into what some might wish it to have been. I hope that by documenting the facts surrounding these light stations, their history can be transferred to the future intact. Although folklore has an important place in culture, its role should not be that of displacing fact.

Historians may bemoan the lack of footnotes in this book but, as it is intended primarily for the general reader, ease of reading was a priority. References are listed in the back of the book and I am available to discuss the research with anyone who might have such an interest.

Long Island's Lighthouses: Past and Present covers the history of 24 light stations, and an untold number of men, women and children, over a period of over 200 years. Although it contains a great deal of information, it is not the end of the research, since much more information is likely to surface on the subject.

I hope that you will enjoy the book, and that it will inspire you to further explore the lighthouse heritage of Long Island, and the rest of America. I can often be found leading a tour, giving a lecture, narrating a cruise, or just hanging out with other "lighthouse people," so keep an eye out for me as you explore our local lighthouses. I am happy to answer any questions you might have and help you enjoy the vast and wonderful history of Long Island's lighthouses.

Bob Müller
Islip Terrace, NY
Fall 2003

An Introduction to
Long Island's Lighthouse Heritage

The lighthouse heritage of Long Island reflects both its local history and the development of America's aids to navigation. With regard to the latter, the area's lighthouse heritage may be considered a microcosm. From early navigational difficulties to the challenges of modern-day historic lighthouse preservation, Long Island has reflected national lighthouse trends. Observing our local lighthouse history in the context of the larger picture helps us to better understand the depth and importance of the history represented by Long Island's many lighthouses.

The need for navigational aids around Long Island must have been obvious early in American history. Long Island's position in the middle of coastal and transAtlantic approaches to New York posed various navigational difficulties, including sand bars, low lands, unlit shores, and rocky shoals. The many safe harbors and inlets, although valuable for mariners, also posed navigational difficulties. Even during the daylight hours, early Long Island presented few features to help the mariner determine his precise position.

The earliest mentions we see in Long Island's history of navigational aids are the reports of fires set by the natives on Turtle Hill, the location of the present Montauk Point Lighthouse. The British are also said to have used large fires on this high land at the tip of Long Island. These fires were probably used as specific signals, as well as navigational aids.

Because of the long and varied history of the lighthouses built on Long Island over the course of American history, the island's lighthouse heritage can be useful as an example of the evolution of lighthouses throughout America.

Pre-Federal Lighthouses (Pre-1789)

Twelve lighthouses were built in America prior to the formation of a national government. In these early times, lighthouses were funded and maintained by local entities, such as colonies or townships. Although no lighthouses were built on Long Island during this period, we can be fairly certain that the settlers who did live on the island used temporary lights to help mariners at night. These could have been lamps hung upon poles, or even bonfires or torches placed near the entrances to unimproved harbors. The shores of Long Island at that time were quite dark, and the difficult navigation caused by a combination of low light, a tricky coast, and the use of sail power would likely have necessitated some form of aids to navigation. These crude aids helped to guide mariners back home at night, as they continue to do today.

The need for lighthouses on Long Island was evident long before the formation of the United States. In 1756, a young Colonel George Washington traveled across Long Island on his way to Boston to conduct military business. According to local oral history, while on the North Fork of the island, he visited Horton's Point with Ezra L'Hommidieu, who would later help to decide the placement of the Montauk Light for Washington. The two young men spoke of the need for a lighthouse at Horton's Point at that time. It would be 100 years before that light would be built.

Early Federal Era (1789–1820)

Not long after the formation of a strong central government under the Constitution, federal lighthouses began to be built. The importance of safe navigation to the economic growth of the young nation was evident early on. This was shown when the First Congress passed the Lighthouses Act of 1789.

The issue of federal support for lighthouses was probably first raised by James Madison on April 21, 1789, when he made a case for duties "necessary for the support of light-houses, hospitals for disabled seamen, and other establishments incident to commerce." On May 5, James Jackson of Georgia proposed a six-cent-per-ton duty that would go to "the support of lighthouses and beacons for the purposes of navigation," "the encouragement of American shipping," and "raising a revenue." John Laurance of New York encouraged specific provisions on June 2 and, on July 1, HR-12 was introduced by the grand committee.

Discussion of the bill began on July 16, 1789. In a harbinger of things to come, some Southern delegates saw the bill as an infringement upon states' rights. On July 17, an amended bill was drawn up, and on July 20 the bill was ordered to be sent to the Senate.

As in the House, there was much debate in the Senate. An amended bill was agreed upon on July 31 and delivered back to the House on August 3. On August 6, the Speaker of the House and the Vice President signed the bill. The following day, August 7, 1789, President George Washington signed the bill into law.

The first Long Island lighthouse to be built under the provisions of this new law was at Montauk Point, completed in 1796. The light at Eaton's Neck was the next lighthouse project of Montauk Point builder John McComb, Jr. This light was completed in 1798. Little Gull Island received the next lighthouse, a 50–foot tower that was to help traffic through The Race, a waterway west of Fishers Island. In 1809, the Sands Point Lighthouse was built after petitioning by local residents.

Over the first 31 years of federal control, four lighthouses were built on Long Island. Of these, three remain standing. The original Little Gull Island Lighthouse was replaced with a taller tower in 1869.

The Reign of the Fifth Auditor (1820–1852)

In 1820, control of the U.S. lighthouse system became the responsibility of the Fifth Auditor of the Treasury, Stephen Pleasanton. This era of American lighthouse history is noted for its poor planning, shoddy workmanship, ineffective aids to navigation, and political intrigue.

When faced with accusations of the service's inadequacy, Pleasanton always claimed that the nation's lighthouse service was not only fine, but that his thriftiness saved taxpayers a great deal of money. But the fact that most of the lights built in this era required a great deal of repairs and often too-soon replacement, and that the lights displayed were often of poor quality, might negate any such gains.

In his 1838 report on the area's lighthouses, Lieutenant George M. Bache commented on the administrative system used to build lighthouses, noting that "[i]t cannot be denied that, under this system, many buildings have been badly constructed," noting even that some of the lighthouses represented "striking instances of the misapplication of the public money." Addressing the inevitable economy defense, he added, "[a]ll these works, built under the economical system of contract, and intended to be permanent, have not stood the proper test of true economy." He also stated that it was "worthy of remark, that the oldest buildings are now in the best condition," pointing out Montauk Point, Eaton's Neck, and Little Gull on Long Island, and stating that those lights built before 1800 afforded "a striking contrast to many of those of very recent construction."

Nonetheless, this era was one of great growth and expansion. Many lights were built in the U.S. during these 32 years. On Long Island, the rate of expansion increased by 150 percent, with six lights being built in 32 years.

As with the rest of the country, the Long Island lights built under Pleasanton's supervision were poorly planned and constructed. Only one of these six lights still stands—at Execution Rocks. The lights at Old Field Point (1824), Plum Island (1827), Fire Island (1827), Cedar Island (1839), and North Dumpling (1849) did not suffer ill fates due to any environmental circumstances. Their fates were sealed with the signing of cheap contracts, the use of poor materials, and the institution of shoddy workmanship. Documents from the era, including some very detailed reports on the lighthouse system, clearly point out the inferiority of these lights. Ironically, it is the Execution Rocks tower, the one with the most difficult offshore location, which still stands. The keeper's quarters at Old Field Point and part of the base of the original Fire Island light also survive from this era.

In addition to inadequate planning and construction of the structures themselves, the lighting apparatuses were ineffective. More often than not, the Winslow Lewis patent lamps specified in the contracts were poorly built. The parabolic reflectors were rarely parabolic, often being closer to a much less effective spherical profile. The finish on the reflectors was often thin, and would be worn out by polishing with the prescribed Tripoli powder, and the reflectors were easily dented. The lamps inside the reflectors were often improperly placed, so that much of the light would scatter, rather than concentrate into a beam. And the exhaust tubes of the lamps were often too short, with the result being a buildup of residues on the reflectors and a further hindrance of the effectiveness of the lights.

United States Light-House Board (1852–1903)

The inadequacies of the Pleasanton era caused an investigation of America's lighthouse system in 1851. A board was established to investigate the lighthouse system on March 3, 1851. The result of this investigation was a complete reorganization of the nation's lighthouse administration. A nine-man Light-House Board was organized by an act of Congress on August 31, 1852. The Board met for the first time on October 9, 1852. Placed under the Treasury Department, the Board's first *Annual Report* included recommendations for "[a]n entire reform" of the financial handlings of the service to avoid waste, stronger control of contracts and work, the establishment of 12 inspection districts, and strict recordkeeping by those employed in the lighthouse service. The Board's intent was summed up as follows:

> By the gradual introduction of a better description of illuminating apparatus, the superiority of which is no longer questioned, by adopting a system of construction founded upon scientific attainments and practical knowledge, by improving the models and employing better materials in our light-vessel, and by introducing a rigid system of accountability, supervision, and inspection in every branch of the service, the board expects to place the light-house establishment of this country on a proper footing of efficiency and economy.

Composed of an array of men who understood maritime navigation, engineering, and other relevant fields, the Light-House Board was responsible for the period in which America's, and Long Island's, lights went from a third-rate system to the best in the world.

On Long Island, the mid- to late 1800s were the Golden Age of lighthouses.

Of the 17 Long Island lights built during these 51 years, only five no longer exist. Four of those losses were a result of human action: the original Lloyd Harbor Light was destroyed by a fire in 1947; Shinnecock Bay was toppled by the government in 1948; Long Beach Bar was burned by arsonists in 1963; and Cold Spring Harbor was dismantled in 1965. The fifth light, at Gardiner's Island, was lost due to erosion after about 40 years.

The lights built during this period that still stand include Horton Point, Fire Island, Cedar Island, Plum Island, Old Field Point, Little Gull Island, North Dumpling, Stepping Stones, Stratford Shoal, Race Rock, Latimer Reef, and Orient Point. Improvements were made at other stations, including Montauk Point, where the tower was raised and modified in 1860 to accept a Fresnel lens, and Sands Point and Execution Rocks, where keepers' quarters were built.

Not only were the lighthouses of this era built better, they also had more powerful and more effective lighting systems. In 1855, the Fresnel lens began to be seen in Long Island lantern rooms, and in many American lighthouses. By the start of the Civil War, all of Long Island's lighthouses were using the Fresnel lens. All seven orders (sizes) of Fresnel lens would find homes on Long Island, including those of a classical design, bivalve design, and at least one lens that combined the two types.

The most striking examples on Long Island of the seriousness and ambitiousness with which the Board addressed its job were the coastal lights. The Shinnecock Bay and Fire Island towers built in the late 1850s would stand majestically over the south shore of Long Island like no structures before or since. The quality of planning and construction of this era might be best illustrated by the island's remaining two unrestored lights. Both the Plum Island and Cedar Island lights have been subject to neglect and erosion over the years, and the interior of the Cedar Island Lighthouse was even burned completely away. Yet these lights still stand, awaiting the chance to once again serve the Long Island community.

The Lighthouse Board Under the Commerce Department (1903–1910)

No lights were built on Long Island during this period.

The Bureau of Lighthouses (1910–1939)

The Lighthouse Board was abolished in 1910, and was replaced by a single civilian head. During the years of the Lighthouse Board, the military had retained most of the control of the nation's aids to navigation. The Bureau of Lighthouses marked the return to civilian control.

Only one lighthouse was built on Long Island during this period. The Huntington Harbor Light (1912), which replaced the Lloyd Harbor Light, would be the last federally funded lighthouse built on Long Island. This lighthouse still stands and is currently under restoration.

U.S. Coast Guard (1939–Present)

In 1939, the U.S. Coast Guard took over the responsibility of aids to navigation. This meant that, once again, the lighthouses were under the control of the Treasury Department. Those Lighthouse Bureau personnel who wished to continue on as keepers were given the option of remaining as civilians or converting to military status within the Coast Guard. The response was about evenly split.

Maintenance of aids to navigation still resides with the Coast Guard, and is likely to remain so for the foreseeable future. Many of the lighthouses have been automated or replaced with skeletal structures. With the advent of automation, many of the structures have suffered from neglect and vandalism. In recent years, the Coast Guard has entered into agreements with private organizations that allow for the Coast Guard to maintain the light, while the organization maintains and/or manages the structure that holds it. On Long Island, this is true for the Huntington Harbor, Horton Point, Long Beach Bar, Montauk Point, and Fire Island lights. The Old Field Point Light is owned by the Village of Old Field and the North

Dumpling Light is privately owned.

Types of Lighthouses on Long Island

Many categories of design, construction, and location show the variety of lighthouses in the Long Island area. Below are examples of each. Stations that have had more than one lighthouse will be marked with a 1 or 2 to show which structure is being addressed.

- Stone construction—Montauk Point, Eaton's Neck, Little Gull Island (1), Sands Point, Old Field (1), Plum Island (1), Fire Island (1), Execution Rocks

- Wood construction—Cedar Island (1), Lloyd Harbor, Long Beach Bar, Cold Spring Harbor

- Granite construction—Cedar Island (2), Old Field (2), Plum Island (2), Little Gull Island (2), Stratford Shoal, Race Rock

- Brick construction—North Dumpling, Gardiner's Island, Horton Point, Fire Island (2), Shinnecock, Stepping Stones

- Cast iron construction—Latimer Reef, Orient Point

- Reinforced concrete construction—Huntington Harbor

- Octagonal pyramidal towers—Montauk Point, Eaton's Neck, Little Gull Island (1), Sands Point, Old Field (1), Plum Island (1), Fire Island (1)

- Round (truncated cone) towers—Execution Rocks, Gardiner's Island, Shinnecock, Fire Island (2), Orient Point, Latimer Reef, Little Gull Island (2)

- Square towers—Lloyd Harbor, Huntington Harbor, Horton Point, Cedar Island (2), Cold Spring Harbor (pyramidal), Stepping Stones, Old Field (2) (beveled), Plum Island (2) (beveled), Long Beach Bar (beveled), North Dumpling (beveled), Stratford Shoal (beveled), Race Rock (beveled)

- Towers integrated into the keepers' quarters—Stepping Stones, Lloyd Harbor, Huntington Harbor, Old Field (2), Horton Point, Long Beach Bar, Plum Island (2), North Dumpling, Race Rock, Stratford Shoal, Cedar Island

- Towers that included keepers quarters—Orient Point, Latimer Reef, Cold Spring Harbor

- Separate towers—Montauk Point, Eaton's Neck, Little Gull Island, Sands Point, Old Field (1), Plum Island (1), Fire Island, Execution Rocks, Shinnecock Bay

- Land-based lights—Montauk Point, Eaton's Neck, Little Gull Island, Sands Point, Lloyd Harbor, Old Field, Horton Point, Plum Island, North Dumpling, Cedar Island, Shinnecock, Fire Island

- Offshore lights—Execution Rocks, Stepping Stones, Stratford Shoal, Race Rock, Cold Spring Harbor, Orient Point, Long Beach Bar, Latimer Reef, Huntington Harbor

The foundations of Long Island lighthouses were made with various materials (including stone, brick, and even pine logs) and techniques, but there are four particular types worth mentioning:

- Cast iron caisson—Cold Spring Harbor, Orient Point, Latimer Reef

- Granite pier—Stratford Shoal, Race Rock, Cedar Island (2), Stepping Stones

- Screw pile—Long Beach Bar (this was changed in 1926)

- Reinforced concrete crib—Huntington Harbor

Conclusion

The variety and history of Long Island's lighthouses make the subject worthy of study and admiration. The differing locations, materials, and construction types make for an excellent representation of the lighthouse history of the United States. The problems and solutions encountered along the way also are telling of the growing pains of our country's aids to navigation. Even today, the struggles to preserve these historical treasures are evident on Long Island, with erosion, neglect, greed, politics, bureaucracy, and vandalism acting as constant antagonists to the many people who put a great deal of time, effort, and money into historic preservation.

Although many of us will travel great distances to see a particular lighthouse, Long Islanders need not go far to see a cross-section of United States lighthouse history. Most of it is right here, waiting to be explored and experienced.

The Lighthouses and Lightships

SONG TO THE BEACON LIGHT

Shine bright, beacon light,
Rival yonder star

The beams above, with a look of love
In the blue heaven afar.

When the sky is calm and clear
And the wave is hushed and still,

Mingle your light with the stars of night
The glow o'er vale and hill.

Shine bright, beacon light,
Far, far away.

Where the wild waves leap and the hoarse winds sweep
There send thy cheering ray

When the tempest thunders louder
And the clouds in wrath are driven

Then shine o'er the sea and thy light shall be
Like a ray of hope from heaven.

Written on Plum Island in 1842 by Sarah Bowditch, the lightkeeper's granddaughter.

The North Shore

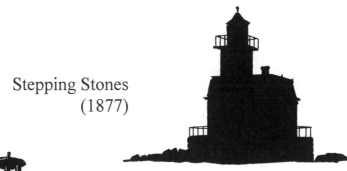

Stepping Stones
(1877)

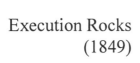

Sands Point
(1809)

Execution Rocks
(1849)

Cold Spring Harbor
(1890)

Lloyd Harbor/Huntington Harbor
(1857, 1912)

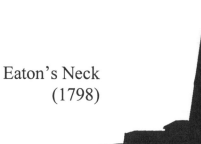

Eaton's Neck
(1798)

Old Field Point
(1824, 1869)

Stratford Shoal
(Middleground) Lightship
(1837) and
Lighthouse (1877)

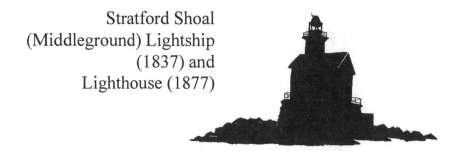

Stepping Stones

The westernmost of Long Island's North Shore lighthouses sits just east of the Throgg's Neck Bridge. Located in the Long Island Sound, between Great Neck and City Island, the Stepping Stones Light has been an aid to mariners since 1877.

Samuel Latham Mitchill, whose monument at Greenwood Cemetery describes him as "Doctor, scientist, citizen, senator," was one of Long Island's more influential citizens in the early 1800s. His 1807 work, *The Traveler's Guide to Nassau Island* (Long Island was originally named the "Island of Nassau"), described a "sandy spot of many acres, with several large rocks appearing here and there above the little water which covers it, [which] stretches far toward the main channel from the bottom of Great-Neck. These rocks are called the *Stepping Stones*."

The great amount of maritime traffic in the area, including ships entering and leaving New York's East River, required that these

National Archives 26 LG 16-61
Stepping Stones Light in an undated photograph.

rocks be marked. Lacking the technology and skills to erect a lighthouse on the rocks, early markers consisted of buoys (in 1827, a black spar buoy marked the site).

This dangerous boulder reef was originally known by the Native Americans as the Devil's Stepping Stones. According to the old legend, the Devil set out to stake a claim in Connecticut by driving out the natives. Local Indians proved too tough and they drove him back to Throgg's Point, where, at low tide, the Devil crossed the rocks in the Long Island Sound. According to the legend, at that time, Long Island's north shore was covered with rocks; Connecticut's shore was not. When the Devil retreated to Long Island, he reportedly brooded over his loss for a bit, then collected rocks around Long Island, deposited them in the Cold Spring Harbor area, and began hurling them at Connecticut. This created the rocky shores that we now see in Connecticut.

In the 1860s, the decision was made to erect a lighthouse near the area where the Devil had long ago crossed the Sound. The original spot chosen was the southern point of Hart Island, located on the northern shore of the Sound. Congress appropriated $6600 for the lighthouse on April 7, 1866, but the government was unable to procure the land. When the landowner was unwilling to sell, the property was condemned. Appraisers put the value of the needed five acres at $25,000, a sum still out of reach of the project's budget.

The 1868 *Annual Report of the Light-house Board* recommended, given the high price of land on Hart Island, the consideration of the erection of a screwpile light "off the point of the island, and below low water mark" with a recommended additional appropriation of $15,000. By 1870, it was determined that the south part of Hart Island was eroding and an expensive seawall would be required to make the point stable. The multiple difficulties with the site ensured that a lighthouse would never be built on Hart Island.

On May 11, 1874, the New York Legislature passed a bill ceding jurisdiction of the underwater area at Stepping Stones to the federal government (less than one acre), and 3.75 acres at the south end of Hart Island "under water and beyond the low water mark."

An appropriation of $6000 for a day beacon on Stepping Stones was made on June 23, 1874, as well as for "the lighthouse on or near the end of Hart Island." In September 1874, the contract for the foundation at Stepping Stones was awarded. Construction began in 1875, with the riprap foundation being completed that year, and work continuing into late December. The relatively sheltered position of the station allowed for construction to continue on further into winter than at some other area light stations built in the same period (such as Stratford Shoal and Race Rock). Work resumed in May of 1876, with the construction being completed by the end of that year.

The new lighthouse was made in a Second Empire style, with a square tower atop the mansard-roofed keepers' quarters. It was the last Long Island lighthouse to be built of brick and stone.

The enrockment around the site, which had been the subject of discord between the contractor, A.D. Cook, and Third District officials, was completed in September 1877, but not before there had been legal actions, delays, extensions, and the discharge of the Assistant Superintendent of Construction.

Findlay Fraser was appointed the first keeper at Stepping Stones, and the light was lit on March 1, 1877, showing a fixed red light from a Fifth Order Fresnel lens. Fraser stayed on until July 15, 1879, when he resigned. Cornelius Douglas, a native of Ireland, was keeper from November 16, 1886 to September 13, 1895, when he transferred to the nearby Sands Point Light.

In the 1890s, there were more problems concerning the rocks surrounding the lighthouse. In 1896, Charles Smedley was awarded a contract for riprap, but a suit was filed against him the following year for failure to deliver and place the stone. In November 1897, Third District Engineer David Porter Heap authorized additional riprap contracts.

In 1908, the Stepping Stones Light Station included a bell struck by machinery every 15 seconds to help mariners in foggy conditions, when the light could not be seen. Ernest Bloom was appointed keeper on April 20, 1910. He was awarded the Lighthouse Service's efficiency pennant in 1911, while a keeper at Stepping Stones. This

Stepping Stones
Light in 1885.

*National Archives
26 LG 16-59*

prestigious award allowed the recipient to fly a special pennant at his station.

On July 28, 1921, keeper Stephen Holm rescued two men whose canoe had capsized near the light station, and took them to City Island. On July 18, 1923, Holm once again came to the rescue, saving two men whose sailboat, the *Mistral*, ran aground and was sinking on the rocks east of the lighthouse. Holm was able to tow the boat to Long Island afterward.

The lens was changed in 1932, from a Fifth Order showing a fixed red light, to a Fourth Order exhibiting a fixed green light. An incandescent oil vapor (IOV) lamp, producing 870 candlepower, provided the light.

Life at an offshore lighthouse could be difficult, especially in the winter, as Keeper Charles A. Rogers found out. An unusually cold spell in February 1934, combined with a blizzard on the 20th of that month, completely surrounded the Stepping Stones station with ice, making it impossible for the keeper to get ashore for supplies for himself, wife, and child. The March 1934 *Lighthouse Service Bulletin* reported that "[a]n exceptionally long period of cold, with ice which prevented his reaching shore, forced the keeper of Stepping Stones Lighthouse . . . to hoist distress signals on March 1." Fortunately, as food stores were running low a "small tanker . . . was able to get close enough to the station to hail the keeper, and get his request" that food be sent. That same day, the lighthouse tender *Hickory* was dispatched and supplies were brought to the station.

U.S. Coast Guard photo

Stepping Stones Light in an undated photograph.

Al Williams, a retired Coast Guard Chief Boatswain's Mate, who was stationed at nearby Execution Rocks in the 1950s, related a story of a fellow Coast Guardsman who possessed an enthusiasm for cleaning and was stationed at Stepping Stones at the time. Reportedly, Stepping Stones was the cleanest lighthouse in the entire area, with even the drip pans under the generators being highly polished.

In 1964, the Stepping Stones Light was automated, with the 1700–candlepower electric light showing a flashing green characteristic. The automation was expected to save $10,000 per year. Its last keepers left behind an 89–year history of duty and dedication. Today, the Stepping Stones Light still helps mariners navigate the tricky waters of the western Long Island Sound.

As this book went to press, the Stepping Stones Light appeared set to be included in the next wave of Long Island lighthouses to be declared excess property by the U.S. Coast Guard. Its future will be determined by whomever, if anyone, takes over the maintenance of the lighthouse from the Coast Guard.

Photo by Nancy Bahnsen

Stepping Stones Light in 2003.

Sands Point

Located on Long Island's famed Gold Coast, the Sands Point Lighthouse is the third oldest standing light tower on Long Island. Its history is an integral part of Long Island, although it is no longer an active light.

The story of the Sands Point Lighthouse begins with a man named Noah Mason, the lighthouse's builder and first keeper. Born in 1755, in Dighton, Massachusetts, Mason was a subject of British government. By the time he was approaching 20 years of age, war was on the horizon. In early 1775, British armed incursions at Lexington and Concord shocked the lives of many New Englanders. Noah Mason was one of the affected and, on May 8, 1775, he enlisted in the new Continental Army.

Mason participated in the building of a fort at Dorchester Heights, Massachusetts, then another on the North River at Tarrytown, New York. He served with General Horatio Gates at the Battle of Saratoga, where he suffered a serious wrist injury. He also

From the author's collection

Early 1900s postcard.

participated in the Battle of Rhode Island before being discharged on September 10, 1778.

After the war, Mason moved to New London, Connecticut, and became a mariner. He married Lucretia Kinnie on December 14, 1786, and continued on in the local sea trade for 20 years.

The next period in Noah and Lucretia Mason's lives owes its beginnings to Samuel Mitchill, a United States Senator from Cow Neck (now Port Washington). Mitchill had been a proponent of a lighthouse on Cow Neck as early as 1790. In 1805, he was aboard the Revenue Cutter *Active*, commanded by Captain Caleb Brewster (like Mason, Brewster was a Revolutionary War veteran). Discussions between Mitchill and Brewster led to a series of petitions being drawn up and distributed. These petitions found their way to Congress later that year. Because of Mitchill's involvement, and his position as one of the area's pre-eminent citizens, the Sands Point Lighthouse would sometimes be called "the Mitchill Lighthouse."

On January 26, 1806, Congress acted on the petitions. Shortly thereafter, David Gelston, the Collector of Customs for the Port of New York, issued a call for proposals to build a lighthouse at Sands Point, New York. Noah Mason submitted a contract bid for the lighthouse and won the job.

On April 1, 1808, five acres on Sands Point (then also known as Watch Point) were procured from Benjamin and Jemima Hewlett for $512.50, for the building of a lighthouse. The boundaries of the property were marked by coastline, a large "Walnut or Hickory tree," a "marked Buttonwood," and a "White Oak tree."

Mason built the 40–foot octagonal pyramidal light tower out of blocks of brownstone, with a wooden stairway, for a cost of $8759.82. There has been some debate about the construction over the years, with some researchers stating that Abashai Woodward was the builder. Based upon the area's lighthouse-building activities of the era, it is possible that Mason built the stone tower, with Woodward supplying the cast-iron lantern.

On September 11, 1809, at the age of 54, Noah Mason became the first keeper of Long Island's fourth lighthouse. The tower exhibited a fixed white light, as it would through at least 1827. The

Masons lived in the wood-framed keepers' quarters, which would undergo many alterations over the years.

The completion of the Sands Point Lighthouse was cause for celebration. According to records of the Towns of North and South Hempstead, "[t]here was a grand civic festival at the place at which the members of the most respectable families in the neighborhood attended. Samuel S. Mitchell [sic] as the founder was honored with an invitation to meet his fellow citizens and was there on one of the happiest occasions that had occurred within the recollection of the numerous company assembled."

Mason served at the lighthouse for many years, witnessing the economic growth of the young nation as evidenced by the increasing shipping on the Long Island Sound. He also witnessed another war with the British, albeit this time as an observer. On September 10, 1814, Mason watched a naval battle off of Sands Point between the British frigate *Acosta* and 30 American gunboats.

While at the lighthouse, Noah and Lucretia took in an orphan child, Susan Ann Smith, who died April 11, 1828, at the age of 15.

National Archives LG 26 14-58
Sands Point Light on May 13, 1919.

Very little is known of this child, or of the three daughters that the Masons raised.

In 1838, at the age of 82, Noah Mason was still going strong, tending the 11 lamps with nine-inch reflectors in the lantern room. Lieutenant George Bache paid a visit that year, noting the station's "great importance to the navigation of the sound, as it serves to lead vessels clear of the Execution rocks." By 1840, Mason was the only surviving Continental Army veteran in the Town of North Hempstead.

The March 13, 1841 issue of *The Corrector* carried notice of the end of Noah Mason's life:

> Another Revolutionary Hero gone. Died, at Sands Point, Long Island on Saturday the 27th, Captain Noah Mason in the 85th year of his age, a soldier of the Revolution. Captain Mason was at the time of his decease the keeper of the Sands Point Lighthouse on Long Island Sound, and had acted in that capacity for thirty-two years past.

Upon Mason's death, Lucretia became the light's keeper, receiving her first, and only, pay voucher as a lighthouse keeper 16 days after Noah's death. Lucretia survived another 14 years, passing on April 16, 1855, at the age of 85. Both were buried on Sands Point.

Although Noah Mason was gone, the light in the Sands Point tower would continue on for many years. By June 30, 1841, Daniel Caulkins, of Connecticut, had taken over as the light's keeper. He later went on to be the keeper at the Navesink Lighthouse in New Jersey, where he died in 1888.

In a report on June 14, 1850, the captain of the ship supplying the lighthouse noted the following: "Light-house is a good building, of hewn stone; and the lantern is good, with large plate glass." The keepers' quarters, though, needed work, as the east end of the house was noted as being "quite leaky." Daniel Caulkins was still the keeper at this time, tending the 11 lamps with 18–inch reflectors.

In February of 1855, "the seawall at Sands Point gave way in an easterly gale." Its poor construction had caused problems for many years. Reinforcement of the seawall was suggested, as was the replacement of the light's nine lamps and 21–inch reflectors with a Fifth Order, 270–degree Fresnel lens.

In 1856, the illuminating apparatus was changed, but to a Fourth Order lens with a 30–second interval flash. This change would have made the job of keeper Benjamin Downing easier, as the single lamp burned less oil than the previous nine and required less maintenance.

On March 12, 1866, John Wesley Seaman became the light's keeper, at the age of 36. At the time, he and his wife had a two-year-old son, Wesley. The light station received a new dwelling in 1868, and other renovations were made: iron stairs replaced the wood stairs in the tower, and a barn and outhouses were made from the materials of old dwelling.

National Archives 26 LG 14-63

Sands Point in 1884.

In 1881, an inspection reported that the "dwelling was crowded with boarders, which the Keeper had received in violation of the Regulations." Seaman was reprimanded, but kept his job.

Keeper Seaman's son, Wesley, became the proprietor of the nearby Sanspareil House and Wesley's son, John Wesley, was born at the lighthouse on October 23, 1888. Keeper Seaman passed on in July in 1895, at the age of 65. His family stayed in the area after his death.

Wesley Seaman's son was killed in the Summer of 1903, at the age of 14 years and 9 months, when he accidentally shot himself while snipe hunting in a rowboat near Sands Point. The report of the incident suggested that he fell while holding his shotgun, accidentally discharging it. He was killed instantly, although his friend, Wyland Trask, 16 years old, rowed the boat and body back to land near the lighthouse. Young John Wesley was described as "an intelligent boy of industrious and excellent habits," who "was highly esteemed by all who knew him, and was a valuable helper in his father's business."

In 1907, the Sands Point tower was still casting light through a fixed white Fourth Order lens, 64.5 feet above mean high water. The height from the base of structure to center of lantern was listed as 46 feet.

In the early 1900s, there was concern about the establishment of a right of way to the lighthouse. This was a problem at many lighthouses, as automobiles and roads began to replace ships and the sea as the main way of transporting goods to many light stations. In establishing these stations, provisions for land access was not the highest priority. This resulted in the lands between the stations and major roads sometimes coming under private ownership, which caused the government to negotiate with local landowners to establish rights of way for access. A right of way for the Sands Point Light Station was obtained for one dollar on November 14, 1911, from Ralph Hill Thomas. This right of way was essentially a continuation of Middle Neck Road.

The year 1916 saw the sale of 6.396 acres adjacent to the light station to Alva E. Belmont, from Helen K. Thomas, for $100. Mrs. Belmont would end up owning much more land in the area.

Thomas J. Murray became the last keeper of the Sands Point Light in 1917. Not long after, it was decided to replace the 1809 tower with an automated light.

In preparation for the discontinuance of the Sands Point Lighthouse, on May 3, 1920, New York State ceded jurisdiction of "a certain piece of land for lighthouse purposes under water at the end of the rocky reef extending northward of Sands Point, Long Island, New York." The intent was to install an automated light on the reef.

On May 31, 1922, Mrs. Belmont received a revocable license form the Commerce Department, for $250 per year for five years, to use a portion of the reservation in a way that would not be detrimental to the interests of the United States. This caused a problem for Keeper Murray, as he was informed on June 22 that he could no longer have visitors on Sundays and holidays during the Summer months.

Courtesy of Suzanne Hall

1937 Christmas card from Lewis Coal and Oil Company, Inc.

The lighthouse was decommissioned in December 1922. It was replaced by an acetylene light, placed on the end of a reef north of the lighthouse, for which the government had previously obtained rights.

New York State Governor Alfred E. Smith wanted to establish a state park at the site, and did manage to have its auction delayed once, but Mrs. Belmont bought the light station on January 31, 1924, for $100,000. By then, the old hickory and buttonwood trees were long gone, so the property was marked partly by "a one inch diameter iron pipe," also using a road, a well, two more pipes, and the mean high water line to mark the property.

The Belmonts did not keep the lighthouse long, selling it, along with their mansion and all of the property, to William Randolph Hearst in 1927 for $400,000. Hearst, in turn, transferred the property to his bank to pay off the mortgage in 1940. In 1941, the old mansion was leveled. The property was then sold again, and subdivided into smaller lots.

Photo by Nancy Bahnsen

Sands Point, as seen on the Society's 2003 Gold Coast cruise.

Today, the Sands Point Lighthouse is still privately owned. Over the years, construction has destroyed most of the historic nature of the site, but efforts are now being made to preserve the 1809 tower and 1867 dwelling as reminders of a noble history of service.

Execution Rocks

Perhaps no lighthouse on Long Island has a more mysterious air about it as the one at Execution Rocks. Much of that mystery comes from its name. According to one legend, as told by William O. Stevens in his book, *Discovering Long Island:*

> During colonial times, when punishments were cruel and judges were merciless, prisoners condemned to death used to be taken out to this isle and chained to a ring set in the rock at low water mark. They were left until nature had taken its course.

The above legend is usually told as a Revolutionary War tale, with the British chaining Americans to the rocks. In some versions of this story, Indians are said to have committed these acts against colonists. No evidence has been found of such grisly incidents.

A more likely story is one that has been told by two respected local citizens. In 1807, Samuel Latham Mitchill described some shallow areas that he believed may have been islands at one time: "One of these shallow places, whose rocks are frequently bare at low water, lies off the extremity of Cow-Neck, and occupies several acres near almost the middle of the Sound. From the damage sometimes done to vessels, by this shoal and its rocks, they are called *Executions.*" In *Recollections of and Old New Yorker*, Frederick Van Wyck offers the same explanation. Van Wyck's grandfather, George W. Blunt, was involved in the effort to have a lighthouse built on the rocks.

Whatever the reason for the name of the rocks, there has never been any debate regarding the danger they have posed to maritime traffic in the western Long Island Sound. Early markings included a white spar buoy (1827). On March 3, 1837, Congress appropriated $5000 for "a revolving or double light upon the south side of Execution Rocks." Inspectors were then sent to the site to see what could be done with those funds. Commander Francis H. Gregory's report concluded that $5000 would be inadequate to complete the building a lighthouse, and that at least four times that would be needed. It was suggested that a "floating-light," or "light-boat," be built with the money.

There was then some discussion about what the wording of the appropriation allowed. Commodore Charles Morris, of the Navy Commissioner's Office, wrote on November 1, 1837, in a letter to Superintendent of Lighthouses Stephen Pleasanton:

> Sir: The Commissioners of the Navy have received your letter of the 31st ultimo, and beg leave to call your attention to the fact that the law does not provide for a light-*house* or a light-*boat* on Execution rocks, but a "revolving or double *light*," without specifying either a *house* or a *boat* on which to erect it. Is it not therefore discretionary to make use of either?

Pleasanton responded the next day, stating:

> It is true, as you allege, that the law does not specify whether the light on Execution rocks should be placed upon a *house* or a *boat*; but I think the intention of the law to place it upon a house is manifest, from the facts that revolving lights are never placed upon light-boats; and, indeed, it would be altogether impracticable; and double lights are often placed in light-houses; that is to say, one set of lamps above another, several feet apart, by way of distinguishing them from others in their neighborhood.

> Whatever may have been the intention of the law, however, it will not be in our power to build a light-boat with the appropriation of $5,000, as it will require double that sum to build a boat for that situation.

By December, it was decided by the Secretary of the Treasury that the appropriation did not apply to a light boat. That, combined with Pleasanton's statement that the appropriation would not be enough for a sufficient boat, caused the subject to be suspended in December 1837, pending further action by Congress. That action would not come until ten years after the initial appropriation.

In 1838, George Bache's report on the area's lighthouses contained a discussion of the need for a "light-house or light-boat on Execution rock." The "extensive trade" in the area, with its corresponding maritime traffic, and the fact that "the Sand's point [lighthouse] . . . cannot be depended on when the weather is thick and boisterous" made the need seem obvious. Bache noted that a lighthouse or lightship had been suggested prior to his report, and went on to describe why he thought a lighthouse would be better.

The principal reasons were that a lighthouse can house a better light; a lighthouse will not stray from its location, as a lightship can in bad weather; a lighthouse can be put right on top of the rocks, giving a better indication of their position; and over time, a lighthouse is more economical because of its sturdiness (meaning less maintenance) and smaller crew. Bache's estimated cost for 25 years was $102,500 for the lighthouse, and $115,000 for the lightship.

Prior to the establishment of the lighthouse at Execution Rocks, the Sands Point Light was responsible for aiding ships between Eaton's Neck and Throggs Neck, complemented by a buoy that marked "the east end of the shoal off the Execution rocks." At the time, it was considered the duty of the Sands Point Light to "lead vessels clear of the Execution rocks, which are three-fourths of a mile to the northward and westward of it."

By the late 1840s, the technology and know-how to build offshore lighthouses was developing in America. On March 3, 1847, Congress appropriated $25,000 for a lighthouse, which was to be built on Execution Rocks. The lighthouse plan selected for the site was a stone truncated cone, designed by noted engineer/architect Alexander Parris (the alternative plan was for a screwpile structure). There was a great deal of discussion between Parris, Pleasanton, local captains and pilots, and others regarding the exact location. Parris' initial recommendation, on the largest of the boulders on the reef, was eventually selected.

The construction of the light was completed in May 1849, but not without problems. Contractor Thomas Butler, who had won the job with the lowest bid, is said to have lacked the ability to accomplish the task, and subcontractors did much of the work.

When completed, the lighthouse was a whitewashed tower, in the shape of a truncated cone. Argand lamps with reflectors provided the light.

Sands Point Keeper Daniel H. Caulkins was given the responsibility for the Execution Rocks Light. Two assistant keepers aided him. On June 15, 1850, Captain Howland brought his supply ship to visit Caulkins at Execution Rocks. He reported that stones on the east side of the station had been carried to the west side by the

National Archives 26 LG 11-53
Execution Rocks Light between 1867 and 1899

sea. He also noted that the "[h]ouse is very leaky; wants to be well cemented in the joints, and the windows ought to be made tight." He also recommended "greater protection from the sea" consisting of "a base of heavy blocks of stone nearly as high as the door of the light-house." The illuminating apparatus at the time consisted of 15 lamps with 21–inch reflectors. Red shades around the lamps gave the light a steady red characteristic.

On March 17, 1851, William Craft became the keeper at Execution Rocks, but resigned on August 19 1852, not long after Congress put America's lighthouses under the charge of the newly-created Light-house Board. At this time, 13 Winslow Lewis lamps with 21–inch reflectors emitted the light from the tower. Over the next several years, Keepers E. H. Weed, Benjamin Baker, Andrew A. Constant, Joseph Brundage, and Moses H. Odell kept the light at Execution Rocks.

Almost from the start, there were concerns about the lighthouse's foundation. A plan was developed to help protect the site in 1853, and in 1854 a breach in the sea wall was reported. In 1855, while Joseph Brundage and Underhill Lockwood were responsible for the Execution Rocks Light, it was noted by Captain George Dutton, a Third District engineer, that "[t]he foundation is insecure. The stones thrown to the eastward of the tower to protect it from the heavy gales from that quarter have been washed to the west side, and the vessel filled with stones for the same purpose is breaking up. The landing wants considerable repairs, as does also the gallery round the outside of the tower, and the plastering inside. I would recommend that the whole be attended to at the earliest moment possible, and at the same time a larger bell, with suitable striking machinery, be substituted for that now in use, which is much too small, and can be heard but a very short distance."

The early part of 1856 was stormy, with many gales. One of these claimed a boat at the station, and a storm in November 1858 claimed another boat while damaging the breakwater and dock. A storm in April 1867 would claim yet another boat.

By this time, Execution Rocks was showing a fixed white light visible for 12 miles. Its multiple lamps and reflectors had been replaced by a single lamp with a Fourth Order lens in 1856.

After the Civil War, as many stations in the Third District were being improved, a decision was made to erect permanent keepers' quarters at the site. In 1868, a new "protecting pier of stone, with an entirely new keeper's dwelling thereon" was built. There was also "a complete overhauling and improvement of the tower, providing it with a new lantern and iron deck-plate, and iron windows." It was also noted that the "fog-bell will be replaced by a trumpet operated by a hot-air engine." In the 1866 *Annual Report*, the station's fog bell, rung by hand, had been described as "entirely useless."

With the station renovated, it became of greater importance to protect the site. The old enrockment had settled, and no longer afforded protection from "the severe storms of winter and the heavy pack ice brought against it by the tides." On July 15, 1870, $8000 was appropriated for "protecting" the site and work promptly began.

Undated Photo of
Charles Finch Sherman.

Courtesy of Cathy Robbins

On May 7, 1873, at the age of 43, Charles Finch Sherman became keeper of the Execution Rocks Light. One week later, Vincent Emmons was assigned as his assistant. On November 24, he received another assistant: his wife, Mary Lucy (Edwards) Sherman. Both Charles and Mary were children of former Cedar Island Lighthouse keepers (Charles' father, Lyman G. Sherman had been succeeded by Mary's father, Nathaniel Edwards). Both would remain at Execution Rocks until June of 1882. Charles passed away nearly 15 years after leaving the station, in January of 1897.

Mary Sherman was just one of several female assistant keepers at Execution Rocks in the 1800s. Others included Alicia Odell (1859), Clarissa Miller (1867–1869), Jane Williams (1869–1871), and Ellen Fraser (1871).

In the 1870s, the fog signal at Execution Rocks was a "Third-class Daboll trumpet, operated by an 18-inch Ericsson hot-air engine, in duplicate." This apparatus, during the year ending June 30, 1875, had operated 368¾ hours, using 5798 pounds of coal, 182 cubic feet of wood, with eight pounds of pressure, sounding for seven seconds, at 15–second intervals.

Severe winter storms in 1877–1878 damaged the 1870 enrockment on the northerly and northeasterly sides. This was a recurring problem at Execution Rocks.

In 1879, $15,000 was appropriated, and a first-class Daboll trumpet replaced the former third class signal. "[C]orrespondingly enlarged engines and fittings" were also installed at that time. Fog signals have never been completely reliable, and there have been times where the absence of a signal has caused problems. One such occurrence happened at Execution Rocks in March, 1882, when the lack of a fog signal caused a "disaster" for the schooner *Martha Welsh*.

In June of 1890, the American Brotherhood of Steamboat Pilots petitioned for a lightship at Execution Rocks, but this was never acted upon. That year, though, the light at Execution Rocks was given a red sector to warn mariners of the south side of Hart Island.

The year 1891 was a busy one at the station. A new fog signal building, with an attached coal shed, was built, and a cistern was built in the basement of the tower to provide water for boilers to power the automatic steam sirens, which would be installed the following year. Also during 1891, the poor relationship between the keeper, John J. Kennedy, and his assistant, Alfred J. Brandis, resulted in charges and countercharges between them. Both were removed from the station in October 1891.

The season following the departure of Kennedy and Brandis, the light was changed from a fixed white light to one flashing every ten seconds, and steam sirens replaced the Ericsson hot-air engine and Daboll trumpet. The new sirens must have been quite effective as, on

From the author's collection

Postcard showing 1891 fog signal building.

September 21, 1893, the New York State Board of Health wrote a letter transmitting a protest regarding the fog siren from the Westchester County Medical Society. The sirens were disabled in early 1895, and replaced (presumably with lower power sirens) and put back into action in 1897.

By 1894, the southwest wall of the keepers' quarters had "settled dangerously," so it "was taken down, the loose stone upon which it rested was taken out and replaced, the voids were filled with concrete, and the wall was rebuilt." In 1897 a new lantern and deck were installed on the tower, and the lens and clockworks rotating mechanism were overhauled. The next year a covered walkway from the dwelling to the fog signal house was built.

On May 15, 1899, the brown band around the center of the tower was added. It had been solid white for the preceding 50 years, but would retain its new daymark into the 21st century.

In 1902, approximately 200 tons of riprap were put at the site to help protect the station. This was a problem for many years, with hundreds of tons of riprap having previously been put down in 1870, 1878, 1892, 1896 (600 tons), 1897 (200 tons), 1899 (500 tons), and 1901 (400 tons).

On August 17, 1913, keeper George L. Costello and second assistant keeper Frederick C. Lovatt assisted a group whose motorboat had been disabled, later bringing them and the boat to Huckleberry Island. By this time, the lighthouse was using an incandescent oil vapor lamp in place of the former oil lamp, increasing the candlepower emitted from its lens approximately four-fold.

On February 4, 1920, the steamer *Maine* wrecked at Execution Rocks. The ship, built in 1892, was one of the early passenger ships on the Long Island Sound to use a screw propeller instead of side paddlewheels. She was driven stern first onto the station, nearly hitting the lighthouse, by a combination of full moon, tide, snow, high winds, and a pack of ice. The ship eventually broke up, reportedly snapping and cracking loudly, and was a total loss. According to the chief engineer, "[I]t sounded like the Fourth of July but certainly didn't feel like it." The *Maine's* passengers, including

14 horses, were saved, but not before the drinking water had run out and they had had to resort to melting snow.

Few things were as frightening at a small, offshore light station as fire. In the early 1900s, fire twice threatened the station. Just before noon on December 8, 1918, the engine house caught fire. The engine had been running several hours, powering the fog signal, when Keeper Peter Forget noticed the change in the engine's speed. He sent out a distress signal, and while they waited for help, the men on the station—two keepers and two sailors temporarily stationed there—worked to control the fire. Navy patrol boats and soldiers from nearby Fort Slocum arrived to help about 1pm, and a fire boat arrived near 2pm, with the latter being the final piece needed to extinguish the fire. No lives were lost in the blaze, and the damage was repairable. A few years later, fire once again broke out in the engine room, but it did less damage and the station was repaired and improved.

U. S. Coast Guard photo

Aerial view showing 1920 oil house.

Photo by the author

Execution Rocks Light in 1999.

First Assistant Keeper Walter A. Story and Second Assistant Keeper Leonard Hainsworth were "commended for meritorious service rendered on May 29 [1921] in saving the lives of two men whose canoe had capsized during a sudden windstorm and in recovering the canoe."

In 1966, the Coast Guard described the light as sitting in 37 feet of water, three miles north of Sands Point, exhibiting a 1/2–second white, 600,000 candlepower flash (the light had been electrified by this time) every 10 seconds, from a height of 62 feet above the water. The station's fog signal sent a one-second blast every 20 seconds from a diaphragm type foghorn. The station also included a radiobeacon antenna, and a distance finding station.

The lighthouse at Execution Rocks was automated in 1979, at which time its Fresnel lens was removed. Today, because of its name and offshore location, Execution Rocks is Long Island's most mysterious lighthouse. Despite the relatively mundane reason for its name, the lighthouse retains a very important place in the local community as the only remaining Long Island lighthouse from the era when Stephen Pleasanton oversaw aids to navigation in the United States.

Cold Spring Harbor

When a lighthouse is moved from its original foundation, it is usually cause for great fanfare, with crowds, ceremonies and, in modern times, even live internet feeds. But few people know of the Long Island lighthouse that was moved in 1965. Today, the Cold Spring Harbor tower remains the only Long Island lighthouse to be moved from its original site.

Jutting 1500 feet out from the eastern shore of Centre Island is a muddy shoal that poses an obstacle for maritime traffic entering Cold Spring Harbor. Getting around this shoal requires that the mariner stay close to Lloyd's Neck, on the eastern side of the channel.

This harbor is largely famous for its whaling fleet. Cold Spring Harbor's fleet owed its existence to the Jones family, which had been in the area for some time (Major Thomas Jones, a "privateer" who had been born in Ireland in 1665, moved to nearby Oyster Bay in 1695). The major's great-grandsons were the founders of the Cold Spring Harbor whaling fleet.

The Jones Brothers, as they have often been referred to, started out in the mill industry, gaining a reputation

Undated postcard

From the author's collection

for fine textiles by the 1820s. They also operated grist mills and a cooper's shop. By 1827, the Cold Spring milling business was suffering from overseas competition. This is when, and perhaps why, the Jones Brothers began to explore the whaling business.

In 1836, the Jones Brothers bought their first whaling ship. It was the bark *Monmouth*, formerly of Sag Harbor, which was purchased for approximately $20,000. The 100–foot boat set sail on its first whaling trip out of Cold Spring Harbor in early July 1836, returning May 4, 1837, with 1700 barrels of whale oil. This early success must have encouraged the Jones Brothers.

In 1837, they bought the *Tuscarora*, a larger, square-rigged ship from New London. The success of this ship prompted the Joneses to incorporate in 1839, creating the Cold Spring Whaling Company. The company consisted of these two vessels until 1843, when two more were bought. Five additional vessels were purchased between 1844 and 1852, bringing the total to two barks and seven ships.

The loss of two of the fleet's vessels greatly hurt the operation. The *Richmond* ran ashore off the Bering Strait on December 2, 1843, and the *Edgar* was lost in June 1855, just south of the Arctic Circle, when it was overturned by a sudden change of wind while "cutting-in" a whale.

With the deaths of Walter R. Jones (1855) and John H. Jones (1859), the Cold Spring whaling business was left without its two most important leaders. Two of the whaling ships, the *Sheffield* and the *Splendid*, were away when John died. Upon their return in 1860, the whaling industry of Cold Spring Harbor ended. Each of the vessels had covered its expenses and made profits, but the loss of two of the nine vessels resulted in a net loss over the 23 years and 37 completed whaling voyages out of Cold Spring Harbor.

Whaling was not Cold Spring's only maritime activity. The Jones Brothers, probably with others, also built ships in the early to mid-1800s. And they purchased a sidewheel steamboat, the *American Eagle*, in 1842 or 1843. First, it operated out of the Fulton Market Slip in New York, making runs to New Rochelle, Glen Cove, Oyster Bay, Cold Spring, and Huntington. In 1844, Cold Spring

Harbor was made the home port for the steamer, until her sale in 1849.

Despite the shipping associated with grist and woolen mills, shipbuilding, whaling, and a regular steamboat operation, Cold Spring Harbor operated without a lighthouse to guide ships around the large shoal at its entrance. It was not until 1874 that Congress was petitioned, by Henry Warren and others, for a light in Cold Spring Harbor. An examination of the site by the engineer and inspector of the Third District resulted in the recommendation of "two range-lights on the mainland." This recommendation was approved on March 3, 1875, and $20,000 was appropriated for the purpose.

Acquiring the land necessary to establish these lights was difficult. In 1876, efforts were still being made to establish range lights on Lloyd Neck, formerly known as Horse Neck, but it was reported that "[t]he owners of the lands where the lights would be located are opposed to its occupation for the purpose indicated, believing that it must result to their injury." Further complicating the matter was the fact that the proposed locations of the range lights, although fairly close together, were actually in different counties (Queens and Suffolk). This necessitated duplication of much of the work required for obtaining the land. By this time, consideration had begun regarding the establishment of an offshore lighthouse, but the appropriation for the range lights was "not sufficient to erect a structure on the shoal called the Middle Ground" (note: there have been many shoals in the United States, and several on Long Island, referred to as Middle Ground).

The Lighthouse Board's *Annual Reports* for the next two years carried the same exact report as 1876. In early 1879, plans to erect two cast iron towers were drawn up. Also in that year, the New York State Legislature ceded jurisdiction, and negotiations for the land were in progress with the landowners. Within two years, a title investigation determined that the price for land would be too high, and that if the lights were to be established, condemnation of the site would be necessary.

In March 1881, a letter from General J.C. Duane (the same J.C. Duane who had been one of the engineers for the Shinnecock Bay and Fire Island lighthouses as a lieutenant in 1857–1858) to United States Navy Rear Admiral John Rodgers, Chairman of the Lighthouse Board, stated that the range light issue was "in abeyance awaiting the result of the question of cutting a channel through from Lloyd's Harbor to Cold Spring Harbor." The letter also mentioned the inability to procure the land for the front range light that had so long been sought for the site.

By 1888, "still further unsuccessful efforts to obtain title to the site on the land" resulted in the proposal to "erect the light-house on Middle Ground Shoal in Cold Spring Harbor in 11 feet of water." Architectural plans had already been made.

In June 1889, Third District Engineer David Porter Heap accepted the proposal for the construction of the lighthouse. In July, the Secretary of Treasury approved it as well. Construction proceeded quickly and, by 1890, a "structure, consisting of an iron cylinder filled with concrete, surmounted by a square wooden tower containing the light and fog-bell, was built on the southeast end of the middle ground, entrance to Cold Spring Harbor. The light was first shown on January 31, 1890."

William S. Keene was assigned as the station's first keeper, but only remained until his resignation on February 17. Samuel L. Turner took over for Keene, first as an acting keeper, then receiving his per-manent appointment December 28, 1891.

U. S. Coast Guard Photo

Not long after the establishment of the light, a petition requesting a change in the light's characteristic was submitted. By May, the change had been made: "a red sector was fitted in the lantern, covering Buoy No. 17 and Center Island around to Plum Point."

Turner had a tough time in 1900. A letter in June of that year reported the "[i]nfirmity of Keeper (Turner)." In November, Third District Inspector Shepard recommended the dismissal of Turner for insubordination. On January 4, 1901, Turner was replaced by Adolph Obman.

The 1907 Light List described the station as having a fixed white light with a fixed red sector, 40.5 feet above mean high water. The fog signal was a bell struck by machinery every 30 seconds.

On April 3, 1908, keeper Chester Rowland drowned. Arthur Jensen, an assistant at Execution Rocks, who would later be known for his many years as the keeper at Eaton's Neck, was assigned to replace Rowland on April 10. Although Jensen was only stationed at Cold Spring Harbor for eight months, he had the honor several times to be visited by President Theodore Roosevelt, whose "Summer White House" at Sagamore Hill was not far away. Roosevelt, a well-known outdoorsman, would visit the lighthouse by rowboat with his children.

U. S. Coast Guard Photo

56

US Lighthouse Society Photo
Keeper Albert Possel's boat.

Jensen was offered an assignment as assistant keeper at the Eaton's Neck Light in early April 1909. Having been married the previous October, and his wife now pregnant with their first child, he accepted the opportunity to leave the offshore station for one where he could be with his family.

On February 25, 1918, in a southwest gale, the Cold Spring Harbor Light was damaged. A letter from Keeper Louis P. Brown stated the following:

Last night while a south to southwest gale was blowing, a cake of ice about 1 mile square, from 4 to 8 inches thick, came out with tide and wind from Cold Spring and struck this station with such force it jarred the lantern doors open, also throwing a number of articles from shelves, oil cases and cans, dishes, pots, and pans. Everything on the station was working, as I have been watching the ice the past two weeks; more so in stormy weather. I dumped the fire in our stove and put out the light in lantern, just using a hand lantern; some articles I put on the floor to keep them from falling and breaking.

The light in lantern was put out at 1:45 a. m., February 26, and was lit again at 2.55 a. m.; the light was out 1 hour and 10 minutes. There is still one mile and a quarter square of heavy ice in Cold Spring Harbor at present.

In the 1940s, when Albert Possel was the keeper, the light was produced by an incandescent oil vapor lamp and Fourth Order lens, producing 2900 candlepower from its white sector and 870 candlepower from its red sector, which covered Plum Point and the shoal off of Centre Island Point. In bad weather, the fog bell rang once every 30 seconds.

Photo by Robert M. Scroope

The Cold Spring Harbor tower in its present location.

The light was automated in November 1948, and maintenance of the Cold Spring Harbor station, along with that at Lloyd Harbor, was made the responsibility of personnel at Eaton's Neck.

In 1965, the 75–year-old tower was removed from its foundation, and scheduled to be destroyed. A local woman inquired about the possibility of obtaining the tower, and it was sold to her for one dollar. It was then put on a barge, brought to Center Island, and dragged across marshes to her property. It has been there ever since. A skeletal tower replaced the old wooden tower, atop the 1890 caisson, and this is how the original site still appears.

Today, the wooden tower is still privately owned, and looks out on its old foundation. It remains the only relocated Long Island light, and a secret to most.

Lloyd Harbor
Huntington Harbor

The story of the Lloyd Harbor Light Station is a tale of two very different lighthouses in two very different, albeit nearby, locations.

The first Lloyd Harbor Lighthouse was built on the end of a sand spit at the entrance to Lloyd Harbor. The harbor had long been used by sailing vessels for protection from the dangerous seas of the Long Island Sound. In 1838, George Bache recommended the establishment of "[a] small beacon-light" to help ships enter "Lloyd's harbor, Huntington bay." He went on to describe the area:

> Huntington bay, from its position and accessibility, is a place of general resort in heavy weather; but as the northerly winds here drive home, vessels, when practicable, seek a better shelter in Lloyd's harbor, in which, although it is a place of no commerce, upwards of seventy vessels have been counted at the same time. This harbor is difficult to make at night, owing to the low sandy point at its entrance; upon which it is respectfully recommended that a light be placed.

Bache's "low sandy point" was the southernmost tip of the east side of Lloyd's Neck, south of what is now Target Rock National Wildlife Refuge.

On August 9 1853, U.S. Navy Captain Hiram Paulding sent a letter to Secretary of the Treasury James Guthrie:

> SIR: I have the honor briefly to address you on a subject of importance to the interests of commerce as well as to the cause of humanity.
>
> Lloyd's harbor, on the Long Island sound, is the only refuge in stormy weather, for many miles, for the numerous coasting and other vessels that navigate the sound at all seasons. The light on Easton's [sic] neck guides them to the bay of Huntington; but the approach to Lloyd's harbor, where alone they can find a safe anchorage, is dangerous and extremely difficult, from the existence of a low sand-spit on one and a rocky shoal on the other side of the channel. It is suggested that a beacon, or some other conspicuous

landmark, should be erected in such locality as may be adjudged best.

Having been respeatedly [sic] requested by the watermen who navigate the sound to give my aid in bringing this subject to the notice of the government, I have considered that I could in no way more properly do so than by addressing myself to your excellency. That a more perfect knowledge may be communicated to the department, and upon which an appropriation may be asked of Congress, I would most respectfully propose that a commission of two or three officers be appointed to examine the location, and report to the department over which you preside.

I would take leave further to remark, that in the intervals of service for the last fifteen years my residence has been in the vicinity of Lloyd's harbor; and my professional calling has often led me to consider the importance of a beacon or some other guide by which the harbor could be approached in stormy weather.

I have the honor to be, with the highest respect, your most obedient servant,

H. PAULDING
Captain U. S. Navy

In 1861, Commodore Paulding would order the destruction of the Gosport Navy Yard, near Norfolk, Virginia, and the ships there, to keep the facility out of Confederate control (the Confederates would refit one of those ships, the *Merrimack*, as an ironclad gunboat and rename it the *CSS Virginia*; this ship would later encounter the Union ironclad *Monitor* in one of the nation's most famous battles). *New York Tribune* editor Horace Greeley would refer to this shipyard's destruction as "[t]he most shameful, cowardly, disastrous performance that stains the annals of the American Navy." Paulding would later become a Rear Admiral, in charge of the Brooklyn Navy Yard.

Paulding's letter regarding Lloyd Harbor was obviously heeded, as the following letter was sent to Navy Lieutenant T.A. Jenkins, Secretary to the Light-house Board, on October 21, 1853:

SIR: I have just returned from an examination of Lloyd's harbor, Huntington bay, L.I. It has always been, and is still, a great harbor of refuge for vessels navigating Long Island sound in stormy

61

or easterly weather. A light, say of the fourth order Fresnel, would be of the greatest service in making it, and in my opinion is very much needed. If one is erected, I think it should be placed on the end of the sand point, north side of the harbor. By referring to the coast survey chart of Huntington bay, you will see that the water is bold to it. The point is formed by the wash of the sea; is of coarse sand and gravel, and at times entirely covered by water.

The letter from Captain Paulding, U. S. N., to the honorable Secretary of the Treasury, and enclosed to me by the Light-house board, is herewith returned.

Very respectfully, your obedient servant,

A. LUDLOW CASE
Inspector of Lights, &c.,
Third District

The opinions of Paulding and Case prompted Congress into action. Congress appropriated $4000 in 1854 for the establishment of the lighthouse. On July 26, 1855, Samuel and Hannah Denton sold 2½ acres on the "South Point of the East Beach of Lloyd's Neck" to the federal government for $250. The purchase also included "the right of way to and from it." This was an important inclusion, as it would avoid the need to negotiate a right of way with local landowners later on.

Lieutenant J.C. Duane, engineer for the lighthouse project, submitted his plans and estimated cost in early 1857. When completed later that year, the Lloyd Harbor Light was a square brick tower, 34 feet tall from its base to the focal plane of the light. A Fifth Order lens showed a fixed white light from 48 feet above sea level. Attached to the tower was a white, two-story, wood frame keepers' quarters, with a brick foundation. There was no fog signal at the station.

On June 4, 1857, John S. Wood was appointed as keeper. However, he appears to have never actually tended the light, as Abiatha Johnson was appointed on August 11, prior to the completion of the lighthouse.

Ten years into the light's life, it required some work. In 1867, a new lantern deck was installed, along with an iron railing. The

National Archives 26 LG 12-62

The original Lloyd Harbor Light in an undated photograph.

interior of the cast-iron lantern was lined with wood, and the windows in the keepers' quarters were all given shutters. A shed for fuel and a small cellar under the dwelling's east room were built.

On November 22, 1870, a gale damaged the station. The following year, a granite seawall was erected to protect the site. This seawall was damaged in 1872 by ice, but was repaired. By 1873, erosion at the point led the Light-house Board to ask for $2000 to help protect the station. The erosion threatened "the destruction of the site." In 1875, an enrockment was built at the lighthouse site with the appropriation requested in 1873.

With over three decades of exposure to the sea and storms, the Lloyd Harbor Light was ready for some extensive repairs by 1880. In that year, "the roofs of the dwelling and the kitchen were reshingled." The floor of the porch was also rebuilt, as were the steps and railing leading up to it. In addition, "the station was repainted throughout and put in thorough repair."

Keeper Johnson died in 1885 and Robert McGlone was appointed acting keeper on September 26, 1885. McGlone received his permanent appointment on July 9, 1886.

63

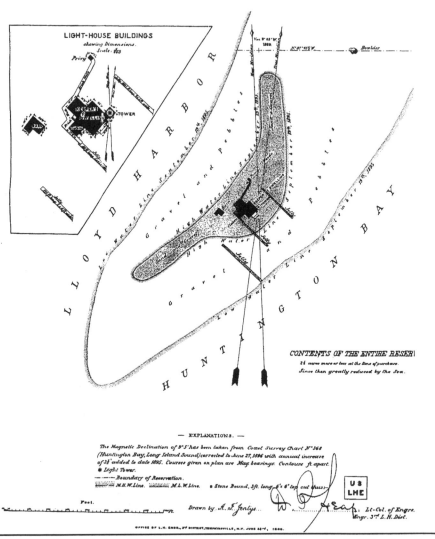

LLOYD HARBOR

LIGHT STATION,

N.Y.

Lat. 40°54'54" N.
Long. 73°26'06" W.

Kind of Lights .... Bay and Harbor Guide.
Order of Light .... 5th.
Characteristic of Light .... F. Red.
Base of Tower above water level .... 6 ft.
Focal Plane .... 40 ft.

Site Purchased .... July 24th 1855.
Deed Recorded at Oyster Bay, Queens Co., N.Y. 1855
First Buildings, when built .... 1857.
When rebuilt or renovated .... 1873.
Area of Reservation to M.H.W. line 1A.0R.27.79P.
Area enclosed .... by Water.

Reservation Surveyed September 19th, 1895, by Ad. F. Jentys.

Scale, 1/1500

LIGHT-HOUSE BUILDINGS
showing Dimensions.

CONTENTS OF THE ENTIRE RESER[
24 acres more or less at the time of purchase.
Since then greatly reduced by the Sea.

— EXPLANATIONS. —

The Magnetic Declination of 9°5'has been taken from Coast Survey Chart N°368
(Huntington Bay, Long Island Sound) corrected to June 27, 1896 with annual increase
of 3' added to date 1895. Courses given on plan are Mag. bearings. Contours ft. apart.
※ Light Tower.
———— Boundary of Reservation.
▨▨▨▨ M.H.W. Line.   ▨▨▨▨ M.L.W. Line.   ▪ Stone Bound, 3 ft. long, 6"x 6" top cut thus.

U S
LME

Feet.

Drawn by A. F. Jentys.

Lt.-Col. of Engrs.
Engr. 3rd L.H. Dist.

OFFICE OF L.H. ENGR., 3rd DISTRICT, TOMPKINSVILLE, N.Y. JUNE 22nd, 1896.

From National Archives microfilm. Record Group 26. Roll Number Red 3
The Lloyd Harbor Light Station in an 1895 survey.

During 1890–1891, the dwelling was again "thoroughly overhauled," and the chimney was rebuilt from the roof up. A leak over the front door was fixed with the installation of some new flashing. The following two years saw work completed to make the foundations more secure. The encroachment of the sea was continuing to be a problem, especially near the dwelling's southwest corner.

Tragedy struck the McGlone family in 1900, when Mrs. McGlone died during childbirth. Augusta Harrigan, a 31–year-old local woman, then came to care for the keeper's six children.

By 1900, changes had taken place that affected the light station. Since the light's construction, ships had become stronger, and many were using propellers instead of sails, making Lloyd Harbor's safe haven less of a need. Also, Huntington was developing commercially and this, combined with a dangerous rocky reef at the entrance to Huntington Harbor, indicated a need for a light there. The light on Lloyd's Neck, although not very far from the entrance to Huntington Harbor, did not meet the growing demand for a stronger aid.

In 1905, the Light-house Board submitted the following in its *Annual Report*:

> The Board has received evidence that the interests of commerce and navigation require the establishment of a light at the entrance of Huntington Harbor and Lloyd Harbor, when the present Lloyd Harbor light can be discontinued. After careful examination of the matter, the Board is of opinion that the establishment of a light at the point named will not only be useful for Huntington Harbor, but will also serve every purpose now served by Lloyd Harbor light, and that a tower showing a flashing light and having a bell fog-signal, should be erected at the entrance to Huntington Harbor when the present Lloyd Harbor light should be discontinued. It is estimated that this work can be done for $40,000, and the Board recommends that an appropriation of that amount be made therefor.

The report was not acted upon in 1905, and the Board issued the same recommendation in 1906. On March 4, 1907, Congress did appropriate the funds, then "[s]oundings and borings were made at the site and preliminary plans and specifications approved."

By 1910, the contract had been awarded, the contractor was "assembling the material," and $1116.32 had been spent on the project. By June 30, 1911, $7195 had been spent and completion of the light was expected by the end of December.

On June 16, 1912, the new light and fog signal station were placed in service. The Bureau of Lighthouses, which had replaced the Lighthouse Board, described it in a thorough manner:

Purpose.—Lloyd Harbor Light Station, N.Y., was reestablished in its present position June 16, 1912, for the reason that the light in the old location simply marked the entrance to Lloyd Harbor, while in the new position it marks the entrances to both Lloyd and Huntington Harbors. The old reservation is retained as a shore station for the keeper.

Site.—The station is located on the southwest side of Huntington Bay, north shore of Long Island, at the entrances of the harbors mentioned above. The structure is on a submarine site, the depth of water being 6 feet at mean low water and the rise and fall of the tide 7 feet 6 inches. Borings made over the site previous to commencing the work indicated sand and gravel, with an under stratum of clay at one of the borings. A diver examined the site just before the crib was placed and all high places were cut down and stone and other obstructions were removed.

Structure.—The structure consists of a reenforced [sic] concrete crib 26 by 30 feet in plan and 16 feet high, which was constructed on shore, towed out to the site and sunk in position by admitting water to the inside pockets. As soon as the crib was sunk, riprap 3 feet deep and approximately 100 feet square was placed on the bottom, and was subsequently raised to a height to afford complete protection from ice. The pockets were then filled with concrete, after the water had been pumped out, and upon the upper surface of the crib was constructed a concrete pier whose top is 10 feet 9 inches above mean high water, and this in turn supports the dwelling and tower, both of concrete. Upon the top of the tower is placed a fourth-order, octagonal, straight-bar, cast-iron lantern whose focal plane is 30 feet 10 inches above the top of the pier.

Illuminating apparatus.—The illuminating apparatus consists of a fifth-order lens showing a fixed red light of 90 candlepower, the focal plane is 42 feet above mean high water, and the light is visible

8 nautical miles in clear weather. The light is furnished by a standard fifth-order one-wick mineral-oil lamp.

Fog signal.—This apparatus consists of a 1,000-pound bell operated by a No. 4 fog-bell striker.

Quarters.—The quarters are only intended for the keeper while on watch and consist of a concrete dwelling of one story, containing a living room and bedroom.

The Bureau had created a new form in 1911, Form 60, "to be filled out for new stations as established, and for present stations which have not heretofore been described." This form contained even more specific information about the new station, noting, among other things, its distance from the nearest town (three miles to Huntington), the thickness and size of lantern glass (1/4 inch thick, 34 inches by 36 inches), the lens' manufacturer (Henry-LePaute), how the light's red color was produced (the lamp's chimney was ruby-colored glass), the fog bell's characteristic (one strike every 15 seconds), how long the fog signal would run on one winding (3 ½ hours), and the manufacturers of the stove and water pump (Sears, Roebuck and Company; and Gould, respectively).

The total spent on the new lighthouse by June 30, 1912 was $32,551.41, well below the 1907 appropriation. The old lighthouse on Lloyd Neck was "retained as a shore station for the keeper."

Keeper Robert McGlone was transferred to the new light. At the time, his daughter, Isabelle, born in 1897, and one son were still living at home. The two children spent most of their time at the new lighthouse, with father and son sleeping in the bedroom and Isabelle on a cot in the kitchen. The two children helped their father—who was afflicted with arthritis—tend the light. According to Isabelle, "[i]n our spare time we would dig clams and sell them to a fisherman who took them to Connecticut. We were also able to gather oysters when the 'Perrogie' tide pushed the oyster beds closer to shore. I also caught and cleaned fish and sold them to a neighbor for one cent a piece."

Isabelle McGlone's memories of childhood at the original lighthouse were not as happy as those of many "lighthouse kids." Isabelle remembered "assigned tasks that kept us hard at work." She

Photo by Nancy Bahnsen

The second Lloyd (Huntington) Harbor Light, in May 2003.

"was well schooled in the procedures of lighthouse keeping," filling lamps, climbing the tower, opening the "heavy steel trap door," lighting the lamp, polishing brass and cleaning the lens. During the winter, it was very cold: "Winds howled across the bay and shutters clattered all night."

Keeper McGlone passed away in 1916, and Isabelle left the lighthouse, with no regret. "Looking back on my life at the lighthouse I can truly say there was little pleasure. It seemed as though there was always work to be done and I was more than ready to tumble into bed as soon as the lamp was lit at sundown. I did miss the delights of childhood. Bleakness and drudgery is what I remember."

Robert McGlone was replaced by Marvin Burnham. Marvin, his wife Elizabeth (a sister of Plum Island keeper William Maynard Chapel), and their eight-year-old son Charlie, stayed at the station until 1924. In 2002, Charlie's son, also named Charlie, was able to visit his family's old home, for the first time. The visit brought back memories of his grandfather saying that "he used to sit on the john and fish," as well as his father's stories of rowing ashore to ride his bicycle to school.

On June 26, 1924 the old Lloyd light and 2.5 acres property were deeded to New York State. The federal government reserved "the right of access to the land and water adjacent to Lloyd's neck for the purpose of taking gravel for the use of the Lighthouse Service." The Lloyd Neck property was subsequently transferred to the Town of Huntington on March 21, 1928.

Augusta Harrigan had remained at the old lighthouse after McGlone's children had all left, not leaving until 1925. During this time, she had reportedly kept the building spotless, and kept an old single-barrel shotgun to scare off "suspicious characters." After her departure, the building became the object of vandalism.

In 1935, Art Bouder arrived at Lloyd Harbor Light Station, with his wife, Harriet, and son, Art Jr. In 1936, Bouder bought a new Chevrolet for $600, and kept it, according to Art Jr., "at the Millbank Estate." They stayed until 1938, when Art Jr. had to start school. Art Jr. would go on to a career in the Coast Guard, and was stationed at nearby Eaton's Neck in 1953. According to family lore, Bouder once rescued Professor Albert Einstein. As the story goes, the famous professor and a lady friend were sailing not far from the lighthouse when their sailboat overturned. Although no evidence of this episode has been found, Einstein did much sailing around Long Island at that time and was undoubtedly spotted by many of the island's lightkeepers.

Louis Anderson was a relief keeper at Lloyd Harbor, and at Cold Spring Harbor, during 1936–1937. One of his most vivid memories at both stations was the fog signal, which required winding every few hours as long as the fog lingered. If the fog stayed for days on end, Anderson relates, "you didn't get much sleep." Anderson also recalls that the most impressive boat in the area at that time was William K. Vanderbilt's exploration ship, the *Alva*.

On November 12, 1947, the original Lloyd Harbor Light, which had stood for over 90 years, was lost in a fire. According to newspaper accounts of the day, hunters occupying the site caused the fire. They had created a fire in one of the fireplaces, and lost control of the blaze. All that remained after the fire was the brick tower and foundation of the keepers' quarters. The week following the fire, *The Long Islander* published an article about Augusta Harrigan, noting that she considered the fire "a clean escape from neglect and its scurrilous maltreatment at the hands of tramps, campers, and filthy nobodies."

Photo courtesy of Huntington Lighthouse Preservation Society
The Huntington Harbor Light after completion of exterior restoration.

Photo by the author

The rear of the Huntington Harbor Light in July 2003.

In 1949, the concrete lighthouse was automated. In 1967, the Coast Guard issued a notice that indicated it was going to discontinue the lighthouse, but local recreational and commercial boaters protested and the government relented.

By 1985, the Huntington Harbor Light was in bad shape. The Coast Guard was considering demolishing it. Fortunately, a group of local citizens formed Save Huntington's Lighthouse, Inc., that year and began a long effort to stabilize and restore the light, eventually getting a lease from the Coast Guard. The lighthouse was listed on the National Register of Historic Places in 1989, as a result of the group's efforts.

On July 2, 1998, Save Huntington's Lighthouse's Board of Directors met at the lighthouse, the first time they were able to do so. In 2003, Save Huntington's Lighthouse, having "saved" the lighthouse, changed its name to the Huntington Lighthouse Preservation Society. The society began conducting free tours of the lighthouse, making this the only offshore Long Island lighthouse to be open to the public on a regular basis. Working with the Coast Guard, and the local community, the group continues to make progress in the effort to preserve the station's history, and make it available to the public.

Today, the Huntington Harbor Light casts its beam from a 300mm lens. The original fog bell, which bears the inscription "Jersey City, NJ 1911" sits on the lantern deck, alongside the modern fog signal.

The lighthouse at Huntington Harbor is a fine example of the variety of lighthouses on Long Island. Its unique style, construction, and history give it an important place in the story of Long Island's lighthouse heritage.

Eaton's Neck

Unlike its very similar and slightly older sibling at Montauk Point, the Eaton's Neck Light- house has not enjoyed a life of fame and fortune. The tower, plain white and sans keepers' quarters, is surrounded by faceless government housing. The Eaton's Neck tower does not adorn calendars, t-shirts, company logos, and coffee mugs. It is not visited by tens of thousands of people each year, nor does it appear on many people's lists of "places to visit."

Despite the Eaton's Neck Light's relative obscurity, it is one of Long Island's true historic sites, and shares its sibling's long life of service to the maritime community. It also boasts one feature that no other Long Island lighthouse can claim: a Fresnel lens in its lantern room.

Eaton's Neck received its name from Theophilus Eaton, a Londoner who arrived in America in 1639. In 1646, he bought the land now named for him from the Matinecock tribe, whose chief was Asharoken. The land had been part of the First Purchase of the settlers of Huntington, but the efforts of the Town of Huntington to regain the land from Eaton failed.

The Reverend Joshua Hartt, a part-time surveyor, noted in 1795 that Eaton's Neck included, "a great reef of rocks dangerous to shipping," adding that "many vessels have been wrecked. Hereabouts, it is expected a lighthouse will be built for the advantage of seamen."

Of a visit to the area in May 1804, Timothy Dwight, president of Yale College, remarked on Huntington Bay:

> Its mouth is formed by two peninsulas, or, as they are here termed, *necks:* Eaton's, on [the] east; and Lloyd, on the west. On the former of these is a lighthouse. Few places more demand such a structure or furnish for it a more commodious situation. The rocks which project from this neck and are a continuation of its base into the Sound have in several instances proved fatal to seamen. Captain Keeler, a worthy and intelligent inhabitant of Norwalk, returning from the West Indies after a prosperous voyage, entered the Sound

Photo by the author

Eaton's Neck Light as it appears today.

on the 16th of January in the year 1791. I then resided at Greenfield and distinctly remember the day, and never saw a winter day which was more pleasant. In the evening there arose a tremendous storm. The brig was driven upon these rocks, and every person on board perished.

According to other sources, Benjamin Keeler's brig *Sally* ran aground in late December 1790. This wreck was not discovered until wreckage drifted onto Lloyd's Neck. Ten people were supposed to have been aboard, but only six bodies were ever found.

In late 1797, the Chamber of Commerce of the City of New York asked John McComb, Jr., the builder of the Montauk Point Light, to visit Eaton's Neck and assess the site. He did so in December 1797, submitting a report on the 23rd of that month. His observations were as follows:

First, I would mention Mr. John Gardner's polite attention to me and readiness to assist, and in agreeing to furnish the land for the intended Light House—at the same—mentioning if it was not for that particular purpose, and that the public were much in want of a Light at that place, as stated by you—that he would not dispose of a few acres their for ten times its value—as the Keeper must pass back and forth through the rest of his farm whereby he might experience much inconvenience and damage by their frequently leaving the gates open, and also bringing more people ashore than would be at times agreeable. The lowest price he will take for six acres is Two Hundred and Fifty Dollars. He also agrees in the same proportion to furnish two or three acres more if wanted for the accommodation of the Keeper which must be laid off to the eastward of the 6 acres already pointed out. Mr. Gardner begs me to mention that he should sell the land under certain restrictions, viz. that no other settlement should be made or any other family reside their [sic] except that of the Keeper, also that he would wish to have the recommending of a Keeper himself, or that he would undertake to have the Light attended whereby he might be able to provide a man himself, that would make a careful attentive Keeper and one that could work for him whenever his business at the Light House would permit as he wishes to make the Keeper and family who may reside there as much attached to his interest as possible as an indifferent or dishonest person might commit or suffer many depridations to be committed on his stock or other property at that end of his farm and out of his sight.

The land is of a light sandy soil and of the quality covering with young red ceader [sic] and small oak bushes, which should by no means be cut off, especially near the bank, as the hill would soon be gullied if the bushes were cut off and the sod turned up, besides rendering the Keeper's situation very bleak and disagreeable. About two acres of it would make a tolerable good garden in a wet season. The hill is composed of a loose sandy soil, then with coarse gravel and clay and then coarse gravel and sand. The ground at 400 feet from high water mark is 73 feet high, it then gradually rises for 350 feet farther than 4' 6". Their [sic] is a hollow a little to the eastward of the spot for the dwelling house where a well may be sunk which will be from 40' to 50 feet deep.

The reef of rocks stretched along shore about ½ a mile and runs out in a northeasterly direction, I am informed, nearly two miles with oppenings [sic] through for vessels of a moderate burthen, but within a ½ or ¾ of a mile of the shore their [sic] is not more than from 8' to 12' water at common tides, which rises here sm. 6' to 8 feet.

There is no materials to be had at or near the spot for the buildings. When brought they must be landed to the westward of the reef and may be carted up by making a circuitous Road for the Purpose of about ½ a miles [sic] in length. Huntington Bay affords excellent harbor for small against almost every wind, and a very good harbor for large vessels ag. northeasterly winds in sm. 3 to 5 fathom water.

I am, Gentlemen, very respectfully
Your most oblig'd and Hum. Servt.
JOHN MCCOMB, Jun.
New York 23 Dec. 1797

A letter from noted patriot (and then Senator) John Sloss Hobart to Ebenezer Stevens, Esq., noted that the U.S. Senate had passed "the Act for the erection of a Lighthouse on Eaton's Neck" on March 6, 1798, with "the amendments noted in the margin" and expected the House of Representatives to pass it shortly. Hobart had lived on Eaton's Neck on land purchased by his father.

On March 14, 1798, Congress appropriated $13,250 for the building of a lighthouse on "the headland of Eaton's Neck, on Nassau Island." The New York Legislature ceded jurisdiction over the ten-acre site on April 6, and John and Joanna Gardiner sold the ten-acre site to the government on June 16 for $500.

John McComb, Jr., submitted his proposal for the Eaton's Neck Light on June 29, 1798. On July 2, President John Adams signed the order officially designating the site for the lighthouse.

On July 5, 1798, William Miller, Commissioner of Revenue, wrote a letter to the Secretary of the Treasury, Oliver Wolcott, Jr., reporting on the request for bids for "the Erection of a Stone Light-house on Eatons Neck." Six proposals had been received by Collector Joshua Sands by the June 30 deadline. The low bidders were Mr. McComb and Mr. Moore, both at $9750. Miller reported: "In point of character they are both as respectable as can be desired, but from the variety of public works executed by Mr. McComb with reputation for fidelity & skill, I am inclined to give him the contract."

McComb's specifications called for the form to be

[o]ctagonal the foundation of which to be sunk Eight feet below the Bottom of the Water Table or surface of the Earth and to be commenced of the Diameter of Twenty four feet where the Wall will be seven feet thick." At the bottom of the water table, the wall's thickness would decrease to five feet, then to four feet at the top of the water table, where the diameter would be 18 feet. The height was to be "fifty feet to the Top of the Stone Work, under the floor of the Lanthorn where the Diameter will be Ten feet six inches & the wall Two feet two inches thick." The tower's outside walls were to be built with "large hewn or hammer dressed Stone" with two windows on the east side and three on the west side. "A complete and sufficient Iron Lanthorne in the Octagonal form is to rest thereon the eight Corner Posts or Stanchions of which to be built in the Wall to the depth of six feet where they are to be well secured by Eight Large Iron Anchors.

Part of the agreement was also for a dwelling for the keeper, one and one half stories high, with a full cellar. The first floor had two rooms, with a fireplace in each. An oil vault and a well with a bucket and rope were also part of the deal. The lantern was originally

Photo courtesy of Vivian Jensen Chapin

Eaton's Neck Light in 1935.

equipped by McComb with "four Copper Lamps to contain twelve Quarts each with hooks to support them."

The cost for all this work was $9750. It was to be paid thus: $5000 when the agreement was signed, $2000 "when the first story beams are Laid," $2000 "when the Lanthorn is completed," and $750 when the "described work is perfected."

Over the years, there has been some debate about who was the first keeper. Some reports have indicated that John Squires was the first keeper, and others have claimed it was John Gardiner's son,

John H. Gardiner. Correspondence in 1805 and 1806, at least, clearly point to John Gardiner.

When the tower was first built, its daymark was alternating vertical stripes of black and white. It was changed to all white sometime later, and has remained white to this day.

In 1838, the tower's 12 lamps and reflectors, showing a stationary light, were considered "of service to vessels passing it, or entering Huntington bay for shelter." The 50–foot tower, atop a bluff, held the light at 134 feet above the Sound. The keeper's quarters were wood framed, and a separate "stone oil-cellar" was used for oil storage.

One of the worst disasters in the area occurred on Monday, January 13, 1840. The steamship *Lexington* was a 220–foot long sidewheeler that regularly made runs between New York and Stonington, Connecticut. At 3 p.m. on January 13, she left New York with a cargo of bales of cotton, 91 passengers, and 39 officers and crew. By 7 p.m., the ship was nearing Eaton's Neck and the passengers had just been served dinner while being entertained by a comedian, Henry T. Finn, and an actor, Charles Eberle. The pleasantries were interrupted when someone yelled "Fire!" Benjamin F. Thompson, in the 1918 edition of his work, *History of Long Island from its Discovery and Settlement to the Present Time*, gave an account of the *Lexington* "conflagration":

> At seven o'clock in the evening, when she was about opposite Eaton's Neck, L. I., and nearly in the middle of the Sound, going at the rate of twelve miles an hour, the cotton near the smoke pipe was discovered to be on fire, and the wind blowing fresh, all endeavors to extinguish the flames were found ineffectual, and the boat was headed for Long Island. But the tiller ropes were soon burnt off, which rendered the vessel unmanageable.
>
> The alarm and consternation were now so great, and the consequent confusion so universal, that the boats, three in number, besides the life boat, were no sooner lifted out, and let down into the water, than they were swamped by the crowd and the rapid motion of the vessel.
>
> The engine also gave way, and the boat, which had now become unmanageable, was drifted about at the mercy of wind and tide,

while the fire was sweeping over her, in the most terrific manner imaginable.

The fire being amid-ships, cut off necessarily, all communication from stem to stern, where the passengers were collected, bewailing their awful condition, not knowing the fate of their friends, and fully aware that to remain longer on board, was certain destruction, the flames spreading with terrible rapidity, and involving the whole vessel in one sheet of fire.

The lurid light of the blazing wreck shown far over the cold and heavy waste of waters, showing with fearful distinctness the dreadful scene. The greater number, therefore, threw themselves into the sea, laying hold of any floating body within their reach, while others, not so fortunate, were instantly drowned. Some who hesitated to precipitate themselves into the water, clung to some portion of the burning wreck, in the hope of prolonging for a few moments their miserable existence.

The night was cold in the extreme, and the surrounding darkness was rendered more terrific, by the glare of the burning mass. The cries of distress, mingled with the deepest supplications for relief, were such as cannot be described—the anguish of hopeless despair. The captain, it is believed, was suffocated in the wheel house, at an early stage of the fire, and out of the whole number on board, four only were saved, while one hundred and twenty men, women, and children were lost.

The steamer *Statesman* was one of the ships that went in search of survivors, returning to New York on the January 17, 1840. On board the *Statesman*, Joseph J. Comstock gave an account of the effort to retrieve survivors, bodies, and wreckage. Despite searching 90 miles of shoreline, with help from "others on shore who came down by land," only five bodies were recovered, along with 30 pieces of luggage and the *Lexington's* lifeboat. Comstock described the wreckage:

> From Crane Neck to Old Man's landing, twelve or fifteen miles east, including the deep bays adjacent, is covered with pieces of the wreck, among which I noticed her name upon the siding, nearly in full length, large pieces of her guards, and portions of almost every part of the boat, all of which is mostly burned to coal. We found one of her quarter boats, from which three of the bodies now in our possession were taken; she is very slightly damaged.

The boat is at a place called Miller's Landing, and here we learned that a man had come shore on a bale of cotton, alive, fifteen miles to the eastward of this place, to which I immediately repaired. Here I could effect no landing, owing to the large quantities of ice drifted in by the stormy northerly wind. We, however, crowded the steamboat in near enough to the shore to converse with persons drawn to the beach by our signals, and from them learned the fact that Mr. David Crowley, second mate of the Lexington, had drifted ashore upon a bale of cotton on Wednesday night at 9 o'clock, after being forty-eight hours exposed to the severity of the weather—after which, he made his way through large quantities of ice, and swam before gaining the beach, and then walked three-quarters of a mile to a house—his hands are little frozen—his feet and legs considerably so—he is not able, however, to be moved for the present; this I have been told by a person who saw him this day. . . .

I saw Capt. Manchester [the *Lexington's* pilot] at Southport on Wednesday night, who perfectly corroborates Capt. Hilliard's [the only passenger saved] statements, which shows how collected each must have been in their perilous situation.

We left Crane Neck, for New York, at half past 5 P.M. Arrived at New York at 9 A.M., after a passage of fifteen and a half hours—came fifty miles through the ice.

Captain Stephen Manchester would have another experience near Eaton's Neck less than seven years later, when the steamship *Rhode Island* lost her tiller in a violent storm on Saturday, November 1, 1846. Captain Manchester managed to steer the ship near shore, and dropped anchor. By noon on Sunday, people were gathered at the beach. An attempt was made by five men to get ashore by launching a lifeboat, but the boat was immediately swamped. The men got back to the ship and, being whalers, recommended the use of whaleboats for rescue. This message was sent ashore in a bottle, which "was retrieved from the waves by a large dog." Whaleboats were brought from Huntington and all 150 passengers, and the crew, were saved.

Benjamin Downing was appointed keeper of Eaton's Neck on April 24, 1843. At that time, the light from the tower was emitted from 12 lamps with nine-inch reflectors. Downing kept a record of ships passing the Eaton's Neck station. One week in the Summer of

1849, he noted "3 ships, 25 brigs, 134 schooners, 262 sloops, 5 propellers, [and] 56 steamboats" passing in daylight. That year, a volunteer life-saving station was established on the site—the first on Long Island. The lighthouse keeper was put in charge of the station.

Captain Howland brought supplies to Eaton's Neck on June 17, 1850. Of the tower's 13 Winslow Lewis lamps with 15–inch reflectors, Howland commented: "Lighting apparatus we placed in about as good order as we knew how; for years past there has been complaint upon complaint about it; two years ago the keeper [Downing] did not want me to do anything to them, and last year left word with his family (he being about) for me to do nothing to them; consequently, they have been carried up and down to New York to be repaired; and then, as he said, they were not half done. In consequence of these reports, I have been very particular in making repairs, that there might not be any cause of complaint."

Leonard Mott was appointed keeper of Eaton's Neck on March 5, 1851, but declined the appointment. George S. Gardiner was appointed on the 17th of that month, remaining a little over two years. On April 29, 1853, Edward Floyd was appointed keeper, drawing a salary of $350 per year.

The Henry-LePaute company of Paris shipped a new Third Order lens and lantern for the Eaton's Neck Light on April 20, 1857. On July 22, 1857, Third District Engineer Morton reported that the Eaton's Neck tower would require some masonry work before the installation of the new lantern. The new Third Order lens, which still occupies the tower's lantern room, was a fixed lens, with a reflector plate on the landward side of the lens. Above the central lens were 17 prisms; below it, ten prisms.

On April 4, 1861, U.S, Navy Commodore Hiram Paulding wrote a letter from Washington, D. C., recommending the removal of the keeper and installation of Platt Scudder of Huntington as keeper. On April 13, Darius Ruland was appointed keeper and would remain for nearly five years. In 1876, Ruland would officially take charge of the life-saving station and do so until his retirement in 1894.

The 1867 *Annual Report* called for a fog signal at the station. According to the report, "[a]fter a severe snow-storm, early last

Photo by the author

The Third Order Henry-LePaute lens in the tower's lantern room

spring, three vessels were found wrecked at the mouth of this harbor, which disaster would probably have been avoided had the entrance been defined by a powerful fog-signal."

During 1868, as many Third District light stations were being renovated, the station underwent some important alterations. The *Annual Report* carried an account of these repairs:

> The parapet of the tower has been covered with cast-iron panels, and a cast-iron deck-plate put around the lantern. The wooden stairway in the tower has been replaced by iron steps and landings built inside of a cylindrical brick wall. Iron window frames and sashes were substituted for those of wood; an oil-room of brick, provided with closets and shelves, built in connection with the tower; the passage-way between the tower and dwelling rebuilt. The dwelling was repaired and repainted, and an addition built to it, with a cellar underneath. That portion of the dwelling not worth repair was removed and connected with the barn, which was put in repair.

The fog signal requested in 1867 was authorized on July 20, 1868, but was not installed until 1871. It was a steam siren, which used a caloric engine to pump the fresh water used to power in the

EATON'S NECK LIGHT HOUSE, NORTHPORT, LONG ISLAND, N.Y.

Undated postcard from the author's collection

Eaton's Neck with its keepers' quarters.

siren. The signal was used so often (494.75 hours in 1873), that it was using up the station's fresh water quickly. A new well and an "accessory cistern" were built to help provide the necessary water.

On November 18, 1873, another shipwreck occurred not far from Eaton's Neck. The *Florence V. Turner* was returning from Honduras with a cargo of coconuts. She reportedly struck a reef in a bad storm and began taking on water. The captain, his wife, the cook, and the mate tied themselves to the rigging, while two of the crew went out in the ship's lifeboat. Keeper William E. Perrott went to the village during the raging storm to find volunteers to help him launch the metal lifeboat. Captain Edward Scudder, John Soper, Dyke Ruland, Sr., Washington Sills, and a blacksmith from the Eaton's Neck farm volunteered. They set out to the ship. They found the captain, his wife, and the mate alive, but the cook, still tied to the ship, had drowned. The two crewman in the lifeboat were reported to have drowned. Perrott submitted a report on the incident, and on November 24, 1873, Third District Inspector Trenchard submitted the keeper's report of the wreck of the schooner to the Light-House Board.

Between July 1, 1874 and June 30, 1875, the fog signal at Eaton's Neck operated 487.5 hours (for comparison, the signals at Montauk Point, Little Gull Island, and Execution Rocks operated 748, 651, and 368.75 hours, respectively). The signal consumed 70,540 pounds of coal and 51.5 cubic feet of wood. The boilers produced an average of 60 pounds of pressure for the steam siren, which gave off a nine-second blast every 30 seconds.

There had apparently been some problems at the station when, on February 10, 1879, the Secretary of the Treasury authorized the removal of Keeper H. E. Wood, Acting First Assistant Keeper Albert Joy, and Second Assistant Keeper W. W. Matthias. New keepers were appointed that month, but the new First Assistant Keeper, James Walsh, was absent from the station in April and was promptly removed. The next year, Secretary of Treasury John Sherman abolished the Second Assistant Keeper position at Eaton's Neck.

In March 1880, the Third District Engineer General J. C. Duane prepared a description of the station. He noted that the station had no wharf or landing, and that "[l]anding may be made with ease on beach in fair weather" and reported that "[t]he ascent from the beach to station is easy." The nearest railroad station, in Northport, was seven miles away; the nearest steamboat landing, also in Northport, five miles; and the nearest public road one mile. The ten-sided lantern, of iron and copper, included a copper wire attached to the iron lightning rod; the wire being run down the outside of the tower and two feet into the ground. Inside the Third Order lens, a Funck lamp with two wicks provided the light. Duane reported the fog signal to be a "2nd Class Brown's Steam Siren." In addition to the tower and wood-frame dwelling the station included a barn, shop, fog signal houses, coal bin and privy. The quality of the drinking water, collected from rain was reported as "good" and its quantity "ample."

The "character of the water" at the site was causing problems with the fog signal's boilers by 1880. The signal was also still using a great deal of water, and materials were ordered for building another cistern. The new cistern, "50 by 20 feet, with a depth of 8 feet" was built, and a 30 by 100–foot shed built over it. The boilers were also rebuilt.

On October 1, 1880, Michael J. Burke became the keeper at Eaton's Neck. He would remain until October 6, 1909. His many assistants over those years included Richard E. Ray, who served June 30, 1891 to August 9, 1892, and Arthur Jensen, who served from April 6, 1909 to April 11, 1911. Ray would later be the last keeper at the Old Field Point Light, and Jensen would later become the head keeper at Eaton's Neck.

In 1884, a new boiler was installed, and the fog signal was overhauled. A brick engine house, with two 13–horsepower oil engines with air compressors, was built in 1904. The engines and compressors were to power a new fog signal, a "first-class automatic siren . . . operated by compressed air, sounding blasts of four seconds duration separated by silent intervals of forty seconds."

On February 28, 1907, the lamp inside the Fresnel lens was changed. The old oil lamp was replaced by an incandescent oil vapor (IOV) lamp, increasing the light's power.

One of the station's most notable keepers was Arthur Jensen. Born in Drammen, Norway, on August 26, 1875, he came to the United States at the age of 21. Jensen served in the U.S. Navy in the Spanish American War, then joined the Lighthouse Service. He served as an assistant keeper at Execution Rocks from May 24 to August 10, 1908, when he became the keeper at Cold Spring Harbor. He remained at Cold Spring Harbor for a little over six months. He was assigned as an assistant keeper at Eaton's Neck, then transferred to Faulkner's Island, Connecticut. He returned to Eaton's Neck to become its head keeper, and would finish his career at the station, retiring in August 1942.

On August 26, 1926, Jensen and his assistant, Ole Anderson, rescued two men from barges that had broken loose from their towlines in "a heavy westerly storm." The first barge, the *Planet*, broke loose first and ran into the rocky reef. Anderson set out for the barge by himself. He rescued the crewman on the barge and brought him safely to the beach. Another barge, the *Murray Valley*, broke loose that day, with a crewman aboard. This time it was Jensen who headed out to save the crewman. Both keepers were "officially commended for meritorious services."

While at Eaton's Neck, the Jensens (Arthur had married Ingebord Myhre at Oyster Bay in 1908) had three children: Arthur, born in 1917; Alice, born in 1919; and Vivian, born in 1923. Vivian, who now lives in Washington, has fond memories of her time at the lighthouse. The keeper's dwelling at that time was set up for two families. The keeper had a kitchen and living room on the first floor, with three bedrooms upstairs. In the kitchen were a coal stove, kerosene stove, sink, and well water. The privy was behind the house, "a long walk on a cold winter's night." According to Vivian, "the best part of the house was the kitchen, especially in the winter with the coal stove warm and cozy."

The Jensens had a radio in the 1920s, when radios were a new invention. In the evenings, the family listened to *Amos 'n Andy*, boxing matches, and *Fibber McGee and Molly*. Each Spring, Arthur Jensen would paint the tower and cupola. Vivian did not like watching her father paint the red cupola, as it was a precarious position. Each Spring, they also burned the fields, as they stood ready with wet mops to control the fires. The burning of the fields would result in the eating of strawberries in June. Mrs. Jensen would make jam, and the extra berries would be given away to friends and relatives. There were also plum bushes near the water, the fruits of which were tart. Another Spring rite was the arrival of the inspector, "who would go over the station very carefully, even running his finger on the top of the doors in the house." The *Larkspur* and *Tulip* were the tenders that usually visited Eaton's Neck in Jensen's time.

Christmas was a special time for the Jensens. Baking was a large part of the preparations, with "endless cookies, breads, and goodies" being made and often given to neighbors. The girls were quite particular about the family's tree, and guided their brother in the quest for the perfect one. The children always received a book "and other small items" in their stockings. If the weather allowed, the Jensens would visit the Presbyterian Church on Christmas Eve. The children would visit Santa and receive candy. If the holiday was snowy, the manager of the adjacent farm would take the children on sleigh rides.

Vivian remembers her time at Eaton's Neck with great fondness, especially "the family life, the good neighbors, the vast opportunities

Photo courtesy of Vivian Jensen Chapin

Keeper Arthur Jensen at Eaton's Neck, 1935.

for outdoor activities and the sublime realization that there was no place on earth quite its equal." Arthur Jensen retired from Eaton's Neck in 1942 (he had remained a civilian when the Coast guard took over aids to navigation). The Jensens moved to a home overlooking Northport Bay, and the street was renamed Mariners' Lane in his honor. Arthur Jensen passed away in September 1947.

When Arthur Jensen retired, the light at Eaton's Neck showed a fixed white light of 26,000 candlepower, the illuminant being an electric bulb inside the old Fresnel lens. The fog signal was a first-class siren, giving a two-second blast every 30 seconds.

In 1969, the old keeper's dwelling was torn down, and 11 Coast Guard family housing units were built. That year, the station had a mascot, an eight-year-old black Gordon Setter named Inky.

The lighthouse was listed on the National Register of Historic Places in 1973, largely due to the efforts of the Northport Historical Society. Its significance as one of the earliest aids to navigation to guide ships to and from New York, one of the nation's most important ports, was now nationally recognized.

A bad storm in 1992 removed 40 feet of the bluff at Eaton's Neck, adding to the already-troubling two-feet-per-year erosion problem. By 1996, this settling of the hill had caused cracks in the brick attachment at the base of the tower, and the concrete retaining walls around the base of the light. Cracks were also developing in the foundations of the Coast Guard housing and some cast-iron drainpipes had snapped. Due to the erosion problems, a constant need for dredging in the channel at the station, other needed renovations, and budget constraints, consideration was being given to the moving of the station. By 1998, a decision had not yet been made regarding the matter. The Huntington Town Board and Congressman Gary Ackerman had been working to save the station, trying to convince the Coast Guard that the station was necessary for safety, as well as being an important historical site worth preserving.

By February 1999, the group led by Ackerman received word that the station at Eaton's Neck would remain open for the "foreseeable future." As has happened so many times in historic preservation, the cries of the local populace had affected the future of an important site.

Today, the lighthouse, with its Fresnel lens, and surrounding Coast Guard station continue a long tradition of service to the community. Although the tower is not open to the public for visitation, it stands as a strong reminder of Long Island's maritime history.

Photo by Diane Mancini

Fog Bell on display at Eaton's Neck. Made in 1898 by the Chaplin-Fulton Manufacturing Company of Pittsburgh.

Old Field Point

Old Field Point, just west of Port Jefferson Harbor, was the site of the fifth station established on Long Island. The original tower was the first Long Island light to be built under the direction of the Fifth Auditor of the Treasury, Stephen Pleasanton. Today, the site contains one of Long Island's three remaining Pleasanton-era structures.

Prior to the establishment of the first light at Old Field Point, there were no lighthouses on Long Island's North Shore between Eaton's Neck and Little Gull Island. This stretch of coastline included rocky reefs, sandy shoals, and harbors that were becoming busier. More aids to navigation were needed.

An act of Congress on May 7, 1822 stated

[t]hat, as soon as the jurisdiction of such portions of land at Old Field Point, Long Island, in the State of New York, or on some place in the vicinity, as the President shall select for the sites [sic] of a light-house shall be ceded to, and the property thereof vested in, the United States, it shall be the duty of the Secretary of the Treasury to provide, by contract, which shall be approved by the President, for building a light-house on such site, to be so lighted as to be distinguished from other light-houses near the same; and also to agree for the salaries, wages, or hire of the persons to be appointed by the President for the superintendence of the same.

Congress appropriated $2500 on May 7, 1822, and an additional $1500 on March 3, 1823, for the establishment of this station. On January 27, 1823, the land for the lighthouse was purchased from Samuel Ludlow Thompson and Ruth Thompson, using the high water mark, a fence, and a cherry tree among the boundary markers.

The original lighthouse was an octagonal stone tower 30 feet from base to lantern, showing a fixed white light from 67 feet above the water. It was built by Timothy, Ezra, and Elishia Daboll. The construction cost $3999.25, with the extra 75 cents carried to the surplus fund.

Atop the tower, a cast iron lantern contained an illuminating apparatus consisting of nine Winslow Lewis lamps, with 13 –inch parabolic reflectors, which burned whale oil. The keeper's quarters, which are still in existence, were constructed of rough stone, housing five rooms.

Photo by the author

The original keeper's quarters in 1999.

Upon completion of the station, Edward Shoemaker became its first keeper in 1824. He died on December 21, 1826, and his wife took over as keeper. Mrs. Shoemaker was Long Island's first female keeper, serving until she was replaced on June 5, 1827 by Walter Smith. In April 1830, he died. His wife, Elizabeth, took over and would remain as Old Field Point's keeper for over 25 years.

By 1838, the tower was showing signs of problems common to the Pleasanton era. The lantern deck was leaking and the mortar was falling off the walls. The dwelling was also in need of repairs. Its roof required replacement and the walls needed a new coat of cement. U.S. Navy Lieutenant George Bache described the station as being "badly constructed."

The illuminating apparatus was changed in 1839, and again in 1849, with nine lamps and 15–inch reflectors installed on the latter date. The characteristic remained that of a fixed light.

On August 12, 1841, Stephen Pleasanton, Fifth Auditor of the Treasury, wrote a letter to New York's customs collector, Edward Curtis. Pleasanton's letter addressed Curtis' August 9 correspondence regarding the area's lighthouses, including Old Field Point:

> *Old Field Point light.*—As the keeper is represented to be a good one, you may have a small kitchen erected for him adjacent to his house. The fences may also be repaired.

Pleasanton may have been unaware that the keeper at Old Field Point was a woman, but he knew of Elizabeth Smith's reputation as a good lighthouse keeper.

Captain Howland brought supplies to Old Field Point on June 17, 1850, reporting the lighthouse and dwelling to be "in good order" and the lighthouse and illuminating apparatus to be clean. He delivered 231 gallons of spring oil and 124 gallons of winter oil.

In early 1856, the lighthouse was given a Fourth Order lens from the Henry-LePaute Company of France, showing a fixed white light. Shortly thereafter, Mary Foster replaced Elizabeth Smith as keeper. Mary would be the last keeper of the original Old Field Light, staying on until June 21, 1869, a service of 13 years. Mary's time as keeper appears to have been largely uneventful, although a storm in December 1859 damaged the station.

A decision was made to replace the old tower in the late 1860s. The plans used were those previously drawn up for the Block Island Lighthouse. In fact, the submitted plans were exactly those of Block Island, with two lines through the words "Block Island" and "Old Field Point" handwritten above them. This design consisted of a granite keepers' quarters, with a cast-iron tower and lantern atop the roof.

The plan for the new Old Field Point Light was approved in April 1867. By the end of 1868, materials for building the new light were on site, but construction did not begin until 1869. The new lighthouse was completed later that year, at a cost of $11,995.42. By this time, local shipbuilding was in its heyday, with shipyards at Port Jefferson, Setauket, and Stony Brook.

Benjamin Floyd was appointed keeper of Old Field Point on June 21, 1869, but was removed on August 9, when George D. Lee was appointed. Lee was a Civil War veteran, having served with the 102nd New York Volunteers for three years, beginning on October 29, 1861.

Lee's father-in-law, Azariah Davis, kept a record of events at and near the lighthouse, including weather, shipwrecks, numbers of ships sighted, visitors, deaths and illnesses of local citizens, and more. In October 1869, Davis chronicled the end of one sailing ship:

> Fri., Oct. 8— . . . Just as I was lighting the lamp, a small schooner, WM. PITTS of N.Y., laden with sand struck a rock a few

National Archives 26 LG 13-33

Old Field Point in the late 1800s.

94

feet East of the light and at 8 PM was filled with water. Capt.'s name Shand.

Sat., Oct. 9—A beautiful morn, wind very light NNE.

J.R. Bayles was here early this morning to examine WM. PITTS, returned & got Capt. Tho. Hallock to come and get her up, but she is still fast on the rock and full of water. Homie [Davis' grandson, Holmes] and I have been to the Port. I took George Crow (a Scotch man), one of the crew of the schooner WM PITTS to the P.O. The other crew hands were Joseph O'Brien and Mike.

Sun., Oct. 10— . . . [Hallock] could not get the WM. PITTS off. The easterly wind and sea have thumped her much but did not move her from the rock.

Mon., Oct. 11– . . . Schooner WM. PITTS is on her beam ends today and appears to be off the rock, some of her stern is off, her rudder unhung. Capt.'s father came today, and they had a loud meeting.

Tues., Oct. 12— . . . The WM. PITTS IS STILL ON BEAM ENDS.

Wed., Oct. 13—Heavy rain, wind NW & heavy sea on.

The WM. PITTS' masts both fell & she turned her keel up & came on shoar [sic].

Thurs., Oct. 14— . . . They have stript the WM. PITTS.

Fri., Oct. 15— . . . George & Mr. Shand have spent the day at the Port and brought sails home belonging to the schooner WM. PITTS.

Sat., Oct. 16— . . . The elder Shand has had an auction today & sold the remains of the WM. PITTS FOR ABOUT $175, with the exception of the sails.

The *Wm. Pitts* was not the only ship to run aground near the light during Davis' stay, but he recorded more than just shipwrecks. Visitors were listed and counted; trips to and from town were noted; the health of family members was recorded; and local and notable deaths and news were written down. Every day, the weather was recorded. In 1870, Davis counted 850 visitors; with 888 in 1871; 1214 in 1872; and 1363 in 1873.

In 1871, the acquisition of a right-of-way became an issue. As was common at other lighthouses, a wealth of negotiation, legal opinions, and paperwork was produced. The right-of-way was purchased in 1872.

Charles F. Jayne became Old Field's next keeper on April 25, 1874. Azariah Davis was still packing on April 30, when he wrote, "[w]e are loading up the goods to leave the U.S.L.H. and are going to Port Jefferson to live in Mr. F.P. Norton's house attached to the drug store." The Lee family would remain in Port Jefferson for many years, with four members of the family serving as Chief of the local fire department between 1906 and 1988.

In 1879, the need for a barn was mentioned in the *Annual Report*. The "distance of the station from any depot of supplies" gave need for plenty of storage room. The existing barn was "ready to drop to pieces," so $500 was requested to build a new one.

A letter from the Secretary of the Treasury, on January 28, 1886, reported the neglect of the keeper to provide assistance to the schooner *Stony Brook* and its captain, Francis Weller, which had run ashore. Keeper Jayne was exonerated, and it was suspected that Captain Weller may have wanted the keeper's job for himself.

Edgar Stanton Maclay was appointed July 26, 1895 to replace Jayne. The year prior to his appointment, Maclay had published a two-volume history of the U.S. Navy. He had also previously built the 100–room Old Field Inn, which burned in 1899. In May of 1897, Maclay sent a bill to Third District Inspector Snow for furnishing meals to some shipwrecked mariners.

Maclay remained on as keeper until September 1, 1900. In 1901, he was dismissed from a post in the New York Navy Yard for criticizing Rear Admiral Winfield Scott Schley in the third volume of his naval history. He later worked for a Brooklyn newspaper and as a researcher in Washington, D.C.

Richard E. Ray replaced Maclay as keeper of the Old Field Light, and would be the last keeper at the station. Keeper Ray rescued two men who had run their power boat aground near the light in 1923, providing them with clothes, food, and shelter for two days.

U.S. Coast Guard photo

Old Field Point after automation. Note the skeleton tower on the left.

The light was removed from the lantern room in 1933, with a light atop the newly-erected 74–foot skeleton tower put in use. The old Fourth Order Fresnel lens was replaced by a DCB-10 aerobeacon.

An act of the 74th Congress on May 28, 1935, authorized the conveyance of the station to the Village of Old Field "for public-park purposes." The conveyance was made on August 9 of that year by Assistant Secretary of Commerce J.M. Johnson. The Coast Guard reclaimed the lighthouse on January 5, 1942, as part of a World War Two naval defense area, and relinquished it at the end of the war.

The 1869 lighthouse regained its light in 1991. It currently houses a Vega VRB-25 optic that shows an alternating green and red flash.

Today, the Village's constable works and lives in the lighthouse, with the Coast Guard maintaining the optic. The tower, originally white, is now black. The station is in generally good condition, with the 1824 keepers' quarters and 1902 oil house still standing. The old keeper's dwelling, used as the Village Hall, is a rare reminder of the Pleasanton era on Long Island.

Photo by the author

Old Field Point in 1999.

Stratford Shoal (Middleground) Lightship and Lighthouse

The Stratford Shoal Light Station, like that at Execution Rocks, stands guard over a treacherous offshore area, midway between the Long Island Sound's north and south shores. Unlike Execution Rocks, however, the Stratford Shoal Light is not always identified as a Long Island lighthouse. Throughout the history of this station, there has been some confusion regarding its state of residence, sometimes listed as New York, and sometimes as Connecticut.

It is said that when Adrian Block sailed up the Long Island Sound around 1614, what is now Stratford Shoal was a series of small islands. Given the shifting sands around Long Island, this would not

U.S. Coast Guard photo

Stratford Shoal Light.

99

be unusual. By the early 1800s, the site contained shoals that posed a hazard to maritime traffic in the Long Island Sound.

On March 3, 1837, $10,000 was appropriated by Congress "[f]or a floating light, to be stationed on or near the Middle Ground, in Long Island Sound, nearly abreast Stratford Point, in the State of New York." Approximately $8500 of the appropriation was spent that year, and a 100–ton ship, framed and planked with white oak, was built in Norfolk, Virginia.

In January 1838, one of the nation's earliest light vessels was stationed off the south side of the shoal in New York waters. At the time, she was called the "Middle Ground floating light," "Stratford Point Light Vessel" or "Stratford Shoal Light Vessel" until 1867, when she received the designation Light Vessel *No. 15* (*LV 15*). The ship had problems right from the start. Her 1200–pound anchor was inadequate, and she was driven off station within eight days. This problem would continue throughout the vessel's stay at Stratford Shoal.

George M. Bache described the site and lightship in his 1838 report:

> The Middle Ground is a dangerous shoal three-quarters of a mile in length, lying about midway between the two shores of the sound; Stratford Point bearing N., distant 5½ miles; Old Field Point S. by W., distant 5 miles. In order to point out the exact position of this shoal, a light-boat was placed off its southeastern extremity in January, 1838 . . . under the charge of a captain and mate, and manned by a crew of four men; ample provision appears to have been made for the accommodation of the crew, and for the stowage of wood and water for four-months' supply, and of oil for one year. The lights are shown from two masts, which are fitted for the purpose—one 40 feet, the other 50 feet in height; each lantern contains a compass-lamp, which is fitted to burn ten wicks.

The 1858 *Annual Report* described *LV 15* as having two fixed reflector lights, at heights of 32 and 40 feet above sea level, and a fog bell. The hull was painted a straw color, with the name of the station "on each quarter in large black letters."

LV 15 was driven from her station by ice three times in early 1868 (once in February, twice in March). The third time, one of her two anchors became fouled in deep water and could not be released, even with the help of a tender. The anchor and 15 fathoms of chain were left in the Long Island Sound.

The 1869 *Annual Report* noted that *LV 15* was "in good condition." That year, new "fire-brick and grates" for the stove were furnished, along with "various small articles of ship chandlery" and other items.

In 1872, the Third District engineer was asked for a report of the cost to replace the lightship at "Stratford Point Shoal, Long Island Sound, New York." After surveying the site, he proposed a lighthouse instead, estimating the cost to be $125,000. The foundation for the new lighthouse was first suggested to be made of "riprap of large irregular blocks of granite from three to five tons each in weight," but in early 1873 further examination suggested that an "iron tubular foundation, or concrete" would work well.

On March 3, 1873, $50,000 was appropriated "[f]or the construction of a light-house to take the place of the light-ship at Stratford shoals, Long Island sound." This appropriation was followed by two more appropriations of $50,000 in 1874 and 1875. Work began in 1873 and expenditures through 1878 would total $140,046.54. On May 11, 1874, the State of New York ceded jurisdiction over "less than one acre" at Stratford Shoal to the federal government for the building of a lighthouse.

In 1874, when a ring of riprap had been completed, the foundation was decided upon as a "granite pier, backed with concrete." During the winter of 1874–1875, the riprap ring filled in with gravel, of which much of the shoal was composed. This delayed the work on the granite pier, but by the end of 1875, the first course of granite was completed and filled in with concrete.

In mid-February, 1875, *LV 15's* long problem with being dragged off station reached a new level, when ice caused the vessel to be driven off station and she ran aground near Orient Point. The lighthouse tenders *Cactus* and *Mistletoe* freed her and brought her to New London for repairs. The following year, she was once again reported off station, this time found near Faulkner's Island, Connecticut.

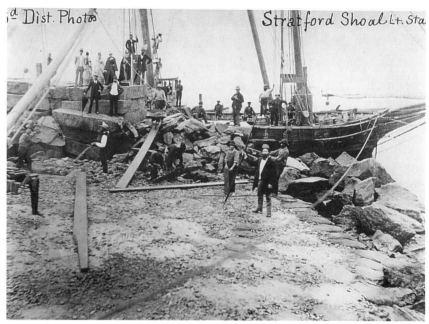

National Archives Photo 26 LG 17-15

Construction at Stratford Shoal, July 29, 1875.

By 1876, the lightship was not in good shape. That year's *Annual Report* stated that "[s]ince the date of last report, no repairs of moment have been made upon this vessel. She is in poor condition, much decayed, and if continued in service will soon require to be practically rebuilt."

By December 1, 1876, the pier of the lighthouse was completed, including the cellar and cisterns. By June 1877, eight courses of the lighthouse's walls had been finished, along with the entire facing of the lighthouse. The lantern was installed in September. The plastering was completed, and the lens, fog bell, and striking apparatus were installed in October and November. On November 8, "in a severe gale, the construction-schooner *Mignonette* broke from her moorings, struck on the rocks, and sunk. The men and most of the materials and utensils were saved, after which the work continued, the men taking up their quarters in the now almost completed building."

On December 15, 1877, the light was lit for the first time. William McGloin, a native of Ireland, had been transferred from *LV 15* (where he had served since February 16, 1876) to the lighthouse on December 4.

The fate of *LV 15* was not glamorous. After a short time as an unused relief vessel, she was sold at auction for $1010. Her final duty was as a floating barracks for workers during the building of the Great Beds Light in New Jersey.

The gravelly shoal that the new light was built upon required a great deal of protection with riprap, as the waves scoured the gravel. By June 1878, over 3000 tons of riprap had been placed, with another 1000 expected to be added.

The new lighthouse held a rotating Fourth Order Fresnel lens in its 8–sided lantern room, with the chain for the clockworks passing through an opening in one corner of the lantern deck, then down and open channel to the floors below. The light exhibited a flash every 30 seconds.

The lighthouse's original illuminating apparatus and fog signal did not remain long. In 1879, the lens was changed to one that flashed every 15 seconds. The following year, it was changed again to show a flash every ten seconds. The 1144–pound fog bell was replaced by a "second-class Daboll fog-trumpet, operated by eighteen-inch caloric engines." At this point, the station was declared to be "in excellent order."

Keeper McGloin was transferred on June 5, 1880. James G. Scott replaced him. Scott remained until September 26, 1885, when he was transferred to Montauk Point.

In 1894, while Richard E. Ray was the keeper, the station received a new lens and the caloric engines were overhauled. The 1895 *Annual Report* mentioned a concern over the fog signal not being powerful enough. It was suggested that the second-class Daboll trumpet might do better if fitted with a Ryder engine and Clayton air compressor. In 1897 and 1898, the caloric engines were replaced with "two Hornsby-Akroyd 3½–horsepower oil engines and improved apparatus to actuate the Daboll trumpet." During the installation of the new apparatus (from December 1, 1897 to January 15, 1898), the station had no fog signal.

Between 1895 and 1902, approximately 1900 tons of riprap were installed around the station to help protect it from the seas and storms. In 1905, a new Fourth Order flashing lens was installed.

Morell E. Hulse was assigned to the three-man station as First Assistant Keeper on April 15, 1905. The Second Assistant Keeper, Julius Koster, had been assigned to the station the previous year. In May 1905, while Head Keeper Gilbert Rulon was ashore, Koster succumbed to the stress of life at an isolated station. Hulse noted that Koster became moody and quiet, and then one night locked himself in the tower and threatened to destroy the light. He did stop it from rotating for a period, before being lured from the tower by Hulse. Koster reportedly tried to take his own life after coming out of the tower, and was dismissed from service not long after.

During Rulon and Hulse's time at Stratford Shoal, the station's third-class Daboll trumpet had a characteristic of six-second blasts, separated by 21 seconds of silence. The lamp in the lantern room at Stratford Shoal was upgraded in November 1912. The old lamp, burning liquid oil, was replaced with an incandescent oil vapor lamp, with 40,000 candlepower.

The third-class Daboll trumpet was removed in 1915. The new apparatus, put into service on February 15, 1915, consisted of

> duplicate first-class automatic air sirens with double mouth horns and duplicate 8 by 8-inch double-acting compressors geared to 18 horsepower single cylinder, horizontal oil engines of the quick-starting type. The air for the sirens [was] . . . passed through a 'reheater' where it [was] heated and expanded by the engine exhaust.

The new fog signal cost $6,000 and was considered to have improved "power and distribution of the sound."

Later that year, the *U. S. Lighthouse Service Bulletin* reported the upgrade, noting the station's location: "Stratford Shoal (Middle Ground) Light and Fog Signal Station, N.Y., is of importance to traffic on Long Island Sound, as it marks a shoal in the direct route of navigation of the numerous vessels plying the Sound." On May 5,

U.S. Coast Guard photo

View from the tower

1921, Keeper Henry R. McCarthy and First Assistant Keeper John J. Horlacher were commended for helping the crew of a boat that had been blown upon the rocks "in a strong northeast gale."

In 1922, keepers McCarthy and J. A. Burk, along with W.G. Gaird, "a workman," helped the four occupants of the powerboat *Gladys*. The boat had been disabled and adrift for 18 hours and those aboard "were in a sick and enfeebled condition from exposure." They were given medicine, clothing, and food, and were stayed at the station until they were able to return to shore.

A radiobeacon was established at Stratford Shoal on March 23, 1927, making it one of five stations in the Third District so equipped. The installation of this equipment cost $2206. In 1932, the radiobeacon's signal was one dot, two dashes, one dot.

In 1931, Keeper Lewis J. Allen was awarded the Service's efficiency pennant for "highest general efficiency" in the Third District for the past year. This entitled him to fly the pennant at his station for the year.

Allen and Assistant Keeper Alfred Auger made a rescue on February 10, 1933 by "[c]hopping away a heavy coating of ice which covered their power boat and its launching gear, and in a strong sea getting clear of the dangerous rocks around the lighthouse." As the *U. S. Lighthouse Service Bulletin* described:

> When the vessel was first sighted in the early morning, the keepers thought that it was having engine trouble and that it would be under way again in a short time. Continued observation showed that something further was wrong, and then the keepers proceeded to the vessel and brought the occupants to the lighthouse when it was learned that they had been without food or heat for 62 hours.

A radio electrician, who was working at the station at the time, made the necessary changes in the radio-beacon transmitting

U.S. Coast Guard photo

Stratford Shoal's Fourth Order lens and clockworks mechanism.

U.S. Coast Guard photo

East side of station.

apparatus so that an emergency call could be made for help. This resulted in an oyster boat coming out that evening and taking the party of 10 ashore.

The ship they had bravely aided was the *Saugatuck*, the occupants of which were in search of a missing boy. The ship's tiller had broken. The boy for whom they had been searching had taken refuge at the Pecks Ledge Light in Connecticut.

In August of 1970, the Stratford Shoal Light was automated, leaving the site without humans assigned to guard it for the first time in 133 years. In clear weather, the light from the tower at Stratford Shoal can still be seen from both shores, as well as the ferry between Bridgeport, Connecticut and Port Jefferson, New York. Whether one views the land under the light as belonging to the people of Connecticut or New York, there is little doubt that the story of the Stratford Shoal Light Station is an integral part of Long Island's maritime history.

The North Fork

Horton Point (1857)

Long Beach Bar (1871, 1990)

Orient Point (1899)

Plum Island (1827, 1869)

Little Gull Island (1806, 1869)

Horton Point

The quaint white lighthouse at Horton Point, perched quietly atop a bluff overlooking the Long Island Sound, leaves little wonder as to why this station was considered good duty by its keepers. Today, it is a destination for lighthouse fans, tourists, and many Long Islanders.

In 1640, Barnabas Horton was one of the earliest European settlers on Long Island. He resided in what was to become the town of Southold. The land upon which the lighthouse sits was the "Cliff Lot" of Horton's 1640 land grant.

Local oral history says that a young Colonel George Washington, on his way to Boston on military business, stopped at Horton Point in 1756. He discussed the possibility of placing a lighthouse at the spot with Ezra L'Hommidieu, who had recently married Charity Floyd, the sister of Declaration of Independence signer William Floyd. L'Hommidieu would later be greatly involved in the procurement of land for, and the placement of, the Montauk Point Lighthouse, as well as many other important Long Island matters. The site was indeed a good one for a lighthouse—a rocky shoal and sand bars off the point had claimed many ships over the years. When the young colonel became the first President of the United States, he did not forget the need for a lighthouse at Horton Point. Washington commissioned the light in 1790, but its construction would not begin until 1856, 100 years after he had first recommended the project.

In 1838, George Bache recommended a "buoy on the northern extremity of the shoal from the westward of Horton's point," adding that "[v]essels not unfrequently ground here."

In a letter to the Light-House Board on November 22, 1853, William Brown, master of the steamer *Bay State*, suggested that a "fixed light upon Horton's point would be of great value to those who navigate the Long Island sound." Brown noted the "existing deficiency of lights upon the Long Island shore between Old Field Point light and Plumb Island light." Petitions for the construction of a lighthouse at Horton's Point were transmitted to the Light-House

Photo by the author

May 2000 photograph showing the anchor of the Commodore,
which wrecked near Horton Point in December 1866.

Board in 1854. One of these petitions was from Connecticut
Congressman Nathan Belcher; the other from L. E. Daboll in New
London, Connecticut.

On August 3, 1854, Congress appropriated $4000 for the proposed lighthouse. This amount was deemed "wholly inadequate" by the Light-house Board. An additional $3500 would be appropriated on August 18, 1856.

Jurisdiction over the site for the lighthouse was ceded by the New York Legislature on January 24, 1855, and the site was surveyed in July 1855. Efforts began that year to purchase the site from its owners, Charles Payne, a retired whaler, and his wife, Hannah. The Paynes had bought eight acres of land for $100 in 1850. They agreed to sell the "Cliff Lot" to the government for $550 after a great deal of negotiating.

The land was purchased and all the paperwork completed by early 1857. On April 4, 1857, Third District Engineer J. C. Duane submitted his plan an estimate for a lighthouse and dwelling on Horton's Point. The cornerstone for the lighthouse was set on June 9, 1857.

William Sinclair, a Scottish immigrant who had been naturalized in 1823 and was previously an engineer at the Brooklyn Navy Yard, oversaw the building of the lighthouse. During the construction, he boarded at the home of John Booth. Sinclair later married Booth's sister, China. He was appointed as the Horton Point Light's first keeper on June 4, 1857, at an annual salary of $400. George Booth was assigned as his assistant on November 14, 1857.

When finished, the structure consisted of a two-story, Federal style dwelling and a 58–foot-high square tower, both made of brick and stone. Connecting the tower and dwelling was a cut-stone arched windway. All were built upon a granite foundation. In the iron lantern room, a Third Order lens cast a fixed white light. The lens was from the Parisian firm of L. Sautter & Company. No fog signal was installed at the station, nor ever would be. Sinclair reported the cost of the lighthouse as $12,212.

A climb to the top of the tower required that the keeper scale the 29 wooden steps on its spiral staircase and two ladders of eleven steps each. When the lighthouse was built, the outside of the lantern could only be reached by a balcony and iron staircase outside the watch room. The iron lantern room was designed with 10 panes of glass. The 10–sided roof was adorned with rainspout covers shaped like gargoyle heads. A Third Order Fresnel lens, which "formed a part of a revolving apparatus" exhibited a flashing white light. From the top of the tower, over 100 feet above sea level, it was possible to see the light at Shinnecock Bay, built about the same time, on the south shore of Long Island.

Albert J. Tillinghast replaced William Sinclair on April 13, 1861, when Sinclair resigned and returned to the Brooklyn Navy Yard. When Tillinghast took charge of the lighthouse, his pay was withheld for a short time due to the misplacement of his appointment papers. This was rectified, and he remained as the keeper at Horton Point for over five years. Barnabas Pike replaced Tillinghast, serving from October 19, 1866 to April 15, 1869.

An oddity in the records appears in the 1867 *Annual Report*, which listed the station as "Horton's Point, Conn." The report described it as having a wooden tower and dwelling, as well as a fog bell, with all being in poor condition. The 1868 report did not refer to the light as being in Connecticut, nor did it make any reference to a wooden tower. It did, however, describe the station as being:

U.S. Coast Guard photo

The southwest corner of the lighthouse in 1934.

. . . in bad condition. The lantern deck (of stone) leaks badly and the water filters through the wall at the base, making the rooms for the storage of oil and other supplies very damp. The roof of the dwelling leaks and the walls and floors need repairs, and all the woodwork requires painting. It is proposed to cover the stone deck of the tower with a cast-iron deck plate; to repair the roof; to provide a proper storeroom, by enclosing a portion of the passage-way from the dwelling to the tower; to repair the barn and fences, and to repaint all the woodwork.

The 1869 *Annual Report* indicated that the conditions were the same, but the 1870 report indicated that an appropriation had been made, and repairs were progressing. By mid-1871, the repairs were completed. Rooms had been added for the assistant keeper and for "the Light-house supplies." The dwelling was repaired and painted, and a cast-iron lantern deck installed. The old lens was replaced by a fixed Third Order lens. The "entire outside brick-work of the tower and dwelling, which was found in a state of rapid decay, caused by the action of the atmosphere and frost, was covered with a coating of Portland cement-mortar." The barn and fences were also repaired.

J. W. Squires had been appointed keeper of the Horton Point Light on April 15, 1869. He remained until 1871. Daniel Goldsmith replaced him on June 1 of that year. On that same day, George Prince was appointed as Assistant Keeper. Goldsmith and Prince had some problems with the quality of water from the station's cistern. It was determined that the water was "not fit for use," and a well was requested.

A report of the "inhumanity" of Goldsmith toward the shipwrecked crew of the schooner *Louis Walsh* was made in early 1873. This report was later determined to be a "fabrication."

George Prince, a Civil War veteran, replaced Goldsmith on February 24, 1877. His salary was set at $560 per year. Goldsmith's son, Daniel, Jr., was assigned as Prince's assistant a month later.

The Assistant Keeper position at Horton Point was abolished on September 14, 1881. To compensate for the additional duties, Prince's salary was raised to $600 per year. Seven years later, Prince's salary was reduced to $560. An oil house was built at the

From the author's collection

Early 1900s postcard.

station in 1891. In September 1896, Prince was discharged for "drunkenness and neglect of duty."

Robert Ebbitts assumed the keeper's position on September 11, 1896. Ebbitts had been born in New York, but moved to Orient with his adopted family when he was a young boy. During the Civil War, Ebbitts served with Company H, 127th Regiment, New York Volunteers. After the war, he served as master of several coasting vessels, then joined the Lighthouse Service. Ebbitts had previously served as Assistant Keeper at Plum Island (February 1892 to June 1893) and Keeper at Cedar Island (June 1893 to September 1896).

In 1903, Ebbitts fell from a ladder and broke his left leg. Stella M. Prince, daughter of former keeper George Prince, filled in for Ebbitts until he recovered.

The lamp was changed in 1907 to an incandescent oil vapor lamp. This greatly increased the power of the light.

Ebbitts was twice criticized by the Lighthouse Board. In 1907, he left some "greasy rags" in the tower. The following year, he had been caught with a lantern room that was not up to the Board's cleanliness standards. He was chided for his "neglect of duty" and warned that

116

"more drastic measures" would be taken if future inspections revealed additional violations.

Ebbitts left the Horton Point Light in May of 1919, after nearly 30 years of lighthouse duty. He remained in Southold, and was one of the area's last remaining Civil War veterans when he died on June 7, 1926. He was 82 years of age.

George Erhardt replaced Ebbitts and would be the last keeper of the Horton Point Light. Erhardt had been an Assistant Keeper at Orient Point, Plum Island, and Plum Beach, Rhode Island, and Keeper at Long Beach Bar. Erhardt, born in Brownsville, New York, has served in the Army's Seventh Cavalry. His first assignment was to care for George Custer's horse, Comanche, after Custer was killed at Little Bighorn. Erhardt also fought at Wounded Knee in 1890.

The tower at Horton Point went dark in July of 1933. An automated flashing green DCB-10 optic atop a forty foot steel skeletal structure in front of the old lighthouse took over the aid to

U.S. Coast Guard photo
The skeleton tower (to the right of the lighthouse) in July 1934.

navigation duties. The Southold Park District was given a five-year revocable license to use the site on November 1, 1933.

Erhardt remained at the lighthouse even after automation. He was responsible for maintaining the automated lights at Horton Point and Shinnecock Bay until his retirement in 1938.

On December 10, 1937, the site, consisting of 7.62 acres, was conveyed to the Southold Park District from the federal government for public park purposes. On January 2, 1942, the Southold Park District was informed that the U.S. Coast Guard would be using and occupying the site for naval defense purposes. Park Commissioner F. W. Stokes responded three days later, indicating that the site had been vacated.

During World War II, the Civilian Defense Corps and various military units used the tower as a lookout. After the war, the lighthouse remained abandoned for many years.

There was talk of demolishing the lighthouse in the 1960s, due to its hazardous condition. The Southold Historical Society and Matt Booth, a member of the Southold Park District commission, prevented its demolition.

Efforts to restore the light began in the 1970s. At that time, a nautical museum was established in the keepers' dwelling, which opened in 1977. The following year, the DCB-10 optic on the skeleton tower was changed to an FA-251.

In 1990, an intense restoration effort got under way, funded by the Southold Park District and Southold Historical Society. An estimate of $30,000 to repair the tower proved too costly, so the restoration was done by mostly volunteer efforts, cutting the cost to $3000. Some of the money was raised by small benefit concerts on the grounds. The tower was repaired, both inside and out, and the FA-251 optic was installed in the old tower on June 7, 1990. The skeletal tower was demolished and the Coast Guard donated a flagpole to be erected on its old base.

The lighthouse has become a popular attraction, and its nautical museum hosts a great deal of information and many artifacts. The Southold Historical Society has tried to reclaim the original Third

Order lens over the years, but it has not yet been located. The Coast Guard has, however, loaned the society an 1850s Fourth Order lens to display. This lens, still on display at the lighthouse, is one of the oldest lenses on Long Island. It was made by L. Sautter & Company, the same manufacturer of the light's original lens. These days the museum contains a myriad of local maritime and lighthouse artifacts, including some of the original keeper's logs.

Marguerite Conway, the daughter of George Erhardt, helped to guide the restoration. One of Ms. Conway's contributions was the suggestion for the planting of the hydrangea bush near the porch of the keeper's dwelling. A photograph of Ms. Conway as a seven-year-old girl in the 1920s showed her and her father standing behind such a bush. This photograph now resides in the museum.

The porch on the keepers' dwelling was restored in 1993. The following year, the lighthouse was listed on the National Register of Historic Places. Other restoration efforts since 1990 have resulted in the rebuilding of the station's oil house, the restoration of the basement, and the establishment of parking on the site. Both the oil

Photo by the author

Horton Point Light in May 2000.

house and basement have been made part of the museum, which boasts artifacts such as the lighthouse's original oil-filling cabinet and several brass U.S. Lighthouse Service pieces.

The FA 251 optic installed in the tower in 1990 had a characteristic of one green flash every ten seconds. The optic was changed again in 1999 to a Vega VRB-25, the new standard optic for U.S. lighthouses, but has retained the same flashing characteristic.

The Horton Point Light's future looks promising. It continues to be a very popular attraction, with its excellent nautical museum, friendly and knowledgeable volunteers, beautiful park grounds, and scenic view. It also continues to cast a light out to mariners in the Long Island Sound, just as George Washington and Ezra L'Hommidieu had hoped almost 250 years ago.

Long Beach Bar

The history of the Long Beach Bar Light Station boasts some of the island's more unusual lighthouse stories: from the screwpile foundation—odd this far north—to its destruction by arson, its "rebuilding," and the recent controversy regarding ownership of the lighthouse replica on the site, it may have the oddest history of any Long Island light station.

In 1868, a petition was received by the Light-House Board for an unlighted beacon on the sand bar known as the "Long Beach bar." The Third District Inspector was in favor of the idea, and it was recommended that a granite beacon be installed on the spot. This recommendation was made in 1868 and 1869 *Annual Reports*.

On July 15, 1870, Congress approved an appropriation of $17,000 for "a lighted beacon on Long Beach Bar, at the entrance to Peconic Bay, eastern end of Long Island." Plans were submitted for a 2½-story wooden lighthouse, to be constructed on a screwpile

Postcard from the author's collection
Long Beach Bar Light on its original foundation.

foundation. By the middle of 1871 the "entire iron and wood-work" were completed.

When finished, the Long Beach Bar Light had a kitchen, "Sitting & Dining Room," an oil room and a hall on the first floor, and two bedrooms and two chambers on the second floor. A wooden tower on the front of the dwelling housed the light about 54 feet above sea level. The metal piles were screwed ten feet into the seabed, then strengthened with metal braces. A walkway surrounded the first floor.

The fixed red light at Long Beach Bar was sent out through a Fifth Order Fresnel lens. The fog signal was a bell, struck every 15 seconds by machinery.

The light at Long Beach Bar was first lit December 1, 1871. The records show an odd series of events concerning the lighthouse's keepers. William Thompson was appointed as its first keeper November 25, 1871, but resigned on December 22. His replacement, Cornelius Oakes, had his appointment revoked on January 3, 1872, and Thompson had to stay on. Lewis Thompson, presumably a relative, was appointed as his assistant on January 12.

In February 1872, ice threatened the station. It destroyed the dock and shook the lighthouse. The attack of the ice became so bad one month later that the keeper and assistant abandoned their posts for two nights "during which no light was exhibited nor fog-bell sounded."

William and Lewis Thompson were replaced by George E. Corey and E. A. Hempstead on April 18, 1872. The latter only remained until September 14, and was replaced by George Fenton.

On June 10, 1872, Congress appropriated $20,000 for "completing the light-house . . . according to the original design." This reference seems to have been made to the protection of the station "by an ice breaker of granite blocks placed in riprap," which had been mentioned in the 1871 *Annual Report*. This protection was completed by mid-1873.

George W. Fenton became the keeper of Long Beach Bar on March 22, 1873. On May 2, Elisha J. Mitchell was appointed as his assistant. The two would serve together for over eight years. The name of Fenton would fill the Long Beach Bar keeper's position for over 22 years.

The New York Legislature granted federal jurisdiction over the land under the lighthouse on May 11, 1874. This land included a 100–foot-diameter circle. The land was not transferred to the federal government and the State reserved concurrent jurisdiction. This concurrent jurisdiction allowed the State to enforce laws on the site "as if such [federal] jurisdiction had not been ceded, except so far as such process may affect the real or personal property of the United States." This cession of jurisdiction, as well as an exemption from state "taxes, assessments, and other charges which may be levied or imposed," was to "continue in respect to said property so long as the same shall . . . be used for public purposes and no longer."

On February 20, 1881, ice threatened the station again. Fenton reported: "Ice packed under the house from the east with flood tide, and broke three spikes [screwpiles], and nearly all of the braces. The ice was two feet thick. Had to steady the lamp lenses by hand to save them." The piles and bracing were repaired, and another 3000 tons of granite were placed to help protect the site. Ice would continue to be a problem at Long Beach Bar.

Elisha Mitchell was removed from his post on December 19, 1881. George Fenton's new assistant, appointed Acting Assistant Keeper on January 19, 1882, was his son, Charles Fenton.

More stone was placed at Long Beach Bar in 1883 "to prevent further injury from ice-fields." A platform and landing wharf were also constructed that year. It seems as though ice once again damaged the foundation, as the 1886 *Annual Report*, in its reference to Long Beach Bar, stated that "[t]he damage done to its foundation was repaired and a safer arrangement was made for securing and landing its boat."

When George Fenton passed away, Charles Fenton succeeded his father as keeper on May 18, 1887. His assistant, appointed nine days later, was W. P. Gibbs, a Navy veteran from Massachusetts. Gibbs remained nearly two years (he was transferred April 1, 1889), and was followed by George P. Porter.

Charles B. Moore, from the nearby town of Orient, replaced Porter as Fenton's assistant on October 14, 1889. As with many keepers in the late 1800s, Moore was a Civil War veteran. He had served with Company H, 127th Regiment, New York Volunteers.

Moore's daughter, Ruth, joined him at the lighthouse. Over the next few months, Charles Fenton developed an affection for Ruth. In time, they were married. They only came ashore for the day of the wedding, then returned to the lighthouse, "to spend their honeymoon at the place both loved the best." Charles and Ruth Fenton spent the rest of Fenton's career at the Long Beach Bar Light.

During Charles Fenton's duty as keeper, ice remained a problem. In 1893, "the landing wharf [was] destroyed by ice." The wharf was rebuilt as a "crib landing wharf, filled with stone, and resting on large cut stone at low-water line, and a plank deck fitted with iron crane for

U.S. Lighthouse Society Photo

Long Beach Bar with its screwpile foundation and 1893 landing wharf.

hoisting the boat, connected with the gallery of the light-house by steps" was also built at that time.

The fog bell's striking mechanism was damaged by a falling weight on March 18, 1899. Until the mechanism was replaced and put into service on June 22, no fog signal was sounded at the station.

An article in the April 1956 edition of the *The Long Island Forum*, by Captain Eugene S. Griffing, told some stories of Long Beach Bar during "Charlie" Fenton's time. Griffing, who remembered "[t]he old Long Beach red fixed light" in his "youthful years as a commercial fisherman out of East Marion," reported that the buildup of rock around the light's foundation had created "a pond in the center which in time became the habitat of fish and crabs." Griffing referred to the station's fog bell "on the southwest porch of the building" as "a welcome sound constantly ringing through a fog" and described the mariner's welcome view of a lighthouse: "Many times I have peered into the distance to catch a glimpse of that light and what a gratifying sight it was on a dark and stormy night, just off the starboard bow. Across the bay was home and good sleep between clean sheets for a couple of nights before returning to the fishing banks and the traps for another week."

The camaraderie between lightkeepers and mariners was evident during Fenton's time. According to Griffing, "[t]hree blasts from a vessel's foghorn or whistle as it passed the lighthouse always brought the keeper out on the porch with his binoculars and Ruthie beside him waving an apron."

Griffing's sister, a church organist, once visited the Fentons for nearly two weeks. At the time, there was an organ at the lighthouse, and Fenton played the fiddle. According to Griffing, "it must have been a very pleasant combination for the Fentons and their guest."

On October 21, 1905, Charles Fenton resigned as keeper of the Long Beach Bar Light. His wife's doctor had forbidden her to remain at the station due to poor health, so the couple decided to live out the rest of their lives on a ten-acre farm they had inherited. Bad weather prevented the couple from leaving the station until November 8.

Photo courtesy of Violet Marquis
William Maynard Chapel (left) at Long Beach Bar,
between 1908 and 1913.

William Janse, who had been appointed Fenton's assistant upon Charles Moore's death in 1902, became Long Beach Bar's head keeper on November 1, 1905. His first assistant was Charles Turnblad, appointed November 17. Turnblad was followed by William M. Chapel, who would become the keeper on May 1, 1909.

In 1915, Keeper George Ehrhardt and his assistant, J. Hamilton, discovered an abandoned motor boat, the *Kitty*, in the vicinity of the station. They "[p]icked up" the boat and "turned it over to civil authorities."

On Saturday, June 13, 1925, William Janse, who had spent seven years at Long Beach Bar, died at his home in Greenport. He had retired ten years earlier. Janse had been born in New York City around 1855. He had also served as an assistant at Plum Island for eight years, and as the keeper of the Stamford Harbor Light in Connecticut. Janse must have been a popular member of the local lightkeeper community, as the pallbearers at his funeral were "William Chapel, Sr. Keeper, Plum Island Light; William Chapel Jr., Keeper Penfield Light; Albert Baker, Keeper Long Beach Light; Mamuel [sic] Freitas, Keeper Orient Point Light; William Baker former Keeper Orient Point Light and Byron Wetmore, former Keeper Plum Island Light." Janse was buried in the Stirling Cemetery in Greenport.

In 1926, the physical appearance of the Long Beach Bar Light was changed, as a reinforced concrete foundation replaced the

U.S. Lighthouse Society Photo

Long Beach Bar after 1926.

screwpiles, and the gallery around the first floor was removed. A central steam heating system was installed in the basement created by the new foundation. The lighthouse also received a new bathroom, with a flushing toilet.

The year 1929 saw another death at Long Beach Bar. Keeper Richard White's wife, Pearl, died on May 11, 1929. Her remains were interred at Torrington, Connecticut, where she had been born and her son, George Weller, lived.

In 1935, when the Cedar Island Lighthouse was replaced by an automated light, William Follett succeeded Gustav Axelson the keeper of the Long Beach Bar Light. Mrs. Follett, not accustomed to riprap, traversed the rocks carefully. When she went back across them a year later, she would never return to the lighthouse, preferring to live ashore.

Life at Long Beach Bar was much more difficult for the aging lighthouse keeper than his previous assignment at Cedar Island. Even launching the boat, which at Cedar Island had meant pushing off the sand, was more demanding. Long Beach Bar had a landing pier, requiring the operation of a hand winch. The increased difficulties required that Follett's grandson, Bill Allen, quit school and stay with his grandfather to help with lighthouse duties.

William Follett and Bill Allen weathered the 1938 hurricane at the Long Beach Bar Light. Waves crashed into and over the lighthouse. The waves and wind, blew over the chimney, blew out windows, and tainted the fresh water supply with salt water. As with other local lighthouses, the station's boats were lost in the storm. The lighthouse did not take as much damage as other, more exposed stations the in the area—the *Lighthouse Service Bulletin* described the "principal damage" as having been at Latimer Reef, North Dumpling, Race Rock, Little Gull Island, and Orient Point—but it must have been nonetheless harrowing.

Bill's younger brother, Warren, spent the summers at the lighthouse, going to school in Rhode Island the rest of the year. When Warren finished school in 1939, he did not want to leave the lighthouse and his beloved grandparents. Grandpa Follett informed Warren that his lighthouse career would soon be over, and that he should get on with his life. He joined the Signal Corps. While Warren was in the military, William Follett retired from his lighthouse career, and passed away not long after.

The 1942 and 1946 *Light Lists* reported an 870–candlepower fixed red light at Long Beach Bar was coming from an incandescent oil vapor lamp and Fourth Order lens. This information conflicts with the first-hand accounts of Warren Allen, who says that, "in 1943 when Bill and I were out to the light to look at the old homestead, there was nothing there. No boats, no oil tank, and nothing in the tower."

The Long Beach Bar Light was officially decommissioned in 1948. Shifting Long Island sands had created shoaling that made it necessary to replace the lighthouse with a lighted buoy further from shore.

On May 21, 1952, the Commander of the Third Coast Guard District declared the Long Beach Bar Light excess property. The decision was made to sell the wooden lighthouse, but the federal government needed to first find out exactly what it could sell. Between 1953 and 1955, this subject was the subject of correspondence between the Third Coast Guard District, the Attorney General of New York State, and General Services Administration. It was agreed by all that the land under the lighthouse had never been the property of the United States, although the State of New York had allowed its use for federal lighthouse purposes.

On October 18, 1955, the General Service Administration's Assistant Regional Counsel, Paul F. Cirillo, recommended to the Real Property Disposal Division "that attempts be made to dispose of the structure for offsite use." This recommendation was not taken, as it was determined that "the cost of removing the building would have been prohibitive" and its sale would have been difficult.

The auction of the lighthouse (Disposal No. 2PS-184) was advertised in the November 3 *News Review* and November 4 *The Suffolk Times*. The property for purchase was described as:

> BUILDING ONLY – 2½ story wood frame structure situated approx. 650 yards southwest from Long Beach Point, off Gardiner's

Bay, Long Island, New York. Structure is erected on a Marine Site surrounded by water.

The Orient Marine Historical Association submitted a bid of $1710 on November 30, 1955. This was a considerable sum, given the fact that the fair value of the building had been determined in February by the General Services Administration to be "zero." The other six bids, submitted by private individuals, ranged from $52 to $212.

The final payment from the Orient Marine Historical Association, Inc., to the General Services Administration was made on February 29, 1956. The Association's Secretary, William H. Gesell, handled the sale.

To many, the sale of the lighthouse to a membership corporation seemed like a good thing. Captain Griffing expressed his sentiment in his 1956 *The Long Island Forum* article when he said that "it's nice to know that, at least, the old structure has been acquired for preservation as a monument to the North Fork's romantic past."

Unfortunately, there was no way to keep the abandoned lighthouse safe. On July 4, 1963, arsonists burned the structure. The loss of the 91–year-old Long Beach Bar Light was considered by some to be "a major tragedy."

Police investigated and rewards were offered, but no one was ever convicted. To this day, 40 years later, there are those in the area who say they know who lit the fire, but that the arsonists' connections prevented their prosecution.

The site was eventually marked as "Lt. Ho. Ruins" on charts. The only remnants of the lighthouse were the dilapidated concrete foundation and the rocks that had been deposited to protect the site.

In the late 1980s, the building of a replica of the Long Beach Bar was proposed. A nonprofit corporation was set up, funds were raised, and a shell resembling the original lighthouse was built on land, then placed on the site in September 1990. Although the new replica incorporated major differences from the original lighthouse, many local citizens were happy to once again see a lighthouse at Long

Photo by the author

Long Beach Bar Light in 1999.

Beach Bar. Perhaps even more welcomed by some was the steady white light that shined from its lantern room.

The East End Seaport Museum and Marine Foundation has maintained the lighthouse since 1990, with the Coast Guard caring for the optic. It has been the only lighthouse on Long Island that allows for overnight stays.

An odd twist to the station's history began in January 2001, when one of the Seaport's founders created a new nonprofit corporation, with a name, address and phone number similar to the Seaport's, and began an effort to wrest ownership of the light from the Seaport. The corporation began raising funds for the Long Beach Bar Light, and eventually gained the backing of a Maine-based lighthouse group. In early 2003, the corporation cut the Seaport's locks off of the lighthouse, posted signs warning trespassers, and began advertising events at the lighthouse. The Seaport obtained an injunction against the group, which is still in effect as this book goes to press. Legal appeals and great expenditures of funds that could otherwise be used for historic preservation and education are expected in this battle.

The Long Beach Bar Light Station's history has been filled with difficulties. From the attacks of ice, and deaths at the lighthouse, to arson and a current struggle for ownership, the station has seen more than its share of problems. Hopefully, one day the site will be free of controversy, and will be a monument to the legacy of which the original Long Beach Bar Light was an important part.

Orient Point

Known to some Long Islanders as the "Coffee Pot," the Orient Point Light guards the end of Oyster Pond Reef. It represents a trend toward the end of American lighthouse construction, of using less-expensive, prefabricated structures to save money. These utilitarian lighthouses represent a far cry from many of the earlier, more stylistic lights.

Prior to the establishment of a manned lighthouse, several efforts were made to mark the dangerous reef. A beacon on the reef was

Photo by the author

The Orient Point Light in 1999.

carried away by ice in 1896, and a "lighted beacon and fog signal," with an estimated cost of $5000, was recommended.

Local Congressmen and citizens had petitioned the government for a lighthouse on the point several times by 1890. Congressman Richard C. McCormick introduced a bill in Congress, H.R. 853, in January, 1896, which provided for "the erection of a lighthouse at Orient Point, Long Island, New York" as well as some minor lights. In February, Acting Treasury Secretary S. Wike reported that the matter had been "referred to the Light-House Board, which has replied that it recommends the establishment of a lighthouse and steam whistle at Orient Point or Oyster Pond Reef, at the entrance of Plum Gut."

On June 4, 1897, $30,000 was appropriated for a lighthouse to replace the old beacon. By mid-1898, plans and specifications drawn up by Third District Engineer David Porter Heap were ready. The plan was to use curved, cast-iron plates, bolted together with flanges on the inside of the plates. The 1899 *Annual Report* of the Light House Board told the story up to that point:

> On October 10, 1898, 48 plates, two lower courses of the foundation cylinder were delivered. . . . On October 26, the second course of plates had been sunk in position when a gale swept them away, breaking 20 beyond repair and damaging 19 others. On April 20, 1899, the iron cylinder plates to replace those broken in the gale were delivered and the work of erection was resumed. On May 31, 1899, the foundation bed was completed ready to receive the cylinder plates. On June 1, 1899, the first course of cylinder plates was erected and the concrete filling was begun. On June 13, 1899, the second course of cylinder plates was erected. On June 30, 1899, the third course of cylinder plates was erected, but not entirely bolted together; the concrete filling was completed to within 3 feet of the top of the second course of cylinder plates. The entire metal work of the superstructure was delivered on July 4, 1899.

When the structure was completed, the interior was lined with bricks, as was the basement. The cast-iron stairs necessary to ascend the structure were set into the brick of the outside walls, and separated from the living quarters by an iron wall. The finished, dark brown lighthouse looked to many like a coffee pot, and earned that nickname.

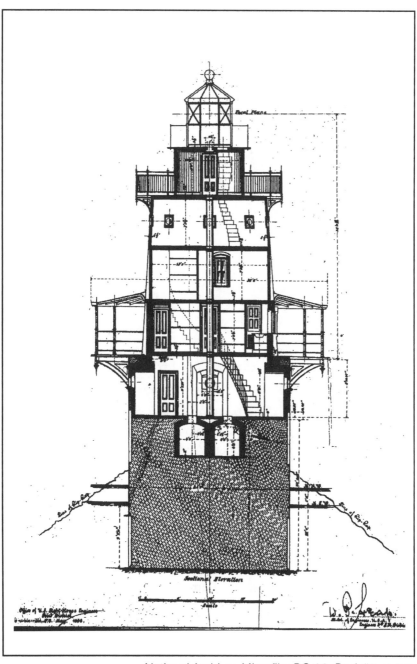

National Archives Microfilm RG 26, Red #5, 3-3-0

Heap's plans for the Orient Point Light.

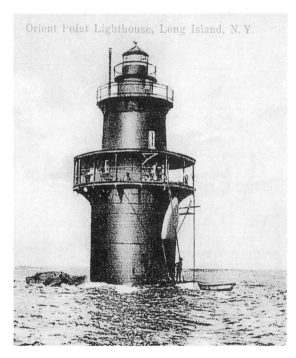

Orient Point Lighthouse, Long Island, N. Y.

Pre-1902 view of the Orient Point Light.

Postcard from the author's collection

By early November, the tower was ready for its lens. On November 10, a red Fifth Order light was established, casting a light from 64 feet above sea level. This proved too dim, and was replaced by a Fourth Order lens on May 1, 1900. One month later, "a blower siren signal was established, consisting of two 2½-horsepower oil engines, a blower, a siren, and a trumpet."

Norwegian native Ole N. A. Anderson was appointed as first keeper of the Orient Point Light on November 1, 1899, earning $600 per year. Silas Stanton replaced Anderson on August 20, 1901. George Ehrhardt, who would later become the last keeper of the Horton Point Light, was appointed as Assistant Keeper on December 31, 1902.

As with all offshore lights, Orient Point required protection from the sea and ice. Between September 1902 and May 15, 1903, approximately 9244 tons of riprap were deposited around the lighthouse to protect it from the elements.

A Daboll trumpet operated by compressed air replaced the original blower siren signal in 1905. The characteristic was a three-second blast, with a 17–second interval.

On June 16, 1906, Jorgen Bakken replaced Stanton, remaining until being replaced by Charles E. Whitford in 1911. Assistant

Keeper John McCarthy passed away in April 1924. He was replaced by John Wallwork, a native of Westerly, Rhode Island. On May 23, a machinist from the Tompkinsville depot, Walter Gill, was on the station repairing the oil engines that ran the fog signal. In the morning, Keeper Manuel Freitas rowed Gill ashore and returned to the station. In the afternoon, Wallwork rowed ashore to pick up provisions and bring Gill back with him. While Wallwork was ashore, the winds picked up and the ebb tide set in, making the seas rough. On the way back to the lighthouse, with Gill aboard, Wallwork's boat was swamped. Freitas had been watching them, and saw them struggle for a moment, then disappear. He launched the station's larger boat, but as he neared the site where they had gone under, he could not find the boat or its occupants. He returned to the lighthouse and called the Rocky Point Life Saving Station and New London, where the tender *Hawthorne* was anchored. The surfmen, in their motorized surf boat, and the *Hawthorne* arrived quickly, but were unable to find any sign of the boat or men. The boat was found the following Monday near Fisher's Island, but the bodies still had not been found a week later.

One Orient Point keeper during the 1920s was William Oliver "Willie" Chapel, son of Plum Island Keeper William Maynard Chapel. Another 1920s assistant keeper was Bill Baker. While stationed there, he became enamored of one of the girls at the Plum Island Light, Elsie Chapel (Willie's sister). Bill and Elsie were later married and ended up living in Medford.

Photo courtesy of Violet Marquis

William Oliver Chapel
at Orient Point Light.

The building of the Orient Point Light, June to September 1899.

Photos courtesy of U.S. Coast Guard Historian's Office

Descendants of Bill and Elsie still reside on Long Island, and are supporters of local lighthouse preservation.

On September 6, 1936, Keeper Marvin Andrews used the station's motorboat to rescue "three persons aboard a sloop which was dismantled near the station." For this rescue, Andrews was commended by the Secretary of Commerce.

The illuminating apparatus was upgraded in 1939, with an incandescent oil vapor lamp installed inside the Fourth Order lens. The characteristic remained a fixed red light.

The station was still considered "operationally necessary" in 1950, when BM1 Forrest W. Suell was the light's keeper. The installation of "sanitary and heating facilities" at the station, with an estimated cost of $11,000, had been under consideration since the previous year. There was, at that time, discussion about operating the light remotely from Plum Island, but the funds for conversion to remote operation appear to not have been available.

On April 9, 1958, the Coast Guard Cutter *Hawthorne* removed the personnel and furniture from the Orient Point Light. The light's last keeper, John R. Kettering, was transferred to Plum Island at his own request, so he could remain near his family in Riverhead. A press release from the Commander of Group New London to the *New London Day* stated that "[p]resent day living standards require adequate facilities and pleasant quarters which are difficult to realize on small cylindrical stations. Modern engineering has solved the problem and realized economy with equal reliability by having the sound of footsteps replaced by the click of micro-switches and solenoid valves." The release also mentioned that Kettering "expressed no regret when he hauled down the flag and closed the door on 59 years of manned attendance."

In 1967, the Orient Point Light still looked like a coffee pot, painted in brown. Its flashing red light was reportedly visible 14 miles, and the fog signal emitted a two-second blast every 16 seconds.

In 1970, the Coast Guard announced plans to demolish the lighthouse. *The Suffolk Times* reported that a "U.S. Navy ordinance disposal team will use explosives to demolish the familiar 'Coffee

Pot.'" It was to be replaced with "a reinforced pipe tower with day marks on the platform sides, which will also have a light and fog horn for navigational aid." An outcry from the community, perhaps the most effective form of historic preservation, caused the reconsideration of the idea. The Coast Guard sent engineers to the site, but did not say much about its future for some time. In October of 1973, work began, without warning, to patch up the 74–year-old lighthouse. Holes in the foundation were fixed, and an epoxy-based paint was applied to the lighthouse after sandblasting.

The Orient Point Light still stands and serves, albeit without its keepers or the covered gallery they once walked upon. Gone also is its all brown color, with the lower part of its tower now dressed in white. Thousands of ferry riders see the old cast-iron light each year as they traverse the waters between Orient Point and New London.

Plum Island

About 110 miles east of New York City lies Plum Island. This island has been known for many things over the years, including farming, fishing, a large fort, an off-limits animal disease center, and a lighthouse. Although the lighthouse is no longer active and has deteriorated, it still represents an important part of Long Island's heritage.

The waterway between Plum Island and Oysterpond Point (now Orient Point) has long been known as Plum Gut. Tidal waters of the Long Island Sound flow through this constriction, creating a rapid tide.

In very early times the island was known as the Isle of Patmos. Later, it became known as Plumb Island, then Plum Island. Some say it was named for beach plums growing there, others suggest that there was a Plumb family involved on the island at one time. It has also been reported that in early colonial times the island was still

Photo courtesy of Jim House

Plum Island Lighthouse in 1995.

connected to Long Island, with settlers taking their livestock across what is now Plum Gut to graze. This seems unlikely, considering the long history of navigation in the channel by large ships.

Plum Island's first non-native owner was Samuel Wyllys, who bought the island from Wyandanch, chief of the Montauks, on April 27, 1659. The price was "a coat, a barrel of biskitt, 100 muxes [a tool for making wampum] and fish hooks."

For over 150 years, the island was used for farming and grazing. Wyllys sold the island to Joseph Dudley in 1686. In turn, Dudley sold the western half to Joseph Beebe. By 1804, it was inhabited by six families, and was known for its excellent land and abundant fish. By 1826, Richard Jerome and his wife, Mary, owned the site where the government decided to build a lighthouse.

On May 18, 1826, Congress appropriated $4000 for a lighthouse on the Plum Island. In 1827, $3650 of that appropriation was spent on the lighthouse, with an additional $170.43 being spent in 1828.

The local Superintendent of Light-Houses, Henry Thomas Dering, issued a call for proposals in the *Sag Harbor Corrector* on August 28, 1826:

> Proposals will be received at this Office, until the 20th day of September next, for building, a *Light-House* and *Dwelling-House* on the west end of Plumb Island in the state of New-York, of the following materials, dimensions, and description: The Light-House to be of stone, the form octagon, the foundation to be of stone, laid as deep as may be requisite, to make the fabric perfectly secure, and to be carried up three feet above the surface of the earth, to the bottom of the water table. The wall to be four feet thick. The diameter of the base from the bottom of the water table to the top thereof; where the octagonal pyramid is to commence, to be eighteen feet, and the diameter ten feet at the top or floor of the lantern. The water table to be capped with hewn stone, at least eight inches wide, and sloped to turn off the water. From the surface to the top of the building the wall to be thirty feet in height, and graduated as follows: The first nine feet from the foundation wall to be three feet thick: the next ten feet to be two and a half feet thick; and the next eight feet to be two feet thick. The top of the building to be arched, reserving an entrance on the side to the lantern, and to have a stone cornice on which to be laid a sope stone or granite stone deck twelve feet diameter, four inches

thick, on one side of which to be a scuttle to enter the lantern, the scuttle door to be framed with iron and covered with copper, the joints of the stone deck to be fitted with lead. The ground floor to be paved with brick or stone, and a sufficient number of strong wooden stairs, with a safe hand railing, to lead from the ground floor to within 6 feet of the top, and an iron ladder from the top of the stairs to the entrance of the scuttle, with steps 2 inches wide; substantial plank floors to be fixed to the stairs on the joists of each story. The Light-House to have three windows, each to have 8 panes of glass 10 by 12 inches, in strong frames with shutters and proper fastenings, painted with two coats of paint, and a substantial pannel door three feet wide and five feet and a half high, on hinges, lock and latch complete, on the lower floor. A complete iron lantern on the octagonal form, to rest on the platform of the pyramid, to be 6 feet 6 inches in diameter and 7 feet high, the eight corner pieces of which to be two inches square above the platform and two and a half inches square below it, to run six feet into the stone work, and to be there secured with anchors. The space between the posts at the angles to be occupied by the sashes, which are to be of iron, moulded on the inside, struck solid, and of sufficient strength so as not to work with the wind; each sash to be glazed with strong double glass 10 by 12 inches, of the first quality Boston manufactory, excepting on one side, where so much of the space as would otherwise be filled with sashes is to be occupied by an iron framed door covered with copper, two feet four inches wide and four and a half feet high. The top of the lantern is to be a dome three and a half feet high, and covered with copper 33 ounces to the square foot formed of sixteen iron rafters concentrating in an iron hoop at the top, which forms the funnel for the smoke to pass out of the lantern into the ventilator in the form of a ball sufficient to contain 40 gallons, and large enough to secure the funnel against rain; the ventilator to be turned by a large vane, so that the hole for venting the smoke may always be to leeward. The lantern to be surrounded by an iron balustrade two feet high, each [rail] or rod to be three quarters of an inch square, inserted in the braces between the eight posts. The lantern and balustrade to be covered with three coats of paint; the door, sashes, window frames, &c. to be well painted, and the building whitewashed and furnished with two electric conductors or rods, with points.

The Dwelling-House to be of stone, thirtyfour feet by twenty, one story of eight feet high, divided into two rooms, with an entry between, the stairs to be in the entry to go into the chambers, a chimney near the middle of the house, with a fire place in each room, iron or stone mantelpiece; cellar under the whole of the house, with sufficient walls of stone, laid in lime mortar, 20 inches thick, six feet deep; the walls of the house to be twenty inches thick, ten and a half feet high from the ground floor, laid up in lime mortar, with split undressed stone, well pointed and whitewashed twice over. The roof to be rectangular, the boards of which to be jointed and halved, and well secured, and covered with good merchantable shingles; three windows in each room, of sixteen lights of 8 by 10 glass each, and one of the same dimensions in each chamber; the doors to be four pannelled, with good hinges and thumblatches to each, and a good lock on the outside door; closets in each room back of the chimney; all the floors to be double and well nailed; the inside walls and ceilings to be lathed and plastered, and all the inside work to be finished in a plain decent style, with good seasoned timber.

A well to be sunk, sufficiently deep to procure good water, at a convenient distance from the dwelling-house, to be stoned & furnished with a curb, windlass & an iron chain, and a strong iron hooped bucket. The whole to be completed by the first of July next.

Separate proposals will be received for fitting said Light-House, within one month after it shall be built, with patent lamps and reflectors, ten butts for keeping the oil and all the necessary apparatus, in the same manner as the Light-Houses in the United States have been fitted up by Winslow Lewis.

No payment made until the whole work shall be completed and approved by the superintendant of the establishment.

HENRY THO'S DERING,
Superintendant of Light-Houses.

The federal government bought three acres "on the South side of the West End or Point of Plumb Island" on August 29, 1826. Richard and Mary Jerome sold the lot for $90. The New York Legislature approved the sale on April 13, 1827, and the lighthouse was built that year.

George M. Bache visited the island during his 1838 inspection of the area's lights, noting that the "Plumb-Island light (revolving) . . . is a leading light to vessels passing up or down the sound, and is useful to those coming into Gardiner's bay, either from the eastward or through the narrow passage between Plumb island and

145

Oysterman's point on Long Island." The illuminating apparatus, consisting of ten lamps, each with a 13–inch diameter reflector averaging two pounds, three ounces in weight, revolved at one half revolution every 66 seconds. The keeper's quarters contained eight rooms, and the entire station appeared "to be kept in good order."

On December 23, 1839, the brig *Pocahontas*, headed for Newburyport, Massachusetts from Cadiz, Spain, struck a rock off Plum Island. When she was discovered, she had lost her masts and was going to pieces on a rocky reef 150 yards offshore. The heavy seas made rescue impossible. All those on the island could do was watch. One man, lashed to the ship, his clothes nearly gone from the violence of the seas, was already dead. In the hours that onlookers observed the situation, two more men slipped beneath the waves. The last man was swept away, but managed to grasp a dangling rope. Eventually, he, too, was washed away. Trunks, papers, and pieces of the ship that washed ashore identified the brig and her captain, James G. Cook. The ship had left Spain for home in October. The papers also revealed the crew list. None of the 12 or 13 crewmen survived. Those bodies found were returned to Newburyport.

In *Historical Collections of the State of New York*, engraver and historian John W. Barber and writer Henry Howe described 1840s Plum Island as being about 800 acres in size with a population of about 75 people. One of those people was Henry Conkling, keeper of the Plum Island Light.

Conkling's granddaughter, Sarah, lived with the family. Her mother, Sally Conkling Bowditch, had died during her birth. Sarah was raised by her grandparents. Beginning in 1840, when she was 16, Sarah kept a notebook for four years. While many modern-day Long Island residents envy the isolated conditions such as at Plum Island in the 1840s, Sarah held no such fondness. The poems in her notebook contained the words of a lonely girl, such as in one writing from 1841:

> Lend me your wings, my gentle dove,
>   O lend them for a while.
> Fain would I spread them wide and fly
>   Far from this dreary isle.

My soul is sick of solitude.
    I long afar to flee
From the ceaseless roaring of the waves
    And the pounding of the sea.

No friends, no pleasures have we here
    The long hours to beguile.
Lend me your wings, my gentle dove,
    O, lend them for a while.

In an untitled poem, she wrote:

Plum Island, thou art not my home,
With thy bleak hills and barren sands,
And shores on which salt sea's foam
    Is dashing ever.

No – thou art not my home – my heart expells
The thought – thou art so bare and lone.
No kindred spirit near thee dwells.
    My home! No, never!

Sarah also related the tale of a shipwreck:

LINES ON THE WRECK OF THE SCHOONER
"SAMUEL CROCKER"
WHICH CAME ASHORE ON THE EAST END OF
PLUM ISLAND, MARCH 28, 1843

The night came on all drear and dark
    And o'er the foaming sea
By the swift wind a little bark
    Was hurried fearfully.

All o'er the blackened face of heaven
    With anxious eyes they gazed.
No star to guide their course was given;
    No friendly beacon blazed.

And higher still the seas did rise,
    And louder sang the gale.

Still onward now the vessel plies
  With torn and shivering sail.

High on a dangerous and rocky shore
  That little bark was driven.
That lonely band must now implore
  The help alone of heaven.

All night they clung in hopeless grief
  Around that dripping deck,
And the stormy morn brought no relief
  To the sufferers in that wreck.

All day the cold and chilling rain
  In torrents down did pour
Their cries for help were all in vain,
  Drowned by the billows' roar.

But e'er that gloomy day was o'er
  One from that little band
Was wafted to the 'eternal shore'
  Of that far-off, unknown land.

Another day. The storm is o'er.
  The danger now is past.
Hope then revives. They reach the shore.
  Rejoice—they're saved at last.

Ah, nevermore will that vessel glide
  O'er the sparkling waves or the yielding tide,
Nor ever again will that sailor boy stand
  On the much loved shore of his native land.

No mother sheds o'er his afflictions warm tears,
  No friend whom he loved, or who loved him, was
  near.
No coffin confined the sailor boy's breast,
  Nor prayer arose from his place of rest.

But they laid him down by the rocky shore
  Where the wild waves dash forever more,
And the stormy wind and the foaming wave
  Sing requiems o'er the sailor's grave.

Sarah did eventually leave the island. On November 6, 1845, she married Benjamin King Mulford. Descendants of Sarah and Benjamin still reside on Long Island.

Henry Conkling remained at the Plum Island Light until he was replaced by S. M. Conkling on November 6, 1846. On August 2, 1849, Sineus Conkling became the keeper of the Plum Island Light.

Captain Howland brought supplies to Plum Island on June 20, 1850. He found the dwelling "in fair order" but the rest of the 23–year-old station was not reported so favorably:

> Tower of the light-house is leaky—always was, I suppose, and always will be. Lantern is in a miserable condition, it being very rusty indeed; sashes large, glass small; lantern apparatus is poor; lantern deck is of rough, unhammered granite; lighting apparatus and lantern not clean. Keeper was formerly a good one, and probably will do better with a new lantern and lighting apparatus; he promised that he would do better, and wished me to make as favorable a report of him as I could. I told him I would. He is a small consumer of oil.

The consumption of oil was important in the penny-pinching Pleasanton years, so the report of him being a "small consumer of oil" was probably Howland's way of trying to put in a good word for Conkling.

William Booth became keeper of the Plum Island Light on May 19, 1853, and was paid $350 per year. This was the same salary Henry Conkling had earned ten years earlier. Booth remained at the light until April 13, 1861.

In 1856, the old Plum Island tower received a Fresnel lens. It was a Fourth Order lens showing a white flash every 30 seconds.

William Whiting Wetmore took over as keeper at Plum Island on April 13, 1861, at the age of 55. This was the beginning of a long Wetmore presence on Plum Island. Wetmore's 1861 salary ($560) was a big improvement over William Booth's ($350).

By 1867, the 40–year-old tower was reported to be "damp and contracted," and the replacement of the tower, lantern, and keeper's quarters was recommended. The 1868 *Annual Report* was more emphatic:

> Both the tower and keeper's dwelling are in bad condition and should be rebuilt. The tower, built in 1827, leaks badly; the masonry is soft and crumbling; the lantern is of the old pattern and with small lights and large astragals, and it leaks badly. It is thought that the old buildings are not worth the money which would be required to put them in good order, and it is therefore proposed to rebuild them.

From January 18, 1868 to May 13, 1869, Austin B. Booth was the keeper. William Whiting Wetmore returned as keeper when Booth left.

A special appropriation for the rebuilding of the station was made on March 3, 1869, and was accomplished in 1870. When completed, the new Plum Island Lighthouse was a granite house with a white cast-iron tower and black lantern on the front of the slate roof. This church-like structure was the last of six nearly identical Fourth Order lighthouses built in the Third District between 1867 and 1870. In addition to the new lighthouse, a fog bell, operated by a Stevens's striking apparatus, was installed at the station.

In April 1871, an assistant keeper was authorized for the station, probably to help operate and maintain the fog bell and associated machinery. Wetmore's 32–year-old son, William Walker Wetmore, got the job, at a rate of $400 per year.

In 1878, the decision was made to replace the slate roof. Shingles replaced the slate and stopped the leaking problems at the lighthouse. At that time, the bell was raised ten feet higher on its tower, with the hope that it would be heard further as a result.

The life of a lighthouse keeper had many aspects that we tend to forget. Two log book entries in 1883, and one in 1887, reported bodies washing up on the beach. One on August 1, 1883 was suspected to be that of Olif Nelson, of Millstone Point, Connecticut. Another body, from November 15, 1883, was thought to be that of Captain H. S. Conway of the barge *Osprey*. In July of 1887, a body was found floating on the north side of Plum Island. Coroner B. D. Skinner oversaw the inquests for all of the above.

Photo by the author

Plum Island Lighthouse in 2001.

By the time William Walker Wetmore's son, Byron George Wetmore, was 15 years old, he was an accomplished fishing guide. Log entries indicate he was especially adept at finding blackfish.

The 1827 keeper's quarters were taken down in 1885, as they were no longer being used. The loss of the building removed all hints of the station's Pleasanton-era beginnings. By 1889, the masonry needed repointing and the plaster had to be repaired.

The Wetmores kept a guest log at the lighthouse. Many visitors signed in; some made sketches of ships or whales; others wrote little limericks that were later crossed out; some commented on Mrs. Wetmore's hospitality and fine culinary skills. An entry on August 23, 1890, by a group who called themselves the "Suicide Club," follows:

> Hurrah for Capt. "Billy"
> His cider will knock you silly
> Climbing up the lighthouse stairs
> If you think that you are tough

Photo courtesy of Nelson Wetmore

Pre-1885 photo shows lighthouse, boathouse, and 1827 keeper's dwelling.

> You will be sure to get enough
> And loose [sic] your city airs

The father-and-son Wetmore team worked together maintaining the lighthouse until the elder Wetmore passed away at the age of 85 on January 3, 1892. The younger Wetmore was then promoted to head keeper. Over the next 11 years, his assistants would include Robert Ebbitts and William Janse, who both would go on to be head keepers in the area.

An entry in the guest book from May 18, 1896 described a trip from Unionville to New London, Connecticut, that ended up at Plum Island:

> One fine May morning, so tis said
> Three jolly young fellows jumped from their bed
> And donning their clothes which was very necessary,
> Started to see New London's 250th Anniversary

Photo courtesy of Carol Smith Charnquist

William Whiting Wetmore, left, and William Walker Wetmore
at Plum Island circa 1880.

They looked and they glared and they stared (and they joked)
And finally ended up in the Manhanset boat
And set sail for Plum Island (to see Uncle Billy
Who has lived their [sic] so long he has seen lots of those gilleys)
They couldn't land at that time, so tis wrote
So they kept right along to Greenport
They made a few calls and saw lots of folks
Then started back for Plum Island in a sail-boat
Now this was a queer thing and twas only by chance
But the captain of this boat was Uncle Billy's Jance,
Now the weather was rough and the water was rougher
But they didn't give a d___ for they were a lot of bluffers.
Did they get wet? Well, I shall never tell
Only this – that the seat of their breeches was wetter than H___

    H. J. Ripley Unionville Conn.
    C. S. Symonds   "   "
    J. C. Monroe   "   "

Symonds may have been the son of Wetmore's sister (hence the Uncle Billy reference). "Jance" was undoubtedly William Janse, the station's assistant keeper at the time.

One guest book entry in 1897 stands out:

Tuesday June 8th Plum Island
Yacht Oneida, after a cruise to Grey Gable, returns to catch fish at
the best place on this coast for that purpose –
    Grover Cleveland   Princeton N.J.
    Ed Benedict,   Greenwich Conn

Cleveland had recently completed his second term as President of the United States. To this day, he remains the only person to serve two nonconsecutive terms in that office.

In 1897, the War Department purchased 150 acres on the east end of Plum Island and established Fort Terry as part of its defenses of the eastern entrance to Long Island Sound. Fort Terry was the westernmost of the five sites in this system of fortifications, the others being at Napatree Point, Rhode Island (Fort Mansfield), Fisher's Island (Fort H. G. Wright), Great Gull Island (Fort Michie), and Gardiner's Point (Fort Tyler).

In 1901, the War Department bought an additional 690 acres, making all of Plum Island, except for the lighthouse reservation, an Army post. Continuing expansion of the fort up to 1914 resulted in an extensive fortification.

William Walker Wetmore remained at Plum Island until October 1, 1903, giving him a total uninterrupted service at the station of over 32 years. When he turned the station over to Richard Curran, the two had to fill out a copy of Form No. 31, which was an account of all of the government property on the site. The form noted that the lens contained a Funck-Heap lamp, with one 1 5/8 inch diameter wick, burning kerosene.

Included in the list were blank forms (including "Form 65—Monthly report of condition of station," and "Form 70—Shipwreck report"), books (including "Fog-signal records" and "Tables of lengths of nights"), brooms, brushes, lamp chimneys, "dry goods" (curtains, covers and towels), "engineers' supplies" (emery paper, machine wipers and polishing paste), fuel, hardware and tools, lamps, lanterns, oils, oil cans, "paints, oils, etc.," soap, stationery, "wick and wick boxes," window and plate glass, and "miscellaneous articles," such as a sailboat, clock, dustpans, lens and pedestal, mops, well pump, sectional ladders, sponges, and a stove. Several other items were written in, including a "prayer book," "hymenal book," "spy glass" and 65 "tags for cans." The conditions of all of these items were noted, as appropriate. When completed, this form was forwarded to the District Inspector.

William Walker Wetmore passed away on July 3, 1909, after a long illness. He was 70 years, 8 months, and 18 days of age.

Curran served as keeper until 1905, when he was replaced by William S. Parks. The station was inspected in September of 1910, and found in poor condition. A follow-up inspection several months later showed no improvement, so Parks was replaced by George Ehhardt. By the time Ehhardt was appointed, the lamp inside the lens had been changed to an incandescent oil vapor lamp.

The Chapel family arrived at Plum Island in 1913. William Maynard Chapel was born July 19, 1876, in Norwich, Connecticut, the son of William D. Chapel and Elizabeth Maynard. For the next 19 years, the Chapel family would occupy the site, with their patriarch serving as keeper of the Plum Island Light. William and his wife, Dora, had six children: Dora (born 1899), Elsie (born 1901), William Oliver (born 1903), Ruth (born 1906), Clifford (born 1907), and Alice (born 1912).

The Chapels were a true Long Island lighthouse family. Keeper Chapel's sister, Elizabeth, married Marvin Burnham, a keeper at Lloyd Harbor. His daughter, Elsie, married an assistant keeper from the Orient Point Light, Bill Baker. His son, William Oliver (Willie) Chapel, followed in his father's shoes, becoming a lighthouse keeper. The younger Chapel served at several stations, including Orient Point and the Cornfield Point Lightship, before becoming the long-time head keeper at Race Rock.

The Chapel family kept busy on the island. Willie, in a letter to his niece, Barbara, in 1976, wrote that they "had a school, movies, churches, gym and various activities furnished by the Army." They

Photo courtesy of Violet Marquis

Undated photo of the Chapel family at Plum Island.

also "had a boat and traveled to Greenport for provisions to compensate for the lack of supplies in the commissary [sic]."

On December 15, 1915, William Maynard Chapel rescued the captain and his wife from the tug *S. L'Hommedieu*. He did so, as the report said "in open boat, without oars."

By 1929, the station consisted of the lighthouse, a brick oil house, a wooden boat house, a fuel house, a steel fog bell tower, and riprap along the shore. The fog bell was mounted on a tower of approximately 40 feet in height, and operated by a clockworks mechanism that required winding every four hours.

William Maynard Chapel, who had retired from the lighthouse in the early 1930s, passed away on May 28, 1941, at the age of 64. He had settled in Hampton, Connecticut, upon his retirement.

In 1941, Fort Terry, which had been nearly unused since World War I, became a training camp. After the war, it fell into disuse and was declared surplus property on June 22, 1948. Suffolk County expressed interest in the site, but it was transferred to the Army Chemical Corps in 1952. It was never actually used by the Chemical Corps, and was turned over to the United States Department of Agriculture (USDA) on July 1, 1954. The Plum Island Animal Disease Center (PIADC) was then established on the island.

Tony Tuliano, a young Coast Guard Fireman Apprentice, was stationed at Plum Island in 1977. His reaction, at first, was not one of excitement: "Being eighteen and yearning for adventure and accomplishment, my immediate response to my assignment was somewhat of a disappointment." Arriving at the station, he was given a short orientation of the building, eventually arriving at the lantern room:

> As soon as you enter the Lantern Room the first thing that grabs your attention is "the Jewel of the House"—the Fresnel Lens. What a fascinating work of functional art. Although showing some damage from a century of service, it was still a breathtaking piece of brass and glass reflecting light from the midday sun. Once the distraction of the sight of the lens and clockworks subsided, you are captivated by the wondrous view of Plum Island, Plum Gut and Long Island Sound. These first 15 minutes as a Lighthouse Keeper are forever etched in my memory.

In time, Tuliano came to appreciate his assignment, and his place in American history:

> When I had the evening watch, I would enjoy climbing up to the light tower early and spend time sitting out on the catwalk with my legs hanging over the edge. The solitude and scenic beauty was soothing to the soul. Time seemed to slow down up there. Passing mariners would wave and it was like I could sense them saying

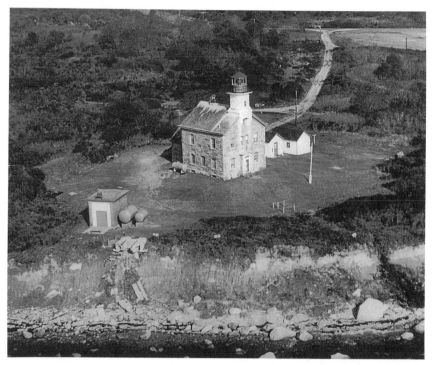

Photo courtesy of Violet Marquis

Undated photo of the Plum Island Light prior to decommissioning.

"thank you for being there." It was not so much them saying it to me, but to the institution of the manned Lighthouse, who's unfailing sole purpose was to guide them safely home. It was times like this that would help me come to realize the true tradition of this Lighthouse and the Keepers before me.

The last crew to man the Plum Island Light consisted of Boatswain's Mate First Class Paul Palumbo, Fireman Apprentice Tom Hazeltine, Machinery Technician Third Class Tom LaFalce, and Seaman Apprentice Gene Price. The crew worked two weeks on, one week off. Palumbo described the "the experience of living at a light station" as "invaluable," and Hazeltine, at the time said, "I wasn't sure about this place when I was assigned, but now I love it," adding that it was his "utopia."

The light was deactivated in 1978, and the lighthouse and land turned over to the USDA shortly thereafter. Unfortunately, the

Photo courtesy of Jim House

The tower, catwalk and lantern in 1995.

USDA allowed the home of the Wetmores, Chapels, and so many others to deteriorate. Over the years, the USDA's attitude would even be defiant, claiming that they were "not in the business of restoring lighthouses," despite the requirements of the National Historic Preservation Act of 1966, which requires federal agencies to preserve historic structures on their property.

The 1897 Barbier & Benard Fourth Order lens ended up in the East End Seaport Maritime Museum in Greenport in 1994, when the Plum Island Animal Disease Center loaned it for display. The lens and operating clockworks have remained visible to the public. In early 2003, the lens was serviced by Jim Dunlap of Lighthouse and Lens Restoration Corporation. In his report, Dunlap, perhaps the nation's most respected lighthouse lens expert, referred to the lens as "a beautiful artifact. It contains all its original prisms, and is relatively rare in that it operates under the power of its weights and clockworks. The lens rotates flawlessly and effortlessly with clockwork gears so pristine they could have been manufactured during the last month, not over 100 years ago." Dunlap's inspection, cleaning, lubrication and painting (in accordance with specifications from the date of the lens' manufacture) were jointly funded by the Seaport and Long Island Chapter of the U.S. Lighthouse Society.

Over the years, there have been many changes to the 1869 lighthouse. The roof is now asbestos-cement shingle; a kitchen and bathroom have been added; some of the interior trim has been removed, as have some of the original doors; the original floors, walls and ceilings have been covered in most places. Neglect has caused leaks to develop in the lantern room, roof, windows and other places. Some of the ceilings have collapsed, and peeling paint abounds. A crack runs almost the entire height on the front granite façade.

Some progress was made toward the preservation of the site in the new millennium, as the Long Island Chapter of the U.S. Lighthouse Society nominated the structure for the National Register of Historic Places in late 2000 (it was approved in 2001) and procured approximately $500,000 worth of rocks to stabilize the eroding bluff, having those rocks transported to the island at no cost.

Photo by the author

Plum Island's 1897 lens on display at the
East End Seaport Maritime Museum.

Little happened from that point on, despite the Society's efforts to work with the USDA.

On June 1, 2003, the Department of Homeland Security (DHS) took over responsibility of the PIADC. In August 2003, a DHS representative contacted the Long Island Chapter of the U.S. Lighthouse Society, prompted in part by letters from descendants of the Wetmores and Chapels, to begin a dialogue regarding the preservation of the lighthouse. Ongoing discussions thus far have indicated a willingness by the DHS to honor its responsibility to the Plum Island Light.

North Fork residents, lighthouse fans, and the Plum Island Light's many keepers and their descendants will continue to watch the situation with the hope that the history of this light station will be respected and preserved.

Photo by the author

Plum Island Lighthouse and eroding bluff in 2001.

Little Gull Island

East of Plum Island lie two small islands, further extensions of the North Fork of Long Island. The eastern- most, and smaller, of these two islands has been home to a lighthouse since 1805. Little Gull Island borders The Race, one of the most dangerous waterways in the Northeast. The Race is a main avenue for the tidal waters of the Long Island Sound. Like Plum Gut, The Race acts as a venturi for these waters, causing them to reach speeds of up to six knots. A rocky bottom adds to the turbulence, and winds, especially if combined with poor visibility, can make matters much worse.

The many shipwrecks in that waterway caused the government to consider action early on. Commissioner of Revenue Tench Coxe proposed the building of another lighthouse in "this quarter of the United States" to Jeremiah Olney, Collector of Customs at Providence (a position he attained after his service in the American Revolution). Olney, in turn, asked the opinion of John Updike, a man whose "long acquaintance with the Long Island & Fishers Island Sounds" enabled him to address the matter. Updike was of the opinion that "another Light House is absolutely necessary for the discretion and safety of the foreign & coasting trade" in the area. Watch Hill had been mentioned by Olney, but Updike felt "that the Little Gull Island . . . [was] the most suitable, and usefull place a Light House" could be built and that "it would guide vessels through [the Race] and bring them in sight of New London Light and be a leading mark for passing up and down the Long Island Sound or into Gardners Bay where is good Anchorage for Ships of the greatest Burthen." He also noted its usefulness for ships bound "for New London . . . or to Sagg Harbour." Updike also mentioned "a dangerous Rock" in the Race "called the Race Rock whereon Vessels have been frequently lost or received Damage in dark Nights, which a Light on the little Gull Island would have directed them clear of."

Updike's recommendation was acted upon, although a lighthouse would be also built on the proposed Watch Hill location a few years later. The two Gull islands, named for the many terns—called Fish Gulls at that time—which nested in the area, were bought from Benjamin Jerome in 1803 for $800. A lighthouse was built on the approximately one-acre Little Gull Island in 1805. Israel Rodgers was appointed its first keeper on July 1 of that year, and would stay on until resigning in November 1809. This whitewashed stone 50–foot tower, made of "smooth hammered freestone" with a wooden stairway, was built to help guide ships through the dangerous waterway, but it would not be an easy task on this desolate, lonely island.

Giles Holt became the second keeper of the Little Gull Island Light Station on December 6, 1809. His seven years at Little Gull would be eventful.

When the War of 1812 came to eastern Long Island, the British paid a visit to the lighthouse at Little Gull Island. On July 28, 1813, they demanded that keeper Giles Holt extinguish the light. The keeper refused, and the British removed the illuminating apparatus from the lantern.

On September 23, 1815, a hurricane hit the area. Keeper Holt was ashore at the time, but his wife and four children were in the

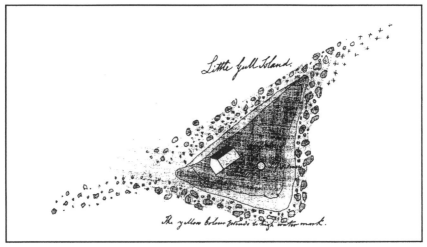

U.S. Lighthouse Society photo

Early map showing original Little Gull Island tower, dwelling, and well.

dwelling quarters on the tiny island. As the storm raged on, the keeper could do nothing but hope and pray that his family would survive the storm. When it subsided, and the keeper returned to the island, he must have had mixed feelings about what he saw. The raging waters of the storm had half undermined the keeper's quarters, leaving it hanging over a bank, and the waters had come within four feet of the tower itself. Fortunately, his family had weathered the storm and was well.

The proven vulnerability of the light station to storms caused the government to erect a 100–foot diameter wall around the tower and keeper's quarters in 1817, when John Rogers was the keeper. Work began in May and continued through August. One of the workers on the wall was a young man named Henry Thomas (Tom) Dering. Tom's father was Henry Packer Dering, local collector of customs, and thereby superintendent of lighthouses, and first postmaster for the town of Sag Harbor. Tom kept a diary during his time on Little Gull Island, beginning with a short history of the light station. He noted that the cost of the first lighthouse was $15,000 and commented on the area:

> The tides around the island are rapid and dangerous and the navigation for boats rude and unpleasant. The well water is brackish and rain water is used for drink. The Great island contains twelve acres of land but is little improved.

Tom also described the wall he was building, which cost $24,500:

> By three commissioners appointed to take a survey of the island it was proposed by them to build a circular wall of 300 feet in circumference and 100 diameter at the top. The foundation sunk on a level with low water mark seven feet thick at the bottom of the wall and 3½ at the top. The outside course of stone laid in mortar and bolted with two copper bolts; the height of the wall 22 feet. On top of the wall a railing four feet high.

Early in the journal, Tom's youthful excitement to be on the island was evident. His mood changed as time passed, however. His August 4 entry shows this: "This wall will soon be finished to the joy of every man on the Island certainly to the joy of Tom Dering." On August 11, he recorded that he "wrote my name in the lanthorn." The last entry in Tom Dering's journal, dated Tuesday, August 19, recorded the inscriptions from two graves on Great Gull Island dating 1814.

Tom Dering would go on to replace his father as the local collector of customs and superintendent of lighthouses. In 1826, he would become responsible for the building of the first Plum Island lighthouse, not far from the island where he had toiled nine years earlier.

The keeper at Little Gull when Tom Dering was the local superintendent was Frederick Chase, a notable Shelter Island resident. In addition to being a ten-year keeper at Little Gull (after being appointed by John Quincy Adams), Chase also served as Justice of the Peace of Shelter Island, Town Supervisor and School Trustee. He had a large farm on the northwest part of Shelter Island and today his family name can be seen in several places on the island. His stay at Little Gull Island lasted from March 8, 1826, until he resigned on August 27, 1836.

In George Bache's 1838 report, the Little Gull Island Light was described as being "of great importance to vessels approaching or passing through 'The Race,' or going into Gardiner's Bay." It's fixed-white lighting apparatus, which had been installed in January, consisted of "fifteen lamps, with parabolic reflectors, which are arranged around two circular tables—eight upon the upper, and seven upon the lower table; the vacant space below being towards Plumb Island. The reflectors are 13½ inches in diameter, and average in weight two pounds six ounces; they are supported firmly by brackets, which project from the tables. The tube glasses are only six inches long, and are so placed that the smoke from the lamps collects upon the upper part of the reflectors." The keeper's quarters at the time was a wooden building with seven rooms. Bache also noted: "At the time of my visit, the light-keeper had been absent four days, owing to sickness; and the lighting apparatus had been apparently neglected by the assistant keeper in charge of it."

In June of 1850, Captain Howland noted that the lighthouse had received a new lantern and illuminating apparatus. It still used 15 lamps, but these were now located within 15–inch reflectors. The captain lamented the fact that the new lantern was not larger, as this would have allowed for even larger reflectors. He also complained of the lack of a crane for unloading supplies, as this "would facilitate our business, for now we have to parbuckle it up very high steps, and it [is] not only slow work but hard work."

By 1855, three years after the formation of the Light-House Board, A. Ludlow Case, Inspector for the Third Light-House District, reported that the lighting apparatus at Little Gull was "very much worn, and I have to recommend that it be replaced by a lens apparatus of not less than a third-order, to illuminate the entire horizon." Little Gull did receive the recommended Third Order lens a few years later, but this lens would only serve until 1869.

Wallace Reeves became Little Gull's keeper on April 16, 1861. His brother, "Captain" Villa Detmold Reeves, was his assistant. Captain Reeves had been a cooper, like his father, making barrels for the whaling industry. The decline of that industry caused Captain Reeves, like so many others, to find other employment. In addition to his lighthouse duties, he also piloted "ferryboats" and "party boats" in the Shelter Island area, and was a constable for Southold Town, Chief of the Greenport Police Department, a member of the Neptune Fire Engine Company and, in his later years a night watchman for the Greenport Basin and Construction Company. Captain Reeves passed away October 12, 1933, at the age of 93.

When the winds of change blew across the Long Island area in the years following the War Between the States, Little Gull Island received a new lighthouse. The new tower was built of large granite blocks, like the other new lighthouses being built in the late 1860s, but it was not to be a small square building like its contemporaries. Little Gull's importance for safety in The Race, combined with the low elevation of the island, dictated that the new tower be tall. Its exposure to heavy winds, rain and, waves made a round construction more feasible. The base for the new tower would be Tom Dering's 1817 wall. You can still see this wall standing, over 186 years after its construction.

Progress on the new lighthouse was slow. This was due to the "lack of room for the employment of more than a small force of workmen, and the exposed position of the station, which renders the

167

landing of materials difficult." The brick-lined tower was built to a height of 81 feet, with four staggered windows to light the cast iron stairway. During the building of the new tower, which was completed in 1869, the light at Little Gull Island was displayed from a wooden "bell-frame."

The new tower was given a powerful Second Order Fresnel lens that mariners would be able to see as they passed between Montauk Point and Block Island on their way to the Long Island Sound. The light's characteristic was set as a fixed white light, as it had always been. It was lit on December 15, 1869.

New keepers' quarters were also built. This was a two-story, mansion-like structure, large enough to house three keepers and their families, made of brownish stone (perhaps from the original tower), with granite arches over the windows and on the building's corners.

The winter of 1874–1875 was a tough one. At Little Gull Island, it damaged the pier, causing a loss of water from the cisterns. The water for the steam sirens, which operated for 651 hours between July 1874 and June 1875, came from these cisterns, making their repair a priority.

The station's lard oil lamp was replaced with a mineral oil (kerosene) lamp in 1883. Twenty-four years later, on February 19, 1907, the lamp was replaced by an incandescent oil vapor lamp. This change of the source of illumination increased the light's brightness a great deal, even though the lens surrounding the lamp was unchanged.

William J. Murray became the keeper at Little Gull Island on December 19, 1909. During his time, he would direct many rescues of stranded mariners. The presence of Fort Michie, which had been established on Great Gull Island during the Spanish-American War, created a great deal of maritime traffic in the area. Among the ships given assistance by Murray and his assistants were the schooners *Pell* (1913) and *Andrew Nebinger* (1915).

Offshore light stations, because of their remoteness, have always been great places to watch the night sky. In the days preceding the glow that arises from Long Island, courtesy of the many streetlights, this must have been even truer. On May 27, 1910, when the sighting

National Archives 26 LG 12-57

Undated photo of 1869 tower and keepers' quarters.

of Haley's comet—seen "very plainly"—was noted in the station's log, Little Gull Island must have been a fine place from which to witness the event.

In July of 1910, the station received a 16–foot power boat. A little over two years later, the tender *Mistletoe* arrived at Little Gull Island and placed mooring buoys for the power boat on the north and south sides of the island. On October 19, 1916, the following entry appeared in the station log: "Keepers power boat breaks away from mooring and smashes up on rip-rap. Lost two in two years. Advice to future keepers. DON'T KEEP YOUR BOAT MOORED OUTSIDE AFTER SEPT. 30th."

Early 1918 was very cold, with much ice gathering around Long Island. On January 20, the keeper noted "Sound full of ice," and on February 9, noted that a boat had landed on Fort Michie, located on neighboring Great Gull Island, for the first time since the 3rd. The surrounding waters had been "choked with ice stopping all traffic."

Two 1500–gallon tanks, and one 600–gallon tank, were installed at the station in August 1921. This negated the need for storing kerosene in cans. As these tanks were installed at Long Island light stations, the oil houses, most of them built about 20 years prior, became tool sheds or storage sheds for chemicals and paints.

Keeper Eugene Merry was replaced by Lawrence Congdon in March 1922. Edgar M. "Ned" Whitford arrived the following June 1 as an assistant, gaining promotion to First Assistant Keeper (1AK) on November 13. Whitford stayed until September 15, 1926, when he transferred to Orient Point, to be the First Assistant Keeper for his brother Charles (He remained there until April 1927, when he became the head keeper at the cast-iron Stamford Harbor Light.)

The year 1928 was eventful at the station. A radio tower was delivered and put up early in the year, with a radio electrician named Wombacher arriving in March to install the radiobeacon and Delco generators. On April 30, lightning hit the station, causing "considerable damage" to the radio equipment, and destroying the telephone line to Fort Michie. That summer, the station received heat and hot water. The keepers undoubtedly welcomed this development, perhaps more than any other.

Photo courtesy of Ed Whitford
Ned Whitford at Little Gull Island in 1923 or 1924.

In October 1929, Little Gull Island and Stamford Harbor switched keepers, bringing Ned Whitford back to Little Gull Island, this time as the head keeper. Whitford would remain until 1942.

New docks, tracks, and cranes were built in July and August of 1931, for the arrival of a new power boat. The new boat arrived on October 29. It was a 19–foot boat, with a four-cylinder engine. Starting it required priming the engine, then spinning the flywheel by hand. The boat, number 541, had "USLHS" on its sides. Because of the many difficulties with the boat's engine, Whitford would eventually dub the boat the *USS Useless*.

The station's status was changed in September 1935, when it was decided to remove families from the island, leaving only the three keepers in attendance. Whitford's family had resided with him at the station for six years, but now moved to Greenwood, Rhode Island. They were allowed to visit, and did so "from time to time." Whitford's son Ed notes that "we traveled back and forth aboard the old Army 'L' boats and of course Dad knew everyone there was to know from Greenport to Fisher's Island to New London." The families of several lighthouse keepers would sometimes meet at the remains of Fort Tyler, off the northern point of Gardiner's Island. Life on the island had been fun for the children, who learned to row a boat before they learned to ride a bicycle.

The 67-year-old plaster on the dwelling's interior walls was removed in June, 1936. Masonite replaced the plaster, but was installed wrong, with the rough side out, "and a mess it was," according to Whitford's log.

On October 20, 1937, an electrician named Gunnel arrived at the station. His job was to install electric lights in the tower and all levels of the keepers' dwelling. The job was complete, with a 500-watt lamp replacing the IOV lamp, by sundown of November 1.

Ned Whitford was still the station's keeper on September 21, 1938, when the infamous hurricane roared through the Northeast. His log entries tell most of the story:

Hurricane swept New England Coast. Started at 1 P.M. and shifted to Southward moderated at 6 P.M. Station badly damaged. Boat house, all boats and equipment, toilets and boat track swept away. South crane listing over to So 45 Degree angle. Heavy seas as high as second floor on dwelling hit pier, twisted and turned completely over large granite block on top of pier, ripping down

The Whitfords' dog, Dixie Dugan, in uniform on Little Gull Island, circa 1937.

Photo courtesy of Nancy Gregg

part of fence and moving cradle out from under one 1500 gal. Oil tank, loosing (sic) all but 600 gal. of kerosene.

High seas tore entire sash out of engine room window over generators causing them to get wet, also flooding engine room and causing several short circuits. Engine room chimney blown over and sky light cover on dwelling blown away. Engine room platform and ladder swept away. Few shingles torn off house and paint house. Part of tower hall gutter ripped up by wind. Considerable damage done to all breakwaters. No telephone connections. Entire island off pier is in an upheaved condition. One and one half cords of wood swept off. Base of stairs off pier to beach undermined. Antenna twisted and tangled with small receiving antenna which broke away when engine room chimney went over and pulled leader pipe over, side of tower hall. Crack in house opened up considerably more. Second floor quarters flooded.

Whitford's family did not hear any news for days (the storm would prompt the family to buy a Stewart-Warner radio to stay in touch). When they did speak to him, he told them that the waves had been passing the six-foot-two-inch keeper at eye level as he stood at the window of the dwelling's second floor. Whitford also related that when the winds first came up, Assistant Keeper Barney Stefanski had his glasses blown off and was unable to help much for the rest of the storm.

The Hurricane of 1938 had hit Little Gull Island hard. The storm waters reached about 40 feet high. Whitford is said to have used mattresses to try to soak up the water on the second floor. The storm swept the island clean and filled the harbor with rocks and sand. Even the *USS Useless* was lost—it was later replaced with a 22–foot power boat.

The U.S. Coast Guard absorbed the nation's lighthouse service in 1939, and on July 1 all of the U.S. Lighthouse Service "pennants and flags [were] replaced by Coast Guard flags." The first Coast Guardsman to arrive at the station was Machinist Mate First Class E. Gaskille. Gaskille replaced Barney Stefanski. Whitford received orders to repaint and reletter the boats in Coast Guard colors in May of 1940.

In July 21, 1941, Whitford took his physical exam for induction into the Coast Guard. Ned Whitford ended up being Little Gull Island's last civilian head keeper, as well as its first Coast Guard Officer in Charge. In September, his long-time assistant, Myron Wescott transferred to Race Rock.

Ned Whitford left Little Gull Island in 1942, and went on to serve at the Cornfield Point Light Vessel, New Haven Harbor Light and aboard the tender *Hawthorn*, before becoming an instructor at the Coast Guard's Aids to Navigation School at Groton, Connecticut. There he became the Assistant Officer in Charge and wrote many of the school's textbooks. He retired in1948. A few months before Ned passed away in 1966, he said, "I have been on the water practically all my life. I have come out of storms where according to the rules in the book and with all my experiences I should be in Davy Jones' Locker."

Photo courtesy of Ed Whitford

Ned Whitford at the U.S. Coast Guard's
Aid to Navigation school in 1944.

U.S. Coast Guard photo

Burned out keepers' quarters on April 22, 1944.

The "majestic old mansion," as Whitford's son Ed calls the station's 1869 keeper's quarters, was destroyed by fire in 1944 and replaced by a bland one-story building. This building was taken down in 2002 by the Coast Guard.

That one-story building would be the home of many more keepers. In 1959, Myrel Stroud was the Officer In Charge at Little Gull Island, with a crew consisting of SN Tom Rysedorph, EN2 Frederick Allen, FN Vincent Strano and SN John Milowski. Also at the station was a nine-month-old pup named Spade, whose mother, Dumpling, lived at the North Dumpling Light, then later at the New London Ledge and Watch Hill lights. The crew at Little Gull at that time worked for three weeks (six hours on, 12 hours off), and then had one week off.

In 1978, the light at Little Gull Island was automated, ending 172 years of lightkeeping tradition on the tiny island. Today, the light and

Photo by the author

Little Gull Island in 1999.

fog signal at Little Gull Island still help local mariners navigate the treacherous waters of The Race. The fog signal in fact, often sounds even when there is no fog. Fortunately, there are few people around to complain about it.

The tower's old Second Order lens is on display at the East End Seaport Museum in Greenport. It is a fine example of an early French fixed Second Order lens (the rarest of imported orders), except for the damage that was done to it when it was reassembled. Its historic hardware was replaced with modern hardware, including Phillips screws (which were not invented until the 1930s, by a man from Oregon).

Although the names of Holt, Dering, Chase, Whitford, and others no longer echo off the granite and stone of Little Gull Island, the lighthouse still stands as a monument to a long tradition of proud lightkeeping on Long Island.

Fisher's Island

Race Rock
(1878)

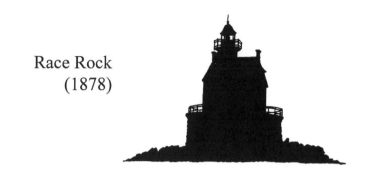

North Dumpling
(1849, 1871)

Latimer Reef
(1884)

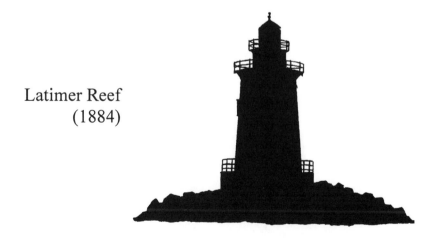

Race Rock

The Race Rock Light is best known for the difficulty with which it was built, and the two extraordinary men who steered its construction. It is also known as the guardian of one of the area's most dangerous waterways.

Much of the Long Island Sound's tidal waters pass through the Race. This large volume of water squeezing through a relatively small passage creates a venturi effect, and can propel the water to speeds of nearly six knots. This rapid tide can make navigating the Race tricky, even with modern ships and equipment.

U.S. Coast Guard photo

Undated aerial photo showing the artificial island
on which the Race Rock Light was built

The difficult passage through the Race, which was also called the Horse Race in early years, was made more treacherous by the presence of a rocky ledge three-quarters of a mile off the western end of Fisher's Island. Prior to the establishment of the Race Rock Light, a variety of unlighted markers were tried, including iron pipes sunk into the ledge.

George Bache's 1838 report included and examination of the possibility of establishing a "light-house on the west end of Fisher's island, at a place called Race point." He noted that in a period of eight years, more than eight wrecks had occurred there, and stated that "much benefit might be derived from a light upon Race point, if the navigation in its neighborhood were free from obstructions; but in addition to the reef which extends for some distance off from Fisher's island, the dangerous rock, called Race rock, lies at a distance of nearly three-fourths of a mile from it." Bache explained that ships using the proposed light for navigation "might be decoyed upon the rocks" and, therefore, did not recommend the building of this lighthouse. He also explained that misjudging the tides in the Race was a danger and recommended that "at night, during the flood tide, a second light be shown from Gull island." This recommendation was based on the remarks of Captain Andrew Mather, commander of the revenue cutter *Wolcott*, regarding his experience in the area between 1829 and 1837. Congress appropriated $3000 on July 7, 1838 for a lighthouse at Race Point, but the project never got underway.

In 1852, the newly formed Light-house Board described the Race Rock as "one of the most dangerous obstructions to navigation on the coast," further adding:

> Various efforts have been made, and numerous appropriations expended, in endeavoring to place an efficient and permanent mark on this point. Buoys cannot be kept on it, and spindles have hitherto only remained until the breaking up of the ice in the spring. To place a permanent mark, of some material which will resist the action of the sea and ice, an appropriation of not less than $7,000 will be required. The urgent necessity for this appropriation will be too apparent, it is believed, to be questioned in any quarter, by a simple reference to the coast survey chart of Fishers' Island sound.

On March 3, 1853, Congress appropriated $7000 for the project, but talk of a lighthouse on Race Point was ongoing. Another request was made for a lighthouse on September, 26, 1853. Leonard Smith, master of the steamer *Chicopee*, of New London, stated that there "ought to be a light house on Race point, the west end of Fisher's Island."

Progress toward constructing a lighthouse on Race Point, and beacon on Race Rock, was being made. On August 3, 1854, $8000 was appropriated for a lighthouse near Race Point. The New York State Legislature ceded jurisdiction "over so much land as may be necessary for the construction and maintenance" of a lighthouse and dwelling, "not to exceed ten acres," on January 24, 1855. A site for the lighthouse was surveyed in 1855, and that year's *Annual Report* included the following on the beacon:

Beacon or spindle on Race Rock.—An examination was made of this position during the last summer, with the view of ascertaining its character and the proper plan to be adopted in the erection of a beacon thereon.

This rock appears to be a boulder, located upon a rocky ledge, about 200 feet average diameter, within the depth of two and a half · fathoms at low water. The depth over the highest part of the rock is five feet at low tide, falling off rapidly on each side to six and seven feet, the accessible solid part of it being about 7 by 10 feet.

It is located about three-quarters of a mile WSW. from Race Point, and between it and the shore is a navigable channel a quarter of a mile wide. It is understood to have had two spindles erected on it within the last fifty years, both of which have been carried away; but they were slender affairs, of only three inches diameter, inserted eighteen inches into the rock. There is not sufficient space on it for a structure of much lateral magnitude, and the examination indicates that a beacon similar in some respects to the one now erecting at Plum Gut would be suitable here, formed of a central shaft of forged iron, seven inches diameter, stepped four feet in the rock, with iron stays around it, secured into the rock with the patent lewis. The shaft to carry a globular or cylindrical iron cage, of conspicuous size, elevated twenty feet above high water.

There can be no doubt that, with the simplest form of structure which may be adopted for this locality, a whole season will be required to secure it on the rock. Nothing having been effected in this respect during the present season, it remains to make arrangements for an early commencement upon the work at the opening of the next.

In 1856, the commencement of work on the Race Point Light was reported to be delayed by difficulty in obtaining a valid title for the site. By this time, the beacon at Race Rock was nearly completed.

Documents over the next ten years do not reveal much about the proposed Race Point Light, but the 1866 *Annual Report* indicated that a lighthouse at Race Rock had been authorized and plans were "under consideration." On July 28, 1866, an act appropriating $90,000 for a beacon on Race Rock was approved.

The 1868 *Annual Report* noted:

The subject of the construction of a beacon to mark this danger has been under the consideration by the board for some years . . . Detailed plans for the construction of a tower of granite have been adopted by the board. It was proposed to lay the foundation upon the bed-rock, twelve feet below low water, by means of a coffer dam. This proposition was based upon soundings made at different times, which indicated that the area required for the proposed structure around the boulder known as Race Rock was very nearly flat, there being a slight inclination outwards from the boulder, this deviation from a horizontal plane not being at any point more than twelve inches. With difficulty these soundings were obtained, by means of an iron rod, from a vessel's boat, the current running at a very rapid rate.

In view of all the difficulties of the proposed construction, it was not deemed safe to rely upon the information gained in the foregoing manner, and a much more careful examination of the site was therefore made. An apparatus was contrived by means of which more reliable soundings could not only be made for the moment, but located and retaken if desired. The soundings could be, and were, referred to a bench mark, and were, therefore, independent of variations in the plane of either high or low water. This apparatus disclosed the fact that the former soundings were insufficient and unreliable for the purpose of a work requiring so much accuracy, and that the area required for the base of the proposed tower was made up of an aggregation of boulders of smaller size than Race Rock itself, and of such number and size as to make the use of a coffer dam impracticable. The project which contemplated the use of one has therefore been abandoned. New plans are now in course of preparation, and it is hoped that ere long something satisfactory may be designed, when the work will be immediately commenced.

The *Annual Report* for 1869 went back to the start, describing the "very serious obstruction to navigation in Long Island and Fisher's Island Sounds," the recent findings about its composition, the 1866 appropriation, and the plan that was to have a light tower on the site, with a "suitable dwelling for the keepers on the south end of Fisher's [Island], distant about three-fourths of a mile from the rock." The report suggested a new approach:

> It is proposed, should Congress see fit to make the requisite additional appropriation, to construct a protecting pier of granite and to erect thereon a keeper's dwelling two stories high and octagonal in plan, with a circular stairway in the center, to be carried a sufficient height above the rook of the dwelling to support the lantern and illuminating apparatus; the whole to be of granite, and fire-proof. A powerful fog signal will be attached. The advantages of this plan over the original one . . . will be apparent. The protecting pier will be of a greater diameter and increased stability, and consequently more effectually resist the force of the storm-waves and pressure of packed floating ice in winter. The attendants upon the light and fog signal will be always be at hand to attend to their duties, which could not be insured if they were compelled to live on the island nearly a mile distant, particularly in the winter, when the ice is brought by the tides in immense packs and with great force through this comparatively narrow channel for passing vessels. The estimated cost of this important aid to navigation...would be $200,000 . . .. The amount now available is, it is believed, sufficient to carry the work above water, and it is proposed to commence the foundation early next spring.

Congress was asked to provide another $10,000 for the project, and did so on July 15, 1870. Unfortunately, the words "in addition to former appropriations" were left out and the original $90,000 appropriation was rendered unavailable, leaving only $10,000 to start the project. The work at Race Rock "was practically arrested for the year."

The contractor selected for the project was Francis Hopkinson Smith, a man who would become a famous engineer, author, and artist. His foreman was Thomas Albertson Scott. In 1870, Smith was 32 years old; Scott was 40.

The Light-House Board asked for another $150,000 in the 1870 *Annual Report*. That money was provided by an act on March 3, 1871 and the *Annual Report* for that year reported that the work was "progressing satisfactorily, about 3,000 tons of granite having been placed in riprap foundation, in addition to which 7,000 tons will be delivered under a contract now in operation." It was expected that the "entire foundation, together with a portion of the supporting pier and landing wharf" would be contracted for and completed within a year. An additional $40,000 was requested, and provided by an act on June 10, 1872.

The 1872 *Annual Report* noted that the "proposals for the construction of the foundation and pier . . . were so excessive in rates, and so much above the amount of the appropriation on hand, that no

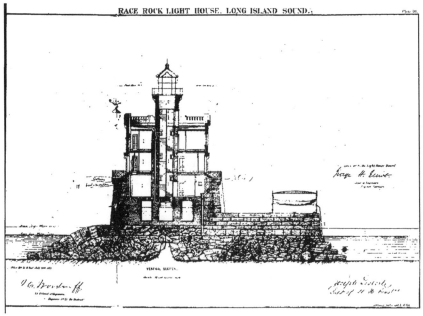

National Archives 3-2R8

Original plan for the Race Rock Light. July 1871.

more than the landing and the enrockment of the foundation, and two courses of the pier, could be contracted for." The previous November, 10,000 tons of riprap had been placed at the site and had weathered "the storms of winter and spring" without any apparent displacement or settling of the rocks. It was estimated that another $75,000 would be needed to complete the pier and lighthouse. Congress appropriated the funds on March 3, 1873.

Work continued in 1872 until early September, "when adverse weather was experienced." By this point, the plan had been modified again. It was decided to build the pier upon a concrete foundation, rather than riprap. Smith and Scott had "made considerable progress" since May, "having completed the laying of the facing or dimension-stone" and begun to prepare to lay the concrete foundation.

In 1908, Smith would describe this point of the project in his book, *Captain Thomas A. Scott, Master Diver*:

> At this stage of the work an important discovery was made; in fact we had been making it ever since work began. Many of the loose rocks forming the artificial island and which, in obedience to the Government's plan, had been thrown into the sea to find their own bottom, were found to have altered their position. Soundings showed that the depth of water outside the edge of the island, instead of being but twelve feet, as shown on the plan, was really thirty feet. We were, therefore, building the island on a pyramid, and not on a level surface. These facts, of course, were known and thoroughly discussed by the Government, and were as fully known to us. But the department had decided to try the experiment of their not settling, rather than incur the additional expense of leveling the whole shoal. The impossibility of placing a granite cone weighing thousands of tons on such a foundation now became apparent. The Government was notified, and after some weeks of investigation, we were asked for a modified plan which would utilize, as far as possible, the work already completed and paid for.
>
> I recall now the days and nights Captain Scott spent over this new problem and the number of models made and abandoned by us as new difficulties and obstacles presented themselves. At last a plan, upon which the lighthouse was finally built, was submitted to the board and approved. It was as follows:—

To chain and drag from the center of the turtle's back by means of heavy derricks erected in a square on four points of the island, all the three to five ton rock that had been dumped in, to replace these rocks outside the circle of the proposed excavation, piling them up as a breakwater until we had reached the original bottom and had uncovered the original Race Rock, a huge boulder weighing some twenty tons, and then to fill this water space with concrete in the form of a great disk up to the level of low water. Upon this concrete disk, in reality one solid stone—the shape of a huge cheese—was to be built the granite cone.

I recall, too, the months of labor devoted to the chaining and dragging from its bed these submerged rocks, jammed together as they were by succeeding winter's storms,—the work becoming more and more difficult as the water deepened. Problems like these are outside a manual; the time must come when a human body and a pair of human hands, backed by courage and brains, must take sea after sea upon his back when working above water, or while breathing through an inch hose when grappling them below the wave break. No money can pay for such labor;—nothing but loyalty to the work and his associates.

The 1874 *Annual Report* showed that things between Smith and the government were not going smoothly:

The work at this station continued until the month of September, 1873, when all active operation ceased. The contractor reported the foundation so far completed as to be ready for the placing of the iron band to be filled with concrete, at the same time submitted a statement of the amount of riprap stone removed from the centre of the island. This statement the engineer of the district [Colonel Woodruff] considered in excess of what he had computed as necessary or possible to be removed. After some correspondence on the subject, the committee on engineering of the board, the contractor, and the engineer of the district, proceeded, to the station, when a survey of the work was made, the amount removed determined, and the matter adjusted. Since settlement of the above question the work has proceeded with the view of preparing the bed for laying the concrete. The necessary removal of remaining stones that interfered with the placing of the iron band, 69 feet in diameter, has been completed, and the band placed. . . . The contractor has erected a shanty on the work for the accommodation of his workmen, &c., and it is hoped he may now push his work forward with more energy and means and equipments than he has heretofore employed.

On May 11, 1874, the New York Legislature ceded jurisdiction over "an area of less than one acre" at Race Rock to the federal government. As with the 25 other properties included in the act, New York retained concurrent jurisdiction.

During the 1874 work season, the construction steamer *Wallace* exploded, leaving several dead, and more injured. The *Wallace* was replaced by the *Screamer*, and work continued.

The 1875 *Annual Report* described the progress:

> The operations during the year have consisted in completing the concrete foundation for the pier, and the laying of the cut-stone courses of the pier and landing-wharf has been commenced. The contractor has not pushed this work during the year with the energy which its importance demands.

Smith, again in 1908, described this part of the project:

U.S. Coast Guard photo

The pier at Race Rock under construction on October 14, 1875.

With the water space cleared, the iron bands to circle the concrete were sunk and laid flat on the sandy bottom, filled with concrete mixed in a soft state, packed into buckets with drop bottoms and thus lowered to the divers below. This was continued until four successive circles of filled iron bands, one on top of the other,—a process occupying months—were laid and the disk struck smooth. The first base stone of the lighthouse,—a mill-stone sixty feet in diameter and three feet thick, hard as an obelisk, and like it of one solid stone,—was now complete.

No other problem confronted us. The succeeding years of work were like those always attending work of this class; there were storms, of course, with high surf, so that the Rock could not be reached and there were set backs of one kind or another, such as loss of shanties, platforms and every movable fixture. But the Captain's work was over, and one of the lasting monuments of his skill and loyalty complete in all its details.

By the end of November 1875, the second course of the pier and landing wharf was complete. Work resumed in May 1876. By the end of September, the eighth course of stone was complete. "After this the progress was slower, owing to the unfavorable weather. The quarters occupied by the workmen were twice damaged by the sea, and on November 21 the crib at the end of the landing-wharf was carried away." Work continued into early December, by which time the tenth course of stone "was set, but not doweled."

Work in 1877, begun on May 1, had some setbacks. Nearly one month was spent "repairing the damages done by the fall and winter storms." Then the concrete delivered to the site was rejected for being "of inferior quality." The pier was completed December 1877, despite progress that the government considered slow and unsatisfactory.

The lighthouse, unlike the pier upon which it was built, presented little difficulty in construction. The entire lighthouse was built during 1878. The 1879 *Annual Report* summed up the project:

This station was finally completed, and the light shone from the tower for the first time on January 1, 1879. The work in all respects has been very thoroughly done.

The final cost for the Race Rock Light Station was $278,716.33.

National Archives 26 LG 14-29

The pier at Race Rock nearing completion.

Neil Martin was appointed first keeper of the Race Rock Light on December 16, 1878, although his status was listed as "Acting" until he received his permanent appointment on February 17, 1881. Martin served at Race Rock until January 14, 1882, when he transferred to Stamford Harbor Light, Connecticut. In October 1882, he then transferred to Penfield Reef and his wife, Jane, became his assistant until her death about four years later. While at Race Rock, Martin's assistants included Joseph T. Adams, Thomas Brock, Thomas S. Carroll.

In March, 1880, the station was described on Form No. 36: "Description of Light-House Tower, Buildings, and Premises." General J.C. Duane was the form's preparer. According to the form, the lantern contained a Fourth Order light, flashing alternately red and white 68½ feet above water. The four-paneled lens revolved once every two minutes, giving a flash every 30 seconds. Two of the panels had ruby-colored glass attached to them to produce a red flash. The cast iron pedestal included an enclosure for the clockworks mechanism, which required winding every six hours. The light came from a Fourth Order mineral oil lamp. The lantern itself was made of cast iron, with wrought iron rafters, a copper roof, three brass ventilators, and brass curtain hooks "screwed into the astragals of the lantern." A wrought iron railing surrounded the lantern's gallery.

The bottom of the tower was ten feet square, and the diameter of the octagonal lantern, seven feet. The walls of the tower were 16 inches thick. Duane described the station's windows as "gothic" and noted that there were three doors to the dwelling, and one to the lantern.

The station was designed for one keeper and two assistants. Its rooms were "2 kitchens, 2 cellars & supply room in basement, 2 sitting & 2 dining rooms 1st floor[,] 5 bedrooms 2nd floor [and an] attic room" One outhouse provided the necessary facilities.

The cellar contained three 50-gallon oil butts, placed on a bench, and one 10-gallon oil can. A 24,000–gallon brick-lined cistern, which collected water from the roof, also resided beneath the dwelling. The station's closets and storerooms were considered "[d]ry and suited" to their purposes.

The station's fog signal was a metal bell weighing 1197 pounds. It was "[s]truck by machinery two blows in quick succession every 20 seconds." The bell was hung in front of the third story tower window.

The nearest town was New London, eight miles away, which could be reached by a small sailboat. Overall, Duane considered the station to be in good condition.

In 1883, a red and white flashing lens, with a "mineral oil" lamp, was installed. This new apparatus showed a flash every ten seconds.

When Neil Martin was transferred to Stamford Harbor, First Assistant Keeper Joseph Adams was appointed Acting Keeper of the Race Rock Light. Thomas S. Carroll, an Army veteran and native of Ireland who had arrived at Race Rock on February 1, 1881, was promoted to First Assistant Keeper. John A. Weller, a Navy veteran originally from England, was assigned as Second Assistant Keeper on January 23. Both Adams and Carroll received their permanent appointments on December 2, 1882.

Carroll had a home in Noank, Connecticut. In January, 1886, Carroll was stranded ashore because of a storm. He eventually decided he needed to return to the lighthouse, but never made it. The waves claimed his small boat, and him along with it. His body later washed up on shore at Groton Long Point. On February 1, John A. Weller was promoted to First Assistant Keeper to replace Carroll, and Moses Hill was assigned as Second Assistant Keeper nine days later.

In 1895, the Race Rock Light was reported as being "of great use to vessels going in and out of Long Island Sound," but that it "would be of much greater use if it had a fog signal." This was considered to be "a source of great anxiety to navigators if not a positive danger." It was thought that $3000 would cover the cost of an appropriate fog signal.

On October 20, 1896, Race Rock's new fog signal began operation. It was a second-class siren, powered by a six-horsepower engine. Due to "unsatisfactory working of the engine," the signal

was discontinued on June 8, 1897. The replacement of the engine with a seven-horsepower Hornsby-Akroyd oil engine was recommended. This change was made, and the signal was re-established on February 21, 1898.

In 1904, Smith and Scott visited the site where they had toiled to establish a lighthouse. According to Smith, in his 1908 book:

Francis Hopkinson Smith, circa 1895.

U.S. Lighthouse Society photo

It is but a few years back since this same old sea-dog—he was gray by this time, with a bald spot on the back of his head and a trifle larger around the middle—boarded his tug in East London harbor—he owned half a dozen of them then—took the younger brother with him and pointed the tug's nose for the Race Rock light, finished twenty-five years before.

Good many holes out there, the sea-dog said, as he plunged her nose head-foremost into the recurrent waves surging in from Montauk, and it git worse before it gits better.

As we neared the isolated pile of masonry, a spot in the waste of waters that all these years had withstood the attacks of the merciless sea, and still holds its light aloft—the figure of a man slid down the iron ladder of the cone and ran to the end of the wharf. Then came a voice.

Anything the matter? Anybody sick?

It was something out of the ordinary for a New London tug to head for the Rock in the teeth of a southeaster.

No,—just come out to see if we could land, the Captain cried.

Gosh!—how you skeered me,—thought some of the folks was tuk bad.

Then another man dropped down the ladder and springing to the boat's davits, began lowering a lifeboat.

What d'yer think, sir, shall we try it? asked the Captain.

Can we land? I asked dubiously.

Land!—of course, he replied with positive emphasis. It won't make no difference to me (he was seventy-four then),—but there won't be a dry rag on you.

I picked up the glass and looked over the joints of the masonry and followed the lines of the wharf and the angle of the cone. They were still as true as when Captain Tom had laid them with his own hands.

Never mind, Captain, I said—I guess you needn't bother.

What a difference twenty-five years makes in some of us!

In 1907, Race Rock's alternating red and white flashes, with a ten-second interval, were accompanied in poor visibility by a third class Daboll trumpet. The trumpet's characteristic was thus: three-second blast, three-second interval, three-second blast, three-second interval, three-second blast, 45–second interval. The trumpet's backup was a bell "struck by machinery a double blow every 20 sec[onds]."

John E. Miller, a retired Brooklyn police officer and son of area keeper Jonathan A. Miller, was assigned to Race Rock as Keeper on October 1, 1911. He remained until May 16, 1912, when he was assigned to Montauk Point.

In 1903, Thomas Albertson Scott had formed T.A. Scott Company, Inc., a marine salvage and construction company. His second son, Thomas Albertson Scott, Jr., born in 1877, became the company's president. In the early morning hours of November 17, 1916, two of the company's tugs were escorting a German commercial submarine, the *Deutschland*, out of New London and through the Race. The submarine and one of the tugs, the *T. A. Scott, Jr.*, collided. The tug sank quickly and took all five of its crew members with it.

In 1922, an inoperative fog signal caused a close call when the steamer *Arizona* grounded at the station. Another grounding at the station occurred nine years later, when the barge *Victorious* broke away from its tug and hit the rocks around the station. Keeper George H. Tooker, and his assistants, Ernest F. Witty and Emanuel Weber, "rescued Captain Hazell by climbing out on the sea-swept rocks and carrying a line out to him, all being in imminent danger of being washed away. The rescue was accomplished under

Thomas Albertson Scott.
U.S. Lighthouse Society photo

hazardous conditions and without injury." For their efforts, all three keepers were commended by the Department of Commerce.

The 1938 hurricane swept away much of the equipment at Race Rock, and spoiled the station's drinking water. The keepers reportedly drank the water from the heating system for several days thereafter. The storm also threw much of the riprap stone around. Some of it ended up by the landing wharf, making landing impossible except at extreme high tide. Three rocks, of about three tons each, were thrown up onto the wharf landing.

William Oliver Chapel, son of long-time Plum Island keeper William Maynard Chapel, became keeper of the Race Rock Light on April 30, 1943. Willie, as he was called, had previously served at the lights at Penfield Reef, Connecticut; Whale Rock, Rhode Island; New London Ledge; and Orient Point; as well as aboard the Cornfield Point lightship.

Chapel had started his lighthouse career prior to the Service's absorption by the Coast Guard. When the Coast Guard took control of aids to navigation, he elected to remain a civilian. During World War II, Chapel was transferred to the Coast Guard, and served two years in that capacity, but was still keeper at Race Rock: "They sent me right back to the light, and that's where I stayed." During the war, he spotted a mine floating near the station. The Navy recovered it, and found that it was a live mine.

Kevin Brennan was 18 years old when he arrived at Race Rock in November 1958. He had previously served on a 40–foot utility boat, *CG40516*, out of New London, performing mainly search and rescue, and logistics, duties. Brennan and three other young Coast Guardsmen were stationed at the light, with one of them on leave at all times. Willie Chapel must have had his hands full with the young men, as Brennan says their youthful enthusiasm created a bit of a "frat house" atmosphere.

While at Race Rock, Kevin Brennan would use a hammock strung between the railing and rain gutter for relaxation. One day, while resting in his hammock, a torpedo suddenly surfaced less than 100 feet in front of the lighthouse. Shortly thereafter, a gray Navy tug showed up, retrieved the torpedo, and carried it away in a special

U.S. Coast Guard photo

Undated photo of Race Rock.

cradle on the aft end of the tug. Kevin had noticed that the end of the torpedo was orange, indicating it was for practice use. This happened several more times during his stay, and Brennan would sometimes see the submarine that fired it off in the distance.

One day, Brennan saw Chapel down on the rocks with a long fish net. He asked Chapel what he was doing, and the head keeper responded that he was going to catch some fish. Brennan "thought he was crazy" but watched the older man for a while. Before long, Chapel caught a blackfish from a spot among the rocks and tossed it up onto the pier. Brennan was impressed, but Chapel told him to wait, as there would be another one. Not long after, the head keeper

Photo by the author

Race Rock in 1999.

caught another blackfish. He then told Brennan that there would be no more for a couple of weeks.

Not long after Brennan's time at Race Rock, Willie Chapel retired, with more than 36 years federal service. He and his wife, Iola, retired to their home in Ivoryton, Connecticut. Upon his retirement, Willie was looking forward to buying a boat and spending much time fishing.

In November 1978, the Race Rock Light was automated and its Fresnel lens removed. The tradition of lightkeeping at Race Rock, which had begun nearly 100 years prior, had ended.

On June 6, 2003, the nomination of the Race Rock Light for the National Register of Historic Places was approved. One of the preparers of the nomination, submitted by the Long Island Chapter of the U.S. Lighthouse Society, was former keeper Kevin Brennan.

The Race Rock Light, unknown to many Long Islanders, continues to guard the Race. Its flashing red light warns mariners of danger, and reminds us of the sometimes indomitable human spirit and the two remarkable men who personified that spirit during the lighthouse's construction.

North Dumpling

On the north side of Fisher's Island, several small islands dot the waters. The largest two are known as the Dumplings. North Dumpling has been home to a lighthouse since 1849.

Prior to the establishment of a lighthouse, a private lightboat had been stationed nearby to mark the entrance to West Harbor, on the north side of Fisher's Island. This boat, maintained by the Stonington Railroad and Steamboat Company, had been there since 1837.

George M. Bache's 1838 report included a letter from Andrew Mather, commander of the cutter *Wolcott*, which mentioned the island:

> An appropriation has been made for a small light on the North hammock, (Fisher's-island sound,) that would no doubt be a very important guide to steamboats running between New York and Stonington, which will soon be the principal route between New

Photo by the author

North Dumpling in 1999.

York and Boston for passengers, and frequently valuable property. It would likewise be an important guide to coasters, as they can often take advantage of the tide, and, if necessary, more conveniently make a harbor by going through this sound.

Bache had received other correspondence about this light. The Customs Collector (and thereby Superintendent of Lights) for the district of New Haven, William H. Ellis, wrote about the proposed light on September 25, 1838. He believed that the $3000 appropriation should be put toward a lighthouse on South Dumpling, as it was "a better site than" North Dumpling. He recommended an additional $3000 appropriation for this lighthouse.

On September 7, 1838, C. Palmer, President of the New York, Providence and Boston Railroad Company, had written in favor of the North Dumpling Light, noting that "[i]n the event of another war, no light in Long-island sound would be so important as this; all the coasting business, in such an event, would pass inside, through Fisher's-island sound. During the last war the harbor of Stonington was more important for the protection of coasters than any other between [New York] . . . and Newport." Palmer included a calculation of the number of people who annually passed North Dumpling, arriving at a total of 121,530 passengers, also adding that an estimated "3,500 transient pass the sound annually."

Bache responded to Palmer on October 20, advising him that "a site preferable to the North Dumpling may be found on the neighboring islet, the South Dumpling" because "a line drawn from the South Dumpling to the light at Stonington, passes through a clear channel; while one drawn from the North Dumpling, in the same direction, will pass very close to the shoals to the northward." Bache added his "opinion that two small lights, one higher then the other, ranging in the channel, and shown from the South Dumpling, will prove a better guide to vessels passing through from the eastward than a single light on the North Dumpling."

Palmer's ensuing response, on October 23, indicated that he had discussed the matter "with a gentleman of great intelligence from Stonington, and also with two of the most experienced pilots that navigate Long-island sound." These individuals agreed with Bache's opinion about the light's location, as well as the use of two lights, since the "arrangement would prevent the possibility of its being mistaken for any other light." Palmer added that the "public interest, as well as our own," would be "much promoted by the early completion of this work." It would be nearly nine years before the government would act on the matter, and the resulting light would not be as Bache had recommended.

On March 3, 1847, Congress appropriated $5000 for the establishment of a lighthouse on North Dumpling. On November 11, 1847, the federal government bought "North Dumplin, or Hammock," from William H. and Margaret A. Winthrop for $600. The Winthrop family had owned Fisher's Island and "the little islands or hammocks thereto belonging" for over 200 years.

Riley Clark was appointed as the light's first keeper on October 18, 1848, but could not be located. Local sea captain Joseph Dayton was temporarily put in charge of the light. The New London Collector of Customs requested that he remain in the position: "The commercial community here and elsewhere has a deep interest in having a Light Keeper who is well acquainted with reefs, rocks and shoals in the neighborhood of the Light House." Despite the collector's request, Alfred Clark was appointed keeper of North Dumpling on December 8, 1848.

A fog bell was on the island when Alfred Clark arrived. He was paid $32 per year by the New York and Stonington Steamboat Line to ring the bell in foggy weather when its ships were scheduled to be in the area.

Little is known of the 1849 lighthouse's design, but its illuminating apparatus consisted of seven lamps with 14-inch reflectors. Red shades created a steady red characteristic.

When Captain Howland visited North Dumpling to deliver supplies on June 29, 1850, he was blunt about the condition of this late-Pleasanton-era light:

> This is, indeed, a poor building—the mason work miserable; rain pours right through the walls—so much so that the keeper says he cannot keep his parlor furnished, because the room is so damp that it spoils his furniture; and this is the south room in the house. Nothing short of digging off the original mortar or sand, and

pointing it with cement or good mortar, will make it tight. Gutters, which were made of light tin, are off. Plank, or sides of the canal, are becoming loose, the lower ends of which were not properly secured. Red shades are altogether too dark; and, to show a light a little distance, the keeper has to raise his wicks so high, and burn so much oil, that he would show a red light without red shades. Everything in and about the premises is neat and clean; keeper is an industrious, and, I presume, an honest man.

Clark was burning 389 gallons of oil per year in the seven Winslow Lewis lamps, according to Howland's calculations.

In 1854, the private fog bell was replaced by a government bell. Upon discovering that the Little Gull Island keeper was getting paid much more for the same service, Clark reneged on his agreement with the steamboat company. The new bell cost the taxpayers $800. The striking mechanism for this bell only worked four times as long as it took to wind it, taking up much of the keeper's time in foggy weather. Eventually, this would lead to the request for an assistant keeper to help mind the station. John Baker, III became North Dumpling's second keeper when Clark resigned in November 1854. Perhaps Clark felt that his $400 annual salary, without the extra $32 he earned annually for the private fog signal, was insufficient. Baker's salary was raised to $500 in April 1855.

In April 1856, Lieutenant George G. Meade, a lighthouse engineer who would later be a Civil War general, completed the design of a striking mechanism for the bell at North Dumpling. Government documents indicate that this new mechanism was installed the following month. At the same time, a 270–degree, Sixth Order Fresnel lens, manufactured by the Henry-LePaute Company of Paris, replaced the old Winslow Lewis lamps.

John Baker tendered his resignation in May 1861, but later withdrew it. By July, John Spencer had been nominated to replace him, and on January 18, 1862, Spencer assumed the keeper's duties.

In July 1863, Hartman Bache and Joseph G. Totten, members of the Committee on Engineering, recommended some repairs for North Dumpling. Both of these men were prominent engineers. A fort named after Totten was being completed about this time just north of Washington, D.C. The fort would be active during the Civil

War. Totten (1788–1864) was known for building forts and lighthouses, with his most notable lighthouse project being the light at Minot's Ledge, Massachusetts. Bache (1798–1872), a grandson of Benjamin Franklin, had been head of the Bureau of Topographical Engineers since 1861. He was involved in the building of many American lighthouses.

By 1867, the station's buildings were "very much decayed" and the lantern was "worn out and of old pattern." The rebuilding of the station was recommended that year, and the following two as well. The 1868 *Annual Report* also requested the replacement of the fog bell apparatus with one that would run 40 times as long as it took to wind it. The mechanism in service at the time only ran four times as long as it took to wind it. This seemed to negate the need for an assistant keeper. The new mechanism was ordered from G. M. Stevens and Company in October.

On April 26, 1869, Henry Spencer replaced John Spencer as North Dumpling's keeper. Almost 15 months later, an appropriation of $15,000 was made for the rebuilding of the station. In 1871, the renovations were completed. The roof of the keeper's quarters was replaced with a Mansard roof and the building also received a new 39–foot tower and lantern, bringing the light 69 feet above water. The station was also given a new barn. At the time, there was a pond on the island, with a sluiceway leading to it, where the keeper moored his boat. The work in rebuilding the station included the installation of granite blocks along the banks of the sluice. Eight years later, a boathouse was built.

Third District Inspector and Navy Captain, A. C. Rhind, recommended John Gunn and his wife as keeper and assistant keeper of North Dumpling in June 1876. Gunn, a native of Scotland, was appointed keeper on July 13, 1876. His wife, Catherine, from Pennsylvania, was appointed as his assistant on January 4, 1878, after passing an examination for the position.

The assistant keeper's position had been authorized in 1872, but in 1886, the position was abolished, and the keeper's salary increased. The Gunns resigned at about this time. The new annual keeper's salary of $600 was much less than their previous combined

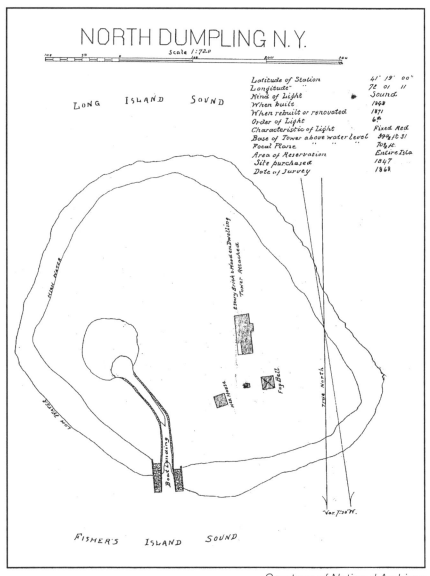

NORTH DUMPLING N.Y.

Scale 1:720

LONG   ISLAND   SOUND

Latitude of Station .... 41° 19' 00"
Longitude " 72 01 11
Kind of Light .... Sound
When built 1848
When rebuilt or renovated 1871
Order of Light 6th
Characteristic of Light .... Fixed Red
Base of Tower above water level .... 39½ ft 31
Focal Plane " " .... 70½ ft.
Area of Reservation .... Entire Isla
Site purchased 1847
Date of Survey 1868

FISHER'S   ISLAND   SOUND

Courtesy of National Archives

1870s map of North Dumpling.

salaries ($500 for him, $300 for her). John A. Weller, a native of England and U.S. Navy veteran, took the job at the new salary, only to have it decreased to $560 as of November 1, 1888. He had been caught out of uniform and reprimanded in August of 1887, but the cause for the reduction in salary was administrative, not as a penalty.

By 1890, the island of North Dumpling included the lighthouse and fog bell tower, with a covered walkway between the two, a boat landing that led to the island's pond, chicken houses, an enclosure used as a coal bin, a work shop, and a large garden. Aside from coal for the stove and oil for the lamp, the station was largely self-sufficient. The island was changing shape, as the high water line on the east side of island was approaching the pond. Eventually, the pond would be lost to erosion.

In 1891, a new fog bell tower and clockworks mechanism were installed at the station. Two years later, the apparatus was overhauled and the station's lens and lamp were changed. A new Fifth Order lens, with a Funck lamp and new pedestal, replaced the former Sixth Order lens in 1892, and a Notice to Mariners was issued.

Keeper John A. Weller resigned in 1895. On September 12, 1895, Joseph Fowler, from South Carolina, replaced Weller. Fowler, who had served at the lighthouse at Watch Hill, Rhode Island from 1890 to 1895, would remain keeper until October 10, 1911. In 1897, Mrs. Fowler, the keeper's wife, was commended for a meritorious act, although it is unclear what that act was.

In 1900, the 1891 fog bell apparatus was changed. Adding a unique aspect to the history of this station, a "telephone plant" was installed at North Dumpling in 1902. The Light-House Board had given permission to the Southern New England Telephone Company to do so in 1900, with no objection from Third District Inspector Shepard and Engineer Heap.

The Fowlers daughter, Ann, met a bugler from Fort H. G. Wright, on nearby Fisher's Island, in 1904. The bugler, Robert Howell (1866–1963), wrote down his memoirs in the 1950s, when he was in his 90s. According to Howell, he had met Ann while he and two others from the fort had hit bad weather in a boat. The keeper's

U.S. Coast Guard photo

Northeast corner of the lighthouse in an undated photo.

daughter had spotted them from the lighthouse and, after helping them back to the fort so that Howell could "put [his friends] . . . in the bake shop to sober up," she brought Howell to the lighthouse to visit her parents. Howell "became a regular visitor and spent a lot of time at the Dumpling, and enjoyed every hour of it."

Howell and Ann Fowler developed a close relationship, spending much time together. They "lobster fished and fished with lure and reel and always had mackerel and flounder, and caught enough one day to give all of the 12th [Company] a big fish dinner."

By 1905, Howell was 42 and Ann, a "stalwart sailor," was 25. The two would spend much time boating and "singing like 2 happy kids." The relationship turned more serious, however, when Ann asked Howell to put down her old and ailing dog. After the dog died, Ann told Howell that she had "only one good friend left" and hugged him. According to Howell: "I knew then I had a job trying to convince her of the folly of falling in love with such a restless individual as I was. I brought up that old bugaboo about youth and old age, but all to no avail. She told me right out in language I could understand that I was the man she had picked out to be the father of her children. What could I say to that? So we just drifted along."

The two witnessed the launching of the 690–foot freighter *Dakota*, one of the largest ships of her kind at the time, at a shipyard in Groton, Connecticut. The *Dakota* would later sink off of Japan in 1907, on her seventh voyage.

One night in November of 1905, Ann Fowler called Fort H.G. Wright to ask for assistance with the rescue "of a schooner that was wrecked on Block Island." She asked for ropes, blankets, dry clothes, "and last but not least a [quart] . . . of good whiskey for a medical purpose." She also asked for Howell to assist her. Of the rescue, Howell wrote:

> She came, was loaded up, thanked all and we left on a voyage of mercy. It took us an hour and a half to get there and we found 8 men in dire distress. Just a few people had braved the strong winter to come and see the distressful situation. We first got the bottle over to the men, she said, "Don't take too much, just a couple of good swallows, and send it back." They did, so we proceeded to put one end of the tackle on their boat and fastened the other to our craft and brought them all safely on board, gave them another swig of whiskey, wrapped them up in the blankets, put the rain coats, dry socks and the low cut overshoes on them and detached the block from the wreck, then headed for the marine hospital at New London. We soon got there and hustled them inside, had them put to bed. We called [Colonel] Davis, told him how well we had done the job and she said she would bring the stuff he had so generously let her have. Col Davis told her to keep that equipment. "I am sure such a Salvage Corps such as yours needs stuff like that quite often." She said, "Col some day I shall come and thank you personally." The old Col said [for her to] "come any time. I too shall be glad to see such a stalwart sailor as you." He also said, "Tell bugler Howell I will put in for a 3 day pass for him. Good night all." We went back to the Dumpling and went to bed tired but happy in thought of a deed well done.

Thirty days after the rescue, Ann called Howell to inform him that Admiral Schley, head of the [Third Lighthouse District] . . .was coming to see and decorate her and would arrive on a certain day at noon. So the Fowlers got busy and prepared a fine dinner for 12 officers, and I can tell you it was some spread. 2 more dutch women from [Connecticut] had come over to assist, and when the 2 ships came up as close to the Dumpling as was safe, they were ready for them. Admiral Schley and 11 officers filed up the hill to the residence, came in and were escorted to the living room and were introduced. Wine was served, smokes to those who cared for them. Pretty soon I stepped to the door and said, "Come and get it," and they came. The Admiral at one end, Miss Ann at the other and I was on her right. The Admiral said, "Now before we start to enjoy this fine repast, I have a job to do and a pleasant one too. Miss Ann the [department] has requested me to present to you this medal, and this five thousand dollars in gold for your bravery in rescuing 8 men on Nov 4th this year." He came to her side, pinned the medal on her breast, and set a chamois skin bag at her place containing 250 20 dollar gold pieces, kissed her on the cheek, went and sat down. She said, "But Admiral I was not alone on that night you mentioned. Bugler Howell of the 12th Co Coast Artillery was my crew and I would love for you to do something for him." "Well I can't give him a medal or monetary reward. What would you suggest?" She said, "If Mr. Howell can pass the examination to qualify as a first class light house tender I would like to have him appointed to this light house." The Admiral said, "I'll do it." Now he said, "You say he will be discharged [March] 21st. I'll make the appointment retroactive to [January] the first and he will have three months and 21 days pay coming. His base pay will be $175.00 per month. $300 a year for clothing, $20 per [month] for Rations which we'll give him. A salary of $220 per month." And with a nice smile he added, "I think you two will be able to live nicely on that. You are now getting $95 per month as [assistant] and from now on your pay will be $125.00 which will remain the same when the bugler comes to take charge." So all fell to and it was a happy gathering. I told them about my early frontier army days, about my romance with Mrs. [General] Custer and my 2 meetings with [General] Fred D. Grant [the oldest son of Ulysses S. Grant]. They sailed away then Ann said to me, "Oh Robert just to think for about an hours work all this good luck as come to me."

Ann Fowler put the money in a bank in New London, with $4000 of it in her name and $1000 in his name, and gave Howell "the deposit book and said that is all yours to do with as you see fit. She was holding me so tight with proofs of love and adoration. I couldn't think of a way to get out of it and not tear her heart to shreds."

When Howell's enlistment neared its end, he had a decision to make:

Well the night before that fatal date [March] 21st came . . . It was 9:30 I was lying there a miserable creature knowing in a few hours I was going to break a woman's heart. She opened the door softly and said, "Robert are you awake?" I said, "I am." She had on a beautiful dressing gown, her pretty hair was down and her eyes sparkled. She pulled a hassock up to the side of the bed . . . and cried loudly. I did too and I often think if I had said to her, "Darling I am not going to leave you, but I am going to stay and be your boss here on the Dumpling as long as I live and dry up your tears. Take me to the fort in the morning, hang around till I round up my affairs, then I'll come back here and make ready for a wedding," what a difference in her feelings there would have been. But the next day when she took me to the Fort there was not much said between us. I said, "I won't say good bye, not yet." She said at parting, "You have 2 choices, you can make me either the happiest woman in the world or the most miserable, which will it be, but anyway good bye for now." I had left the book for the $1000 under my pillow. I thought I couldn't be that mean to take her money and break her heart at the same time. Of course in later years I wondered why I had been such a fool.

In telling the story of his relationship with of Ann Fowler, Howell described himself as "a skunk of the first quality."

When Howell left the area, the light at North Dumpling was a fixed white light from a Fifth Order lens. A red sector covered an area from 900 feet south of the Latimer Reef Light almost to the Race Rock Light.

On October 10, 1911, James J. Barnes became North Dumpling's keeper. In 1915, a power boat with two occupants was stranded on North Dumpling's shore by a strong wind. Barnes brought the boaters safely onto the island.

During Prohibition, it was suspected that Fisher's Island was a hub for bootlegging. Keeper Burkhart was accused of aiding rumrunners by setting up signal lights on the island. North

Dumpling's position certainly would have made it a convenient place for transferring cargo or watching for authorities. No evidence was ever found by officials to indict Burkhart.

The Hurricane of 1938 caused much damage at North Dumpling. The bell tower was destroyed, as were the boathouse and a storehouse, and part of the island was washed away.

Bill Bright was stationed at North Dumpling in 1952. The station's Officer in Charge was Bill Clark, who had been at North Dumpling since about World War II. Life was still fairly rural at the time. There was no central heating; a single stove was used indoors for heating and cooking in winter, and brought outside for cooking during the summer. A hand pump in the kitchen brought water from the cistern to the sink.

Photo courtesy of Bill Bright
Northwest corner of the lighthouse in 1952.

The North Dumpling Light Station was automated in May 1959, with the lighthouse's duties taken up by a 60–foot tower on the southwest side of the island. The 3.755–acre island was put up for auction. It was advertised in the *New York Times*, *New London Day*, *The Suffolk Times*, and Long Island *Newsday* newspapers. The first offering received 34 qualified, and 25 non-qualified, bids, but none were deemed acceptable. The property was advertised again, with 13 bids received this time. The third offering finally resulted in a sale. George Washburn's $18,000 bid won the auction when the sealed bids were opened on July 31.

By mid-August, prior to the closing of title on the property, the "brick dwelling and improvements on the property were vandalized and damaged." Under common law, this was the buyer's problem.

But under the New York State Real Property Law, the buyer was entitled to an abatement. The estimate for damage was $4350, and an adjustment was made in the mortgage.

Washburn, a Manhattan resident, spent little time at the island and neglect and vandalism took their toll. In 1980, David Levitt

Bill Clark at North Dumpling in 1952.

Photo courtesy of
Bill Bright

bought the island for $95,000, then invested more money in the property, repairing and remodeling the island's structures, as well as planting a variety of shrubs and trees. The lighthouse was remodeled, and much of its historic appearance was lost. During the time Levitt owned the island, the light was returned to the lighthouse, and still sits upon the current faux lantern room.

The island was sold again in 1986, to its fifth owner, Dean Kamen, an inventor and entrepreneur. His best-known invention is the Segway scooter. Kamen still owns the island, and is reported to have a sense of humor about his little domain, referring to it as the Republic of North Dumpling, with its own currency and navy (an amphibious vehicle resides on the eastern side of the island). The island also includes a small Stonehenge-like structure, called the Temple of the Four Winds, and a modern windmill.

Although the lighthouse at North Dumpling does not look much like it did in its manned days, it is an active aid to navigation. It will likely remain privately owned for many years to come.

Photo by the author

North Dumpling Light in 1999.

Latimer Reef

The oldest operating cast iron lighthouse in the region, the Latimer Reef Light stands as a sign of the end of the stone lighthouse era in the Long Island area. Sitting upon a reef north of the eastern end of Fisher's Island, it is not usually seen by most Long Islanders.

The reef's name is the subject of speculation, with some reports stating that during the American Revolution a man named Latemore was caught spying on the British fleet near the reef and was hanged. The change to Latimer, according to this theory, came over time. By 1800, less than 20 years after the end of the war, there was reference to "an iron spear about 13 feet long, with a large black ball and white vane at the top, upon the Latimer in Fishers Island Sound." Another possible source of the reef's name may have been the Latimer family, which had settled in New London in 1660. An early member of the family, Robert Latimer, had been involved in the local coasting trade as part owner of the bark *Hopewell*. Several New London Latimers served in the American Revolution.

The 1804 *Coast Pilot* mentioned "an iron spire on top of . . . [Latimer Rock], about 13 feet high, with a white vane." In 1827, the *Coast Pilot* referred to the reef as "Latimore's Reef."

In 1838, George Bache's report on the area's aids to navigation mentioned the existence of a "spindle on Latimer's reef." He also noted a "beacon to be erected on Latimer's reef, near the eastern entrance to Fisher's-island sound. . . . This reef is much in the way of vessels passing in either direction through the sound, or bound into Stonington." Also included in Bache's report was a letter from Andrew Mather, commander of the cutter *Wolcott*, which suggested that the area's navigation would be "improved by a light-boat at Latimer's reef."

In 1857, the reef was still marked by a spindle. Early that year, it was carried away by ice.

Although a lightship was not stationed at Latimer Reef, one was anchored at the nearby Eel Grass Shoal, in Connecticut waters, in 1849. The first lightship (Lightship L) at Eel Grass Shoal was a

U.S. Coast Guard photo

Latimer Reef Light in an undated photograph.

41–ton, wooden vessel. In 1863, she had the station name painted on each quarter in black letters, with a fog bell and horn in addition to her fixed white light. Flashing lights, which were produced by revolving mechanisms, were not used on early lightships.

Lightship L was replaced by *LV 12* in 1871. *No. 12* was a 72–foot schooner rigged wooden vessel with two masts. She had been built with no number in 1846, given the designation *LV 22* in 1867, then redesignated *LV 12* in 1871. In 1872, *No. 12* was transferred to Cornfield Point.

From 1872 to 1877, *LV 25* marked Eel Grass Shoal. The 61–foot vessel had been built in 1827. Prior to being stationed at Eel Grass Shoal, she had been "in Roanoke Sound, North Carolina." When the former station was replaced by a screw pile light, "her services were no longer necessary." She was expected to "probably last for two or three years." Made of wood and schooner-rigged, she had one lantern. By 1876, *No. 25* was "unsound, and too small for the service." The use of this ship for "any considerable time" would require $6000 worth of repairs.

In 1877, *LV 17*, which had been built in 1848 at nearby Stonington, replaced *LV 25*. *No. 17* was a 78–foot wooden sail-powered vessel with two lanterns. *No. 25* was sent to New London to be used as a relief ship. In 1885, *LV 25* was decommissioned and sold at auction.

On October 1, 1880, Charles Edwin Pendleton Noyes was appointed as master of the lightship at Eel Grass Shoal. He had been born April 15, 1831, in Stonington, Connecticut. His wife, Mary Emma (Langworthy), whom he had married on March 12, 1864, was nine years his junior. Charles and Mary had three children: Carrie (born 1865), Emma Jane (born 1868), and Benjamin Franklin (born 1879). Like many lightkeepers of his era, Noyes was a war veteran. During the Civil War, Noyes had served in the North Atlantic Squadron as an Acting Ensign aboard the 137–foot, wooden-hulled sidewheel steamer *Wilderness*. The *Wilderness*, which had been built in Brooklyn as the *B. N. Creary* in 1864, was a reserve ship during the attacks on Fort Fisher, North Carolina, on December 23–26, 1864, and January 13–15, 1865, when the fort was captured. Noyes served aboard her during this battle and in other armed conflicts during the war.

No. 17 remained at Eel Grass Shoal until 1882, when *No. 12* returned to the station. *LV 12*, with Charles Noyes in command, remained on station until 1884.

On March 27, 1883, the New York Legislature ceded jurisdiction and ownership of a site "seven hundred feet in diameter, the center of which shall be the spindle now marking the said site of Latimer's Reef." The act included a stipulation that the jurisdiction and ownership were only for as long as the site was "used for lighthouse purposes and no longer."

In 1884, the lightship at Eel Grass Shoal was replaced by the Latimer Reef Light, located less than a mile southeast of the lightship station. This put the new lighthouse in New York waters.

The new lighthouse was built of cast iron, lined with bricks, on a cement-filled cast iron base. Like the many similar lighthouses that would follow it, the tower was built of curved plates, bolted together through flanges. The base, 30 feet in diameter, was filled with cement, and given a brick-lined basement. The tower itself was 21 feet in diameter at the base, 18 feet in diameter at the top, and contained three floors and an enclosed watch deck. A black cast iron lantern topped the structure, holding the light 55 feet above the water. A central column housed the weights for the rotating lens' clockworks mechanism. A roof covered the walkway around the base of the tower, including the single door, facing west. Cast iron stairs, attached to the outside walls, allowed access to the different levels.

The brown lighthouse with a black lantern was built on the west end of the rocky reef, which was nearly half a mile in length. Its Fifth Order flashing white light was first lit July 1, 1884. A buoy was placed at the east end of the reef at about the same time.

In early June 1884, Third Light-House District Inspector Brown recommended the establishment of two keeper positions at Latimer Reef. The Secretary of the Treasury authorized the positions shortly thereafter.

Noyes, who had been the master of the lightship, was appointed as the first keeper of the Latimer Reef Light on June 12, 1884. His assistant was Samuel G. Gardiner, who had been appointed as Noyes' assistant aboard the lightship on June 2, 1884. Like most of the assistants at Latimer Reef during Noyes' years there, Gardiner did not stay long, transferring on September 9, 1886.

Records indicate that Latimer Reef Light had a change in tower color in 1886. In 1892 and 1899, records once again reported a change in color for the Latimer Reef Light.

In June 1897, Third District Engineer David Porter Heap recommended that Latimer Reef receive a new lamp and lens. He also recommended a change in the order of the lens.

From the author's collection

Pre-1910 postcard.

The lighthouse received a new lens in 1898, with a Fourth Order lens replacing the old Fifth Order. The revolving mechanism was also changed, to a unit using ball bearings in place of the previous unit's wheels. This new design was one of the many improvements made to lighthouse apparatus by Engineer Heap. According to the December 22, 1898 *Westerly Sun*, the new unit worked "with precision and gives much better satisfaction than that of the old design . . . Capt. Noyes . . . will, when this work is done, have charge of one of the finest lights in the world."

In 1907, the lighthouse exhibited a flashing white light every 10 seconds from its Fourth Order lens. A bell struck by machinery every 15 seconds sounded in foggy weather.

William H. Smith replaced Noyes on August 1, 1909. Noyes had served over 25 years at Latimer Reef. He had many assistants over those years, including Samuel Gardiner, George Friend, Manuel Joseph, Joseph Fowler, Christopher Culver, Jr., George Frimm, Albert Warren, Eugene Nash, Charles Oliver, Elmer Rathbun, Adolf Nordstrom, William Tengren, William Mendel, Samuel Leonard, Phillip Roberg, James Barrell, J. R. Carlsson, Henry Spencer, Raymond Cleaves, William Murray, Owen Burdge, W. C. Moore, and Robert Rodger.

Charles Edwin Pendleton Noyes passed away on November 1, 1912, and was buried in Westerly, Rhode Island. His wife, Mary, died January 3, 1920 in Bayonne, New Jersey, and was buried with her husband in Rhode Island.

On March 1, 1914, a bad storm battered Latimer Reef. Keeper Smith reported, "At 9:30 pm., the sea was so high that it broke over the Platform and Pier." His skiff was lost in the storm, as was the woodshed and part of the station's fencing. Making matters worse was the loss of the station's outhouse.

In 1918, the reef was marked on the west end by the lighthouse, with a horizontally striped buoy on the east end. Another horizontally striped buoy sat three-eighths of a mile northeast of the lighthouse, marking another rocky patch.

The 1938 hurricane roared through the area, causing great damage "consisting in general of the destruction of small boats, damage to foundations, the breaking in of windows and doors and consequent flooding, and the destruction of power lines and the derangement of other exposed apparatus." Latimer Reef was listed in the *Lighthouse Service Bulletin* as one of the stations at which "the principal damage occurred."

In 1946, the Latimer Reef Light was showing a flashing white light every 10 seconds. This light came from an incandescent oil vapor lamp casting 24,000 candlepower through a Fourth Order lens. The fog bell sounded once every 15 seconds.

U.S. Coast Guard photo
Undated aerial photo showing exposed location of Latimer Reef Light.

Don Daly was a young Coast Guardsman in 1952. He had relief duty at Latimer Reef for nearly two weeks that year. Unfortunately for him, it was during the winter. The lighthouse was cold; a coal stove on the first floor was the tower's only heat. The two floors above, with sleeping quarters, and the watch deck above them, were unheated. The station had no electricity and no indoor plumbing. The light was produced by an incandescent oil vapor lamp, the clockworks mechanism had to wound by hand, and lanterns were used to read at night. Trips to Fisher's Island were made once a week for showers. According to Daly, "for a 17–year-old from Brooklyn, it was a trip in time back to the 18th century." He would later be stationed at the similar Orient Point Light, but that lighthouse, with electricity, was better duty than Latimer Reef. In remembering his time at Latimer Reef, Daly commented, "I don't remember anything that was good or that was fun at Latimer Reef."

Photo by the author

Latimer Reef Light in September 1999.

In 1983, a 300mm lens replaced the former Fourth Order lens, which had been manufactured by Barbier, Benard, and Turenne of Paris, France. The Latimer Reef tower was painted in 1997, and the white tower with brown stripe, and green railings looked like new.

Today, the Latimer Reef Light's history, and the stories of its keepers, are rarely topics of discussion. Oblivious to its own anonymity, however, the lighthouse continues to carry out its duties as it has for nearly 120 years.

The South Fork

Montauk Point
(1796)

Gardiner's Point
(1854)

Cedar Island
(1839, 1868)

Shinnecock Bay
(1857)

Montauk Point

Photo by the author

Montauk Point tower in 2003.

To many, it seems as though Montauk Point was always meant to have a lighthouse. With a tall hill at the end of a peninsula jutting out into the Atlantic Ocean, the location's suitability for a lighthouse was obvious. The Montaukett Indians realized this long ago, using the elevation of Turtle Hill to display fires for signaling purposes.

Early European settlers also no doubt were quick to see the need for some sort of navigational aid on the spot. This point marked the main entrance in and out of Long Island Sound from the south.

During their occupation of Long Island during the American Revolution, the British were said to have used Turtle Hill as a place for bonfires–one of the earliest forms of navigational aid. The precedent had been set for a lighthouse on Turtle Hill.

In August 1789, the Second Congress put the maintenance of lighthouses under federal jurisdiction. These responsibilities had previously been executed by the states and, before that, the colonies.

In October 1791, New York's Congressional delegation, at the request of Commissioner of Revenue Tench Coxe, asked the New York Chamber of Commerce to provide information for the placement of a lighthouse on Montauk Point. The Chamber, via a special committee, believed "Ezra L'Hommedieu [sic], Esq., of Suffolk County" to be "a proper Person to obtain the information sought after, who undertook to procure a draft, and point out the most proper place on Montauk Point to be fixed upon to erect a Light House at Montauk Point, in the State of New York."

On November 19, 1792, the committee submitted L'Hommidieu's report, dated November 1, and his bill, for seven pounds, six shillings. The report states:

> Gentlemen—I am now on my Return from Montauk point where with the advice of Capts. Rogers, Post and Franks, experienced mariners, and Abraham Miller, Esq., I have fixed upon a spot for erecting a light-house agreeable to the request of the Chamber of Commerce. . . . The hill called Turtle Hill, where the Light-House is to stand, is seventy-five feet above the level of the sea at highwater, and two hundred and ninety-seven feet from the shore. The hill is equally high to the Bank, and the land equally good for a foundation, being to appearance gravel, stone and marl, with

clay, but as the Bank is washed by the sea in storms, we suppose it best to set the Building at this distance. . . . The Proprietors are content to take six pounds per acre for the land, provided the United States fence the same, or such part thereof as shall be improved, at their own expense. They will also grant the privilege of landing on any part of their land, and carting through the same, whatever may be necessary for the Light House. . . . Notwithstanding the height of this hill, above the water, there are others at a distance near the sea, something higher, which will make it necessary in the opinion of the gentlemen with me to have the Light House seventy or eighty feet above the top of the hill, so that the same may be seen over land by vessels which may be to the westward, near the shore. On the north side there is no obstruction. We could see Plum Island, Gardiner's Island and Fisher's Island very plain.

The letter clearly names those involved in the decision for the placement (297 feet from the bluff) and necessary height (70 to 80 feet) of the lighthouse. The fact that the popular story credits George Washington for the placement of the lighthouse is forgivable, as no other figure has had such a mythic place in American history.

Congress appropriated $20,000 for the construction of the lighthouse on March 2, 1793 and, in April 1795, the Treasury Department placed a call for bids. Four proposals were submitted by August from Abashai Woodward of New London, Connecticut; Abraham Miller & Company of East Hampton; Nathaniel Richards of New London; and John McComb of New York.

John McComb, Jr., a Scottish immigrant who had built the original Cape Henry Lighthouse in Virginia in 1791, won the contract for the lighthouse with a bid of $22,300. Construction of the 78–foot tower began on June 7, 1796. Sandstone from Connecticut was shipped to Montauk Point, then hauled to the top of the hill by horse-drawn wagons. Construction continued until the completion of the lighthouse, sans lantern glass and oil, on November 5, 1796. Henry Packer Dering, the local Collector of Customs at Sag Harbor, visited the site on November 8 and reported the lighthouse "together with the Oil Vault and dwelling house compleatly [sic] finished." Just prior to completion, Jacob Hand was appointed as the first lighthouse keeper in Long Island history.

Fate would deal an ironic twist to the start of our local lighthouse history. On December 10, Dering reported to Tench Coxe that "the vessel in which the Oil for the Light House at Montauk was shipped from New Port is on shore at a place called Nappeague." This grounding caused the loss of the lantern glass; replacement panes would not arrive at Dering's office until the following Spring. The oil (which had been stored at Montauk's First House) and glass were delivered in the Spring of 1797, and the light from New York's first lighthouse would be seen in April of 1797. The lamp that emitted this light was probably a spider lamp that used multiple wicks drawing oil from a single pan-like source, or a series of individual oil lamps.

No lighthouse on Long Island serves as such a fine example of the advancing technology of American lighthouse illumination over the years. Argand lamps and reflectors replaced the original lamp, which were replaced by a Fresnel lens with a single lamp, which was eventually replaced by automated electric optics. The full variety of commonly used fuels, and lamp and lens styles, would provide the light from the lantern room atop Turtle Hill over the lighthouse's history.

As Jacob Hand was nearing the end of his time at Montauk Point (he would serve until 1812), he hoped that his son would replace him. President Thomas Jefferson thought otherwise:

> I have constantly refused to give in to this method of making offices hereditary. Whenever this one becomes actually vacant, the claims of Jared Hand may be considered with those of other competitors.

Jared Hand did gain the position, and served for two years.

Patrick Gould became Montauk Point's fourth keeper in 1832, replacing Henry Baker. He would remain until 1849.

By 1837, it was decided to rebuild the keeper's quarters. In the February 18 edition of the *Sag Harbor Corrector*, local Collector of Customs, and thereby Superintendent of Lighthouses, John P. Osborn, issued a call for proposals to build "a Dwelling House, for the keeper of the light house, at Montauk Point." The plans called for the structure:

to be built of hard brick thirty-eight feet front by twenty-two feet deep, one story, nine feet high in the clear, divided into two rooms with an entry between, the stairs to be in the entry to go into the chambers, which are to be four in number, beside the entry, to be lathed and plastered; chimneys in each end of the house with a fire place in each, . . . cellar under the whole house, . . . the walls of the house to be twenty inches thick and fourteen feet high from the ground floor, to be well pointed with cement and whitewashed twice over, the roof to be covered with slate; two windows in each room of 16 lights, of 10 by 12 inches white glass each; to be six dormant windows as large as the roof will allow, three in front and three to the rear; the doors to be four paneled [sic], with good hangers and locks to each, and a strong lock on the front door, . . . the floors to be of good white pine plank, planed grooved and well nailed. . . . A well to be sunk if practicable, if not, a cistern to be dug.

The above dwelling still resides on the site of the lighthouse, located at the bottom of the hill; long used as a storage building.

In 1838, George Bache visited Montauk Point:

No. 9 *Montauk light* . . . is passed by all vessels approaching Long-island sound from seaward, and is a good point of departure for those leaving the sound. It is also frequently made by vessels from the southward bound to the northward and eastward, and by those approaching New-York bay from the eastward. Its elevation is 160 feet, and its limit of visibility . . . is 19 miles . . ..

A new lighting apparatus was placed in the lantern in July, 1838; it consists of 18 lamps with parabolic reflectors, which are arranged around two iron tables—ten upon the upper, and eight upon the lower table; the vacant space below being towards the land. The reflectors are 14½ inches in diameter, and weigh from 3lbs. to 3lbs. 6oz.; the tube glasses in use are too short to project through the holes in the reflectors.

The end of the section contained a general summary of the construction of the Third District's lighthouses and illuminating apparatus. Montauk fared better than most of the area's lights in this summary. This was partially due to the new lamps and reflectors in its lantern room (the inadequacy of the glass chimneys noted above was the only negative comment about this). Lieutenant Bache also noted that in the district, "the oldest buildings are now in the best condition" and that those "erected at the close of the last century, afford a striking contrast to many of those of very recent construction."

On June 1, 1850, Captain Howland's ship arrived at Montauk Point for the annual resupplying of the station. The lighthouse's keeper at the time was John Hobart, and the lantern room contained 15 lamps with 21–inch reflectors, the new lamps and reflectors having been installed in 1849. Captain Howland, reported that:

> This light-house, and, in fact, the whole establishment, I must call in good order, and the lighting apparatus clean. We left our vessel 4 or 5 miles from this light-house, in consequence of the wind dying away and night coming on. Went on shore, made the repairs to the lighting apparatus, which were trifling, and left the oil in the casks for the keeper to cart up and pump off, he not having a team, and none to be obtained short of 6 or 7 miles.

Captain Howland calculated the average use of oil per lamp, based on the amount of oil used since his last visit on June 9, 1849. This average, 32 and three-fifteenths gallons per lamp per year, was less than the 35 gallons per lamp per year that the nation's seacoast lights averaged. Once again, Montauk Point could be proud of its record.

In 1855, keeper Silas P. Loper, who had replaced Hobart in 1849, was drawing a salary of $350 per year. This was equal to the pay received by Lyman G. Sherman at Cedar Island, Edward Floyd at Eaton's Neck, and William Boothe at Plum Island, more than the salaries of Benjamin Downing at Sands Point or Elizabeth Smith at Old Field Point, and less than the pay of Albert Edwards at Gardiner's Island, John Baker III of North Dumpling, or William Ross at Little Gull Island.

December 1856 saw the wreck of the brig *Flying Cloud*, which hit the rocks at Montauk Point. Patrick T. Gould assisted the crew and was awarded a gold medal from the Life Saving Benevolent Association for "his courage and humanity saving from inevitable death" the crew of the ship. Although some sources list Gould as the keeper of the lighthouse at the time, official records indicate that Jason Sorbell was the keeper at the time of the *Flying Cloud's* demise. Gould may have been the keeper of the life saving station, as the heads of those stations were also called keepers. Regardless of Gould's official status, his bravery was most notable.

By 1858, the Light-House Board's overhaul of the nation's lighthouse system was in full swing. Its *Annual Report* for that year showed that a First Order Fresnel lens had been installed at Montauk Point in 1857, showing a fixed white light varied by brighter white flashes (visible three to five miles further than the fixed light) every two minutes.

The June 16, 1860 edition of the *Sag Harbor Corrector* contained the following item under its "Long Island News" heading:

> The work of repairing and raising Montauk Light commenced the first of the week. There are now twelve men engaged in carrying out the proposed arrangements. The Lighthouse is to be built 14 feet higher than at present and a new and superior lantern introduced. Beside this, it is to be strengthened by thickening the walls; two new dwelling houses are to be built for the use of the keepers, so constructed however as to form one building. A tower also is to be raised for a temporary light. A schooner from New York has already landed a cargo of lumber and returned for a cargo of brick.

Montauk Point Lighthouse, L. I.

Postcard from the author's collection

Montauk Point prior to 1903.

This was a major renovation of the lighthouse, intended mainly to extend the tower to let the light be seen further, facilitate the proper display and care of a First Order lens, and strengthen the tower to handle the weight of the new apparatus. The tower's wooden floors and stairs were also replaced with iron construction.

The 1860 renovations also included the large keepers' quarters in which a museum now resides. This was a large improvement over the earlier quarters, and undoubtedly increased the comfort of the keepers and their families.

By 1868, the light station was a well-established part of the Montauk Point landscape. The area surrounding the lighthouse, however, was still quite rural. An article in the Sag Harbor *Corrector* that year included a description of the area by a "correspondent of the Brooklyn *Times* who has been upon a sporting excursion to Montauk." Part of his description of the area near the lighthouse follows:

> The scenery is wild and beautiful in the extreme. In a violent storm it must be truly sublime. From the heaving ocean the eye turns to equally heaving land, covered only by a short grass, on which vast herds of cattle find their sustenance. No sign of human life breaks the strange monotony of the landscape. The notes of the sea bird or the plover alone relieve the sullen boom of the restless waves.

Jonathan A. Miller, a 38–year-old Civil War veteran, became the keeper of the Montauk Point Light on December 3, 1872. He remained until October 15, 1875, and then went on to serve at other area lighthouses.

In 1873, a first class Daboll trumpet was providing the fog signal, powered by "24–inch Ericsson hot-air engines." During 1875, the signal operated 748 hours.

During Miller's last year at the Montauk Point, the lighthouse received some needed work. According to the 1875 *Annual Report:* "Some essential parts of the flashing apparatus at this station have been renewed. The lantern has been entirely reglazed, and the station painted."

Henry A. Babcock became the keeper of the Montauk Point Light on March 2, 1876. Eighteen years earlier, when Babcock was

U. S. Lighthouse Society photo

Montauk Point circa 1884.

captain of the Sag Harbor whaling ship *Washington,* he was returning from a long voyage when the crew sighted what they thought was the light from the Montauk Point tower. The location did not agree with readings Babcock had taken earlier in the day, and, despite protests from some of the crew anxious to get home as soon as possible, he did not give the order to turn north to go around Montauk Point. They continued on, eventually picking up the light at Montauk. The first light they had seen was the new light at Great West Bay, which had been constructed while the *Washington* was away on its voyage. Babcock's confidence in his abilities had saved the ship and crew from disaster. Babcock's nine years at Montauk Point undoubtedly allowed for many reflections of the time he saved the *Washington* and its crew.

James G. Scott followed Babcock as Montauk Point's keeper. He would become a great part of the lighthouse's history. Scott, five feet, eight inches tall, with brown hair and gray eyes, had been born in England. He became a United States citizen on September 30, 1861. He enlisted for a three-year tour of duty during the Civil War. Scott served with Company E, 15th Regiment, New York Heavy Artillery, from January 5, 1864 to August 22, 1865. The end of the war shortened his enlistment.

In 1903, more changes were made at Montauk Point. First, a new Fresnel lens was installed. On June 15, the huge First Order lens was replaced with a smaller, bivalve type lens, manufactured by the famed Henry-Lepaute Company of Paris. This lens, although smaller in size, was still quite powerful due to the layout of its prisms. The first bivalve lens (also known as a lightning lens) to be seen in America had appeared on display in 1893 at the Columbian Exposition in Chicago. That particular lens, originally slated for use at Fire Island, ended up at the lighthouse at Navesink, New Jersey, and still resides there today. Few French bivalve lenses would find their way into U.S. lighthouses, as high tariffs on imported glass turned the lighthouse service to American sources for lenses.

The new Third-and-One-Half Order lens gave off a white flash every ten seconds. The lighthouse continued to use an incandescent oil vapor lamp (similar in principle to the popular Coleman lanterns) as its light source.

The familiar brownish stripe that adorns the middle of the tower at Montauk Point was not an original feature of the lighthouse. From its construction to 1903, the tower was white. About the time the lighthouse received its new lens, a reddish-brown stripe was painted about midway up the tower. This stripe was painted a truer brown in the coming years, but would be returned to its original reddish color in 1999.

In the Spring of 1906, Keeper Scott's eight-year-old grandson Willy came to visit the lighthouse for a couple of weeks. One morning, after a stormy night, Willy assisted his grandfather with the keeper's chores and afterward asked to go walk along the bluff in search of arrowheads and other finds. Upon going outside, Scott and his grandson discovered a wood duck that had apparently been killed the night before. It was common for waterfowl to fly into the lantern room glass, especially on a stormy night. Willy asked his grandfather if he could keep the duck, which showed no outward signs of damage.

Scott had the duck stuffed, then sent it to Willy, who kept it throughout his life as a reminder of his childhood experiences with his grandfather at the lighthouse. In 1992, Willy's grandson, Bill, who now owned the duck, brought it with him when he made a trip from Ohio to Montauk Point. He donated it to the museum and the 100–year-old stuffed duck now resides in the museum as a reminder of days gone by.

Scott's years at the lighthouse, from 1885 to 1910, also saw eight shipwrecks in the area. These included the *Chippewa*, with a cargo that included ostriches and alligators; the *Lewis King*, the crew of which lived at the lighthouse for two weeks until the road damage from the storm was repaired; and the freighter *George Appold*. The *Appold* contained a cargo that included "New England rum, cases of dress goods, and shoes." The shoes were made with copper toes and children whose parents had salvaged the shoes did not like wearing them because they were easily recognized as "wreck shoes." The wreck of the *George Appold*, and the legacy of its salvaged cargo, were the subject of a short poem by historian Paul Bailey, two verses of which follow:

> There were shoes galore along the shore
> In assorted styles of leather,
> But the undertow had scattered them so
> There wasn't a pair together.
>
> It took a year for things to clear
> After the episode,

And even then were women and men
Still walking pigeon-toed.

Scott resigned from his position at Montauk Point on September 30, 1910. On November 1, 1910, he succumbed to diabetes, at age 72. Today, his service at Montauk Point is honored in displays at the lighthouse.

Photo courtesy of Judy Carpenter

John and Hannah Anderson, and Snooks,
at the Princess Bay Light

Scott was replaced by John Frederick Anderson, a native of Sweden who began his lighthouse career on November 1, 1906, as a Second Assistant Keeper to Scott. Anderson had been promoted to First Assistant Keeper in January 1908, then was promoted and transferred to Muscle Bed Shoals, Rhode Island, in October 1908. From there, he was assigned to Bullock Point, Rhode Island, in April 1909, before returning to Montauk Point on October 1, 1910.

The assignment as Head Keeper of the Montauk Point Light was one of great responsibility. The importance of the light, and the many duties necessary to attend to the powerful light, fog signal, and related machinery, required a keeper of great ability. On May 13, 1911, Anderson's performance was evaluated, and recorded in a Department of Commerce and Labor Efficiency Report. Anderson fared well, getting scores of 90 for "Quantity of work," 85 for "Quality of work," and 85 for "Interest manifested in work." The report indicated that his pay was fair for the "grade of work" and "service rendered," and included the following remark: "A reliable man. A little apt to unexpected things but subordinate."

Later that year, Anderson had a problem with one of his assistants. According to him, in a letter to the Third District Inspector's office on November 10, 1911:

> As I reported to the office on October 28th, 1911 that the [assistant keeper] . . . installed a woman with a child as his housekeeper. On the 2nd of Nov. he took her from the station by order of the Inspector. Since then he has received a letter from the office that he could have a relative act as housekeeper but to day he brought the same woman here again, I have heard that he has told outsiders that it is his second cousin, but he told me the first time he brought her here that he did not know the woman, and this time he did not say a word to me about bringing her here.

> The story goes that she has one of the worst reputations of a woman on this end of Long Island, and if such a person is to reside on this station my family refuses to stay with me, so I respectfully wish that this matter will be taken up for consideration, as he is contrary in everything that he will not listen to me.

> Further I wish to state that I have told him time and again to keep his quarters clean but it doesn't seem to matter to him.

Six months later, Anderson was transferred to the Cedar Island Light, an assignment that was "satisfactory" to him. There, he would have no assistants.

Anderson continued his lighthouse career until January 31, 1926, when he retired from the Block Island North Light. In order to receive his retirement pay, Anderson had to obtain a letter stating that his heart problems were "not due to vicious habits, intemperance or willful misconduct." He received this note from the U.S. Marine Hospital in Stapleton, N.Y., and retired at the rate of $438.81 per year. On July 10, 1937, John Anderson passed away.

On May 16, 1912, John E. Miller became Montauk Point's keeper. He was a retired Brooklyn policeman, and son of Jonathan A. Miller. John stayed at Montauk for over 17 years.

Photo by Helen Muller

Montauk Point in August 1939.

In the early 1900s, a second light was displayed from the Montauk tower. A fixed red light, emitted from a range lens mounted outside the lantern room, warned mariners of Shagwong Reef.

The year 1938 saw the availability of electric power at the lighthouse, allowing the installation of a 1000–watt electric bulb inside the Fresnel lens in 1940. By this time, the lighthouse was already a popular destination. A 1939 report showed that almost 16,000 people visited the light that year. It was the nation's most visited lighthouse.

During World War II, the U.S. Army Signal Corps occupied the lighthouse, as part of the Eastern Coastal Defense

Shield. It was at this time that the Fire Control Tower was built near the lighthouse. Spotters in the tower were to direct artillery fire from Fort Hero.

In late 1960, the power of the Montauk Light was increased with the installation of a 2½ million candlepower lamp (the former lamp was rated at 200,000 candlepower). Shortly thereafter, the windup clockworks were replaced with an electric mechanism.

Erosion has been a problem at Montauk Point for many years. Over two-thirds of the original 300 feet between the lighthouse and bluff have been lost since the lighthouse was built. Early efforts to stop erosion failed. In 1945, the Army Corps of Engineers built a 700–foot revetment to halt erosion, but constant wave action and a series of storms overcame the effort within ten years.

A woman named Giorgina Reid became a large part of the history of Montauk Point beginning on April 22, 1970, when she began the implementation of her "Reed Trench Terracing" process on the eroding bluff. Ms. Reid had developed the method at her own home in Rocky Point, and had written a book about the process, entitled *How to Hold Up a Bank*. The method involved terracing the bluff and using plants to hold the soil in place. Perhaps the most ingenious part of her approach was to bury reeds under the soil. This allowed for water retention and provided organic matter to nourish the plants and help them grow healthy root systems quickly.

In the years since 1970, Ms. Reid's methods have been successfully used in combination with a variety of other approaches to help stabilize the bluff and protect the lighthouse. She passed away in 2001, but the work she did for many years acts as a monument to her care, ingenuity, and hard work.

In early 1987, the 1903 bivalve lens was replaced by a DCB-224 optic. This automated electric light consisted of two 24inch drums, each containing a halogen bulb and reflector, rotating to produce a flashing effect. In March of that year, the 190–year tradition of lighthouse keepers at Montauk Point came to an end. This lighthouse, the first on Long Island, was the last to lose its human attendants to technology.

Fortunately, as Coast Guard personnel departed the station, the Montauk Historical Society stepped in. Signing a lease on April 1, 1987, the Society took control of one of Long Island's most well known and beloved landmarks. On May 23, 1987, the lighthouse's museum was opened to the public.

The lighthouse celebrated its bicentennial on June 1, 1996. Several days earlier, on May 26, the museum had received its one-millionth visitor. On September 30, the lighthouse reservation was transferred to the Montauk Historical Society Lighthouse Museum Committee.

Photo by the author

Montauk Point in August 2003. From left to right: WWII-era observation tower, former fog signal building, 1796 tower, and 1860 dwelling.

In 1998 and 1999, extensive repairs and renovations were completed. The brown stripe, which had been Benjamin Moore "Van Dyke Brown" for some time, was repainted a more historically correct reddish brown.

Early in 2001, the optic at Montauk Point was once again changed. The Coast Guard's new standard, a Vega VRB-25, was installed. This new light, smaller and cheaper to maintain, casts a less powerful light than its predecessor. Once again, the lighthouse at Montauk Point became an indicator of lighthouse technology. This change was not without controversy, however, as local mariners, residents, and lighthouse fans lamented the loss of Montauk Point's powerful beams of light.

Since losing its lighthouse keepers, the Montauk Point Light Station has become a popular destination for Long Islanders and tourists. With a variety of displays, including Long Island's largest Fresnel lens collection, the museum in the 1860 keepers' quarters provides a wealth of information about lighthouses. Approximately 100,000 people visit the scenic site each year.

For many years, the lighthouse at Montauk Point has been the symbol of Long Island's rich lighthouse heritage. Under the care of the Montauk Historical Society and the many friends and visitors the lighthouse attracts, it is sure to remain a symbol of our storied past, and the exclamation mark to the Long Island experience.

Gardiner's Island

The stories of the waterways around Long Island often involve dangerous shallows and shifting sands. The history of the lighthouse at Gardiner's Island is a prime example.

George Bache's 1838 report on the state of the area's aids to navigation included an examination of the proposal for a "light-house on the northwest point of Gardiner's island." This examination began with a description of the island, pointing out that "its northern end is the termination of a low sandy beach, from 300 to 500 feet in breadth, which extends three miles into the bay, in a northwesterly direction." Although the west and north sides of the point had deep water, Bache noted that "a shoal extends out to the eastward, upon which vessels coming from that direction, and not knowing their danger, are liable to run." In addition, the point, "owing to the lowness of the land, is impossible to be distinguished at night at any distance."

Bache described the shipping based in the area at the time, which included over 110 vessels "employed in the coasting trade and cod fisheries" and 37 whaling vessels. From court records relating to the grounding of the brig *Malaga*, he found that "in a period of sixteen years upwards of twelve vessels have stranded upon this part of Gardiner's island," including "the brig Malaga, stranded on this point in July, 1836." Other stranded vessels were noted, including Captain Manning's *Gladiator*, of New London, which wrecked in a February storm; two sloops from New London, which went ashore during a violent snowstorm; five sloops from Riverhead: the *Fanny*, *Ocean*, *Ann Maria*, and two whose names were unknown, all of which grounded in the same May storm; Captain Wheeler's sloop *Regulator* of East Haddam, Connecticut in November; and Captain Godfrey's sloop *Canton Crape*, of Newport, another November stranding.

His report on the usefulness of a lighthouse on the point to mariners concluded that "as a light would contribute much to their convenience as well as safety, I would respectfully recommend its establishment."

It would be some time before this lighthouse was built. On March 3, 1851, Congress appropriated $6000 for the construction of a lighthouse on the northernmost tip of Gardiner's Island, known as Gardiner's Point. In August, the government bought 14 acres on the north side of Gardiner's Island from John G. and Sarah Gardiner.

From chart by Darrow & Comstock, Ship Chandlers
Detail of chart showing location of Gardiner's Island Light,
circa 1890.

This would be one of the last lighthouse projects started under Stephen Pleasanton's administration. When informed of the purchase, Pleasanton, known for his thriftiness, wrote "I am happy to learn that you have obtained the site for 400 dollars, a much less sum than we expected to pay for it."

The Light-house Board's first *Annual Report*, submitted January 15, 1853, reported on "objects belonging to the light-house establishment," noting the "action in each case before and since the organization of the board, on the 9th October, 1852." With regard to the lighthouse to be built on Gardiner's Island, it noted the appropriation of funds and listed actions prior to the formation of the Board as "[n]o contract; the deeds approved; sum insufficient." By the time of this report, the Board had "caused the foundations to be examined, and will commence the structure immediately."

By June 1854, temporary quarters for the workers, and a storeroom, were built on the site selected for the new lighthouse. By October, there were concerns relating to the insufficiency of the budget for the project, but work continued on. The lantern and plate glass arrived in November, and the lighthouse was ready to receive a lamp and lens by mid-December.

The lighthouse was completed in December of 1854 and its first keeper, Albert Edwards, was appointed on the 21st of that month. In early 1855, the lamp was lit and Gardiner's Island Light became the first Long Island lighthouse to cast its light through a Fresnel lens.

The Light-house Board's 1855 *Annual Report* described the light station as:

> composed of a keeper's house twenty-eight feet square, of one and a half stories in height, with a cellar, and is connected with a circular tower at the northern extremity nine feet in diameter, surmounted by a lantern, intended to contain a Fresnel lens of the 5th order.
>
> The plan was furnished by the Light-house Board, and the buildings have been constructed in the most substantial manner, of hard-burned bricks laid in cement, with slate roof, and cast-iron lantern. Connected with the building is a cistern, six feet diameter and seven feet deep, and a small frame wash-room ten by twelve feet. The focal plane of the lantern is elevated thirty feet above low water.

The Fresnel lens, although originally intended to be a Fifth Order, was actually a Sixth Order fixed white 270–degree lens. The building plan for this lighthouse was the third proposed; the previous two were not approved.

Josiah P. Miller was appointed keeper of the Gardiner's Island Light on April 21, 1866. He would remain at the station for nearly 27 years.

The lighthouse appears to have been built well, as 13 years after its construction the station was reported as being "in good condition" and without need of repairs. In 1869, a "new stove for warming the tower" was furnished, and it was recommended that a fog bell be

GARDINER'S ISLAND, L.I., NY

Illustration by Paul Bradley

Illustration of the Gardiner's Island Light, from original plans.

installed at the station. The following year, it was recommended that the former Little Gull Island bell be installed there, but it does not appear that the station ever received a fog signal. In 1871, the lantern was modified, and the "tower and keeper's dwelling, inside and out" were painted.

Alfred R. Waud (1828–1891), often considered the best Civil War sketch artist, passed by the Gardiner's Island Light in 1875. He made two rough sketches—the only known illustrations of this lighthouse during its active years. These sketches are currently in the Historic New Orleans Collection in Louisiana.

The 1876 *Atlantic Coast Pilot* mentions the Gardiner's Island Lighthouse:

> Gardiner's Point, easily recognized by the light-house upon it, is the Northern extremity of a long flat beach, which extends in a nearly N NE direction from the main portion of Gardiner's Island for nearly two miles, and is covered only with beach grass.

The light-house, which stands close to the Northern end of the point, is a circular brick tower, twenty-six feet high, painted brown and attached to the keeper's dwelling, which is the same color. It is known as the Gardiner's Island Light-house, and very difficult to recognize, as a light house, until close to it. It has, therefore been recommended that the tower be either raised or painted a different color from the dwelling.

It shows a fixed white light, of the sixth order, from a height of thirty-three feet above sea level, visible eleven miles. Its geographical position is Latitude 41–08N and Longitude 72–08W.

Erosion was a problem near the lighthouse. The long, low, thin, sandy peninsula was subject to the sweeping winds and pounding waves. In time, the seas broke through the peninsula. Erosion continued, and discussions of moving or rebuilding the light began in 1890. In 1893, a "survey of a portion of the island was made to determine the advisability of either moving the old light and dwelling or rebuilding farther from the high-water line, which is approaching the station from the east at the rate of 10–2/3 feet per year for the past three years."

Josiah P. Miller wrote a letter to the *East Hampton Star* on April 29, 1893, describing a storm on April 20:

[T]he wind was blowing a perfect gale and it was evident that we were going to have a full tide. At 10 o'clock in the evening the seas began breaking against the side of the house, and as the tide rose the noise was deafening and no one thought of going to bed that night. When daylight came we discovered that part of the kitchen, the door, yard fence, both stoops, the cellar house and one of the outbuildings had been swept away. The seas broke through the cellar and partly filled it in with stones and sand. My row boat is a total wreck, and all the provisions I had in the cellar have gone to Davy Jones's locker. It was the worst shaking up that old Neptune has ever given us during the 27 years I have kept this Light. The heavy northeast gale of September 10th, 1889, cut a channel through the beach; it is about a mile and a half wide and deep enough for sloops to sail through.

Jonathan A. Miller, a Civil War veteran who had been injured in a naval engagement and had been a keeper at the Montauk Point Light, became the last keeper of the Gardiner's Island Light on July

1, 1893. His letter of employment, dated June 22 and signed by Third District Inspector W. D. Schley, stated that he was to assume the position of "Laborer, Acting Keeper of Gardiner's Island Light Station, at a salary of $560 per annum" pending his appointment as official keeper.

In November of 1893, James W. Covert, the Congressman for New York's First District, requested an investigation of the site, as the sea was undermining the lighthouse's foundation. By the end of the year, Third District Engineer David Porter Heap had submitted a plan for a breakwater to protect the light station. The Light-House Board's Engineering Committee recommended the adoption of Heap's plan in early January 1894, but Heap added some changes and resubmitted the plan in early February.

Commenting on the condition of the station, the January 11 edition of the *Sag Harbor Express* noted: "The attention of Congress has been called to the matter and an appropriation has been asked to repair the damage by the elements. But if Congress adopts its usual course in such cases it will be years before an appropriation is made. Lighthouses have been reported shaky year after year, but Congress usually prefers to have them fall down before making the necessary appropriation for repairs."

A report on the matter appeared in the *East Hampton Star* in early March:

> Gardiner's Island Lighthouse was visited last week by one of the government lighthouse authorities, who made an examination of the structure. He reported that a breakwater would be built to break the force of the tides which now wash against the foundation of the house, the work to be commenced this spring. The breach in the narrow sand strip leading to the light, which was made by the sea four years ago, is now two miles wide and is steadily widening. Frank Miller, the young son of Keeper Miller, was alone in the lighthouse on the night of the last big storm, and passed an experience he does not care to live through again.

By early March, Inspector Schley reported that the lighthouse was still standing, but was too dangerous to occupy. On March 7, the Secretary of the Treasury authorized the discontinuance of the Gardiner's Island Light. Miller received a letter from Inspector

247

Schley, dated March 7, 1894, directing him to extinguish the light until further orders. Miller was told to remove all belongings and supplies to New London aboard a government vessel. He was to frequently visit the station, and make written reports to Schley of its condition. He was also told to keep his sailboat for that purpose.

Although the extinguishing of the light was to be temporary, the lamp and lens were removed by mid-March and delivered to the depot in New London. The lens, made by Sautter & Co., was subsequently described by Heap as being worn out.

Engineer Heap believed the light could be re-established at a cost of $45,000, but by early April, Inspector Schley recommended stationing a gas buoy nearby instead of rebuilding the lighthouse.

With the lighthouse extinguished, several vessels were stranded on Gardiner's Point. The schooner *Henry May*, bound for Sag Harbor from Maine with a load of lumber, required a tug from New London to pull her loose from the sand. The smack *Thomas Rackett*, bound for Greenport, "came to a sudden standstill" in the early hours of March 10. Captain Willard Rackett was able to free her without serious damage as the tide rose. These strandings enraged some of the locals, leading to great criticism of the Light-house Board. The *Watchman* was particularly critical. "Although repeatedly warned in ample season the Board allowed the Lighthouse on Gardiner's point to remain undefended against assaults of the sea, which threatened to cut it off from the main beach and did finally isolate it, and by continued encroachments endangered its safety so that it became unsafe for persons to stay in it during severe storms." The *Watchman* concluded its comments on the matter, saying that it was "unfortunate for the owners of the Henry May that the U. S. Government connot [sic] be brought to book for its culpable neglect of duty in the premises, and be forced to pay the damage of its default."

According to Schley's recommendation, a "gas-lighted buoy was, on May 31, 1894, moored in about 72 feet of water about a quarter of a mile N. by E. from Gardiners Island discontinued light-house." There were many problems with the buoy's gas light in its first season, and it required much attention. In early November, its "disappearance" was reported, but it was found within a couple of weeks.

The lighthouse eventually succumbed to the forces of nature and toppled into the sea. It was never rebuilt.

Keeper Miller was assigned to the new Rockland Lake Light, in upstate New York, on September 1, 1894. That lighthouse, like his previous one, was doomed. The Rockland Lake Light had been built on muddy shoal and eventually sank into the mud, causing it to lean sharply.

Although a lighthouse was never rebuilt on Gardiner's Point, the government did establish a fort on the site. On April 5, 1898, the Secretary of the Treasury, under whose responsibility the lighthouse service existed, transferred "the abandoned light-house reservation at this point" to the War Department.

Fort Tyler took two years and $500,000 to build. It was named after President John Tyler, who had married Julia Gardiner while in office. This was one of four forts built on the eastern end of Long Island at that time, the others being Fort Terry (Plum Island), Fort Michie (Great Gull Island), and Fort H. G. Wright (Fishers Island). Although designed to hold two batteries to protect the area during the Spanish-American War, it was not completed until after the war and never housed a single gun or troop. The reservation was transferred to the State of New York some years later at a cost of $50, in the hopes of making it an island campground. The funds to protect and improve the island were never appropriated, and the ownership of the land reverted back to the federal government.

The fort was reported to have been used as a hideout for bootleggers during Prohibition. During World War II, the site was used as a practice target for Navy bombers despite the objections of local fishermen. In the years since, the little island has eroded further. The site is shown as "ruins" on nautical charts. This is all that remains of Fort Tyler. There are no lighthouse remains. The now-tiny island is marked as a navigational hazard that may still contain unexploded ordnance, and local boaters and fishermen report that it has been rapidly eroding. The American Museum of

Natural History uses the site, along with Great Gull Island, for bird studies.

In 2002, the Long Island Chapter of the U.S. Lighthouse Society contacted retired architect, and noted lighthouse illustrator, Paul Bradley, to see if he could create an illustration of the Gardiner's Island Light from the architectural drawings used in its construction. Bradley embraced the project and recreated the lighthouse in a short time, giving the public its only view of this long-forgotten lighthouse.

Although the Gardiner's Island Light Station had the shortest physical existence of any Long Island light station, its story is still rich with important historical themes. It was the first Long Island light built by the Light-house Board, and the first to cast its light from a Fresnel lens. Its history also contains stories of shipwrecks, a famous family, great storms, Long Island's ever-changing shoreline, and a Spanish-American War fort with a very odd story of its own. The ruins off the northern side of Gardiner's Island recall these themes, and provide a reminder of a lost piece of Long Island's vast lighthouse heritage.

Photo by the author

The ruins of Fort Tyler. 2001.

Cedar Island

Perhaps no other light station on Long Island has experienced as many ups and downs as Cedar Island. From the glory of Sag Harbor's whaling days and the laughter of many children, through erosion, storms, and abandonment, to the current struggle just to remain standing, this light station has had its share of good times, as well as bad.

In the early to mid-1800s, the town of Sag Harbor was generally considered the second most important town on Long Island, second only to Brooklyn. The whaling industry had brought great fortune to the area. To this day, the town touts itself as being "Built by the Whalers."

In 1838, Sag Harbor boasted 20 vessels "employed in the coasting trade and cod fisheries," as well as 29 whaling ships. By comparison, Greenport, at that time the second most popular whaling port on Long Island, had seven whaling ships sailing from port.

Getting in and out of Sag Harbor could be hazardous to mariners. Cedar Island stood between the South Fork of Long Island and Shelter Island, posing a danger to ships entering and leaving the port. The federal government realized this and, on August 20 1838, purchased the three-acre Cedar Island from "the Trustees of the Freeholders and Commonalty of the town of East Hampton" for $200.

In 1839, the government spent $3480 to build a lighthouse on the north side of the island. It was a wooden keeper's dwelling with a tower and cast iron lantern room on top. Like many Pleasanton-era lights it did not fare well. The cast iron lantern was not properly supported, leading this lighthouse, and others like it, to experience structural problems.

On February 2, 1844, Sineus Conkling became the keeper at Cedar Island. He remained until September 1845.

On June 20, 1850, Captain Howland visited Cedar Island. At that time, Keeper Hubbard L. Fordham was in charge of the lighthouse. Howland reported in his log that: "[w]ith the exception of the house being leaky, it is in good order. Lantern is very leaky." He also noted that "[a]n attempt has been made to protect the island from washing away by a wooden fence or breakwater. I am fearful it will not prove effectual."

Photo by the author

Cedar Island Light in June 1999.

On July 1, 1851, the Cedar Island Light had a listed effective range of 12.5 miles. Its nine lamps with 14–inch reflectors cast this light from a height of 32 feet above sea level.

Lyman G. Sherman, a former whaling ship captain who had been born on Shelter Island in 1804, became the keeper at Cedar Island on September 8, 1853. He would remain until April 13, 1861.

The *Annual Report of the Light-house Board* for 1855 stated that the Cedar Island Lighthouse had received a new illuminating apparatus. The lens installed was a 270–degree Sixth Order lens, with Argand lamp, to replace the nine Winslow Lewis lamps and reflectors. The Cedar Island Light was the first Long Island lighthouse to be refitted with a Fresnel lens. Keeper Sherman was likely trained to take care of this new style of apparatus. With the price of whale oil at $2.25 per gallon, the fuel savings associated with the more efficient lamp and lens system must have been great.

The 1858 *Annual Report* indicated that the Cedar Island Light showed a fixed white light from a Sixth Order lens 34 feet above sea level. Oddly, it lists the range as ten miles, 2.5 less than the old lamps with reflectors. The tower on top of the keeper's quarters was painted white.

In April 1861, Nathaniel Edwards, a shipbuilder by trade, took over as keeper of the lighthouse. He had been born in 1799, and married Mary (Polly) Eldridge in 1826. Nathaniel and Mary had a daughter, Mary Lucy Edwards, in 1833. Mary Lucy married Charles Finch Sherman (son of former Cedar Island keeper Lyman Sherman) in April 1855 (and later became his assistant keeper at the Execution Rocks Light in 1873–1874). When Nathaniel passed away on May 21, 1862, his wife took over as keeper until a new keeper was assigned in September.

Hubbard L. Fordham, who had been the keeper at Cedar Island in 1850, returned to his old post and regained his position as keeper of the lighthouse on September 16, 1862. He remained until April 6, 1869, thereby witnessing the building of the new lighthouse.

Congress authorized the rebuilding of the lighthouse on March 2, 1867. An appropriation of $25,000 was made for the purpose.

Fifteen thousand dollars were spent on the lighthouse's construction in 1868, and another $9992.62 to complete the structure in 1869.

The 1869 *Annual Report* stated that the "rebuilding of this station is completed and the old structure removed. A 5th order lens will be placed in this tower as a substitute for the 6th order which was in the old tower." The new lighthouse was L-shaped, with a square tower, made of granite with a hardwood interior. Despite the mention of the Fifth Order lens, subsequent documents would always report the presence of a Sixth Order lens at Cedar Island.

In 1882, a "fog bell, struck by machinery, was established" at the station. The "machinery" mentioned was probably a Steven's Fog Bell Apparatus, as illustrated in the July 1881 *Instructions to Light-Keepers*. This apparatus was, essentially, a wind-up clockworks mechanism that caused a large sledgehammer to strike the fog bell. The bell was suspended from a wooden frame, and the clockworks mechanism was contained in a small wooden structure under the bell frame.

U.S. Lighthouse Society photo

Pre-1910 photo shows original fog bell tower.

On March 23, 1897, Charles Mulford became the keeper at the Cedar Island Light. He was a Civil War veteran who had lost one leg in the war. Popular stories say that some of his wooden legs were still in the attic at Cedar Island when it burned in 1974. Keeper Mulford remained until January 1906.

In 1902, the brick oil house that still resides at the station was built. Many oil houses were built on Long Island about this time, including the extant ones at Plum Island, Old Field Point, Montauk Point, and Shinnecock Bay.

By 1903, erosion, which had been first documented in 1850, had reduced Cedar Island to about 1.5 acres, a loss of half the island in less than 70 years. At this point, riprap began to be placed around the north and west sides of the island to protect it. By 1907, over 6000 tons would be placed. Much of this riprap is still visible at the site.

In 1906, Adolf Nordstrom became the keeper at Cedar Island, for the princely sum of $46 per month. The fog signal at this time was a "[b]ell struck by machinery every 20 sec[onds]."

John Frederick Anderson became the light's keeper in May of 1912, replacing Nordstrom. Anderson, who had been born in Sweden on Christmas Day, 1859, had transferred from Montauk Point, and took a large pay cut to do so. He remained until January 1917, leaving for the Prince's Bay Light in Staten Island.

The Andersons had four daughters and a son. While at Cedar Island, the Andersons received a visit from their three-year-old grandson, Norman Johnson. Six years later, when Norman's mother died, John Anderson wrote to Norman's father asking that Norman be allowed to come live with them at Prince's Bay. The nine-year-old traveled alone, bearing a tag that said: "This boy Norman Johnson is travelling alone from Portland, Ore., to New York to his grandfather, John F. Anderson, whose address is Princes Bay Lighthouse, Staten Island, New York." The reverse side of tag said: "To Officials and Trainmen: Please give this boy, who is travelling alone, every assistance. In case of accident or serious illness notify his father, Emil Johnson at Klickitat, Washington." Norman was sorry that he was not going back to Cedar Island, but

Photo courtesy of Bob Allen

William Follett in the Cedar Island lantern room
with the Sixth Order lens.

was happy to be with his cherished grandparents, who were just as happy to have him.

From 1917 until the light's decommissioning in 1934, William H. Follett was the keeper of the Cedar Island Lighthouse. On July 13, 1919, Follett spotted a boat on fire. The *Flyer* had had an explosion on board. Follett managed to reach the boat, and get the three burned men to the hospital, but none of them survived.

Keeper Follett (who had been an assistant at Hog Island Shoal, Rhode Island and Montauk Point) and his wife Atta, had many good times at the light. During the summers, grandchildren spent time on the tiny island, swimming, boating, and fishing to pass the time. Warren and Bill Allen, grandsons of the Folletts, lived at the lighthouse full-time for a few years until they had to go to school. Then, they would come spend the summers. As Warren recalled at a visit to the lighthouse in August 2003, his first time there since 1934, the boys would often row a boat between the lighthouse and the stone breakwater, an area that is now all sand and beach grass.

As with many light stations, the keeper and his family were important members of the community. Painter Frank B. Fithian, a ninth generation resident of East Hampton, and his wife, Louise, were friends of the Folletts. Frank had given the Folletts a puppy, Brownie, when their previous dog, Mutt, died in 1926 (Brownie remained with the family for the rest of the Folletts' lighthouse-keeping career, passing away shortly after William Follett retired). When Louise Fithian was pregnant in 1922, she chose Atta Follett to be her nurse. When Ellen Fithian was born, with the help of Atta Follett, "Grandpa Follett" was chosen as her godfather.

Photo courtesy of Ellen Fithian Halsey

William and Atta Follett.

257

During Follett's time at the light, the tenders *Tulip*, *Hawthorne*, and *Hickory* would occasionally visit, bringing supplies or inspectors. Warren Allen remembers the duties of each tender. The *Tulip* brought oil, coal, and wood to the area's lighthouses. The *Hawthorne* would bring paint, turpentine, and various supplies for the maintenance of the lighthouses, and also bring the inspectors to visit the light stations twice each year. The *Hickory* was used to maintain buoys.

In 1926, a barge arrived at the breakwater off Cedar Island (today this breakwater is onshore). On the barge was the new steel fog bell tower. The workmen toppled the old wooden tower, breaking it up after it fell off the pier and into the water, then carried the already-assembled new steel tower from the breakwater, through the shallow water inside the breakwater, and hauled it up onto the pier. One of the workmen, a man named Tommy, had to endure the many questions and watchful eyes of Bill and Warren as he worked to secure the tower to the pier. The new tower did not hold the bell aloft as the old one had; rather, it merely served to elevate the weights for the striking mechanism. They were held inside a central steel column.

William Follett kept his personal powerboat at the island, along with a 16–foot sailboat and 12–foot rowboat, which were provided by the U.S. Lighthouse Service. The grandsons would spend much time in the boats, but never piloted Grandpa's powerboat.

Warren and Bill learned important lessons at the light station. One time, Grandma Follett asked the boys to catch her some fish for dinner. The boys came through, using soft shell clams as bait to catch many blowfish; many more, in fact, than were actually needed. The boys cleaned 30 fish for dinner. When Grandpa Follett asked what they were going to do with the rest, they told him they were going to throw them away. The seasoned lighthouse keeper informed them that the Good Lord did not provide the fish for the boys to throw away. Bill and Warren then cleaned the remaining 97 fish. From then on, whenever Grandma asked them to get something, they asked, "how many?"

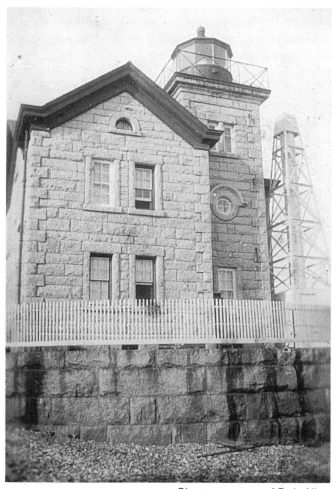

Photo courtesy of Bob Allen

Cedar Island Light, with its post-1926 fog bell tower.

During Prohibition, rum running was as active in the Sag Harbor area as other areas of Long Island. William Follett used to hang a lantern on one of the half-dozen or so cedar trees left on the island if the Coast Guard was in the area. When the grandsons asked what the lantern was for, Grandpa told them it was to keep the deer away. They learned the true reason years later.

In the channel between Cedar Island and Shelter Island, not far from the breakwater, a Coast Guard boat once intercepted some bootleggers. When the rum running boat turned to escape, the Coast

Guard fired on them, stopping the boat and setting it on fire. Water from the Coast Guard boat put the fire out, but all those on board were apprehended. Or so it seemed.

The next morning, Bill and Warren sighted a man clinging to one of the rocks on the breakwater (they had given many of the individual rocks names—this one's was "Fatty"). Bill rowed out and brought the man, Bill Parker, to the lighthouse. He had been shot in the leg, though not seriously. Grandma Follett treated the wound and Bill stayed for a few days to recover. William Follett eventually took him to Sag Harbor. The next Sunday, a large wooden boat dropped off a barrel off the station. In it was the Sunday paper, candy bars for

Photo by the author
Warren Allen at his childhood home in 2003.

the kids, and a bone for Brownie, the Folletts' dog. This happened for three weeks straight. By this time, the kids had come to call the 60–foot boat "the ark," as it looked like what they had imagined Noah's boat was like. One the last visit, Bill Parker called out to them from the back of the boat and told them that they would not see him anymore, as they were moving across the Sound. They later learned that the boat, named *Liberty*, had been sunk in the Sound. To this day, though, Warren is sure that Bill Parker got away safely: "He was just that sort of guy."

When Bill and Warren reached school age, they shipped out to Rhode Island the day before school started, then would return the day after school ended. Warren remembers that leaving the island, and watching the lighthouse fade into the distance, was very sad, but the return the next Summer, seeing the lighthouse enter into view and get larger and larger, was cause for great joy.

Warren remembers his days with Grandpa and Grandma Follett at Cedar Island with great fondness. He believes those many days on the one-acre island were an important part of his life, and regrets that he could not give his children that experience in their youth. In summing up his childhood experiences at Cedar Island, Warren says, with a distant look in his eyes: "We were free."

The 1930s saw several Long Island lighthouses decommissioned. Like the lighthouses at Shinnecock Bay, Horton Point, and Old Field Point, the Cedar Island Light had the lamp and lens removed from its tower. A skeletal tower, which still stands, became the keeper of the light at Cedar Island in 1934. Keeper Follett moved on to the Long Beach Bar Light.

In 1936, Cedar Island was surveyed. By this time, the island had been reduced to less than one acre, with its grove of cedar trees long since washed away by the encroaching waters. The high water line had approached so close as to half encircle the pier upon which the lighthouse was built. It must have seemed that the shifting Long Island sands that had plagued the island for years would soon deposit the old lighthouse into the sea.

The island and lighthouse were sold for $2002 in 1937 to Phelan Beale, a Manhattan lawyer. One year later, in 1938, the infamous

September hurricane struck Long Island, reeking havoc throughout the area. In a bizarre act of fate, this horrible storm would be the savior the Cedar Island Lighthouse had long awaited. The storm filled in the strait of water between Cedar Island and the south fork of Long Island, stabilizing the area sands. Cedar Island now became Cedar Point.

The lighthouse remained in private hands until 1967, when it was purchased by Suffolk County to become part of Cedar Point County Park. After 40 years of private ownership, the lighthouse still was intact, its hardwood interior having the appearance, as one visitor put it, of a mansion. Unfortunately, that changed in June of 1974, just before sunset, when the lighthouse caught fire. Its location at the end of a long sandspit made it too difficult to receive help in time, and the interior and roof of the lighthouse burned away, leaving only the granite shell and cast iron lantern room.

The County sealed the doors and windows and built a new roof. The lighthouse remained in essentially that state for 29 years. Along with the lighthouse, one other building from the light station

Photo by the author

The station's 1902 oil house, prior to restoration.

Photo by the author

Cedar Island Light in 1999.

remains: the 1902 oil house. This building, historically important in its own right, has suffered at the hands of vandals, and many of the bricks that make up its walls have been torn away.

Today, the lighthouse, beaten, burned, and even threatened by damage from trees and vines growing in the spaces between its granite blocks, has a chance to regain the glory of its former years. The Suffolk County Parks Department and Long Island Chapter of the U.S. Lighthouse Society have entered into a stewardship agreement to restore the lighthouse. The joint effort had, by mid-2003, resulted in the light's listing on the National Register of Historic Places and the start of preliminary work inside the structure. As this book went to press, the restoration of the 1902 oil house had begun. The completion of a thorough architectural assessment, including the development of long-term preservation plans and fundraising goals, was expected by early 2004.

For the first time in many years, it appears that the Cedar Island Lighthouse may once again stand proud. Although there are no longer any whaling ships to guide, a restored Cedar Island Light will be a poignant reminder of the area's rich maritime heritage, and an inspiration for visitors and the Long Island community. Warren Allen wishes that his children had had the opportunity to have the sort of experiences that he and his brother did while at the Cedar Island Light. While that may no longer be possible on Long Island, a restored Cedar Island Lighthouse will provide memorable experiences, and important lessons, for many more children.

Shinnecock Bay

One of America's most majestic coastal towers once stood upon Ponquogue Point in Hampton Bays. The loss of this tower illustrates the need for public attention to the well-being of our local heritage.

The importance of marking Long Island's Atlantic Ocean shore was realized early in American history. The establishment of Montauk Point in 1796 and Fire Island in 1827 addressed this need, but there was still a 67–mile stretch of shore between these locations. The actual range of these two lights, especially with their early illuminating apparatuses, meant that a 35 to 40–mile area of the shoreline—much less in poor visibility—had no guiding light to keep ships off the beach and sand bars.

In 1852, when the Light-House Board took over the administration of America's lighthouses, it took a close look at what needed to be done to improve the nation's system of navigational aids. There were so many urgent lighthouse projects across the country that it must have been difficult to narrow them down. But in the Board's first *Annual Report*, in January 1853, a list of eight U.S. lighthouse projects that demanded the immediate attention of Congress was created. One of these eight projects was to build "a first-class seacoast light-house tower, and fit it with the most approved illuminating apparatus, near Great West bay," which we now know as Shinnecock Bay. An appropriation of $30,000 was requested. By November, the estimate had risen to $35,000.

Great West Bay was chosen because of its location almost exactly halfway between Montauk Point and Fire Island lighthouses. The increasing transatlantic shipping of both cargo and immigrants in the area, combined with the many sand bars off the south shore and often rough seas, demanded that this stretch of shoreline receive a lighthouse.

On August 3, 1854, Congress appropriated $35,000 for the lighthouse (another $12,000 was appropriated on August 18, 1856). On January 24, 1855, the New York Legislature granted jurisdiction over an area, "not to exceed ten acres," near Great West Bay. The site was to be approved by the Governor, and a map of the site filed with New York once it was selected. The act provided that, if the government had difficulty obtaining the necessary land, it could file a petition with the Supreme Court in the district in which the site resided. The petition was to include "the names and places of residence of all persons owning or claiming to own or have any interest in said premises, and particularly who of them are infants, persons of unsound mind, or idiots, as far as the same by reasonable diligence can be obtained." The petition was not necessary, as the needed land was purchased from John H. Foster and his wife on June 22, 1855, and from Edward H. Foster and his wife the following day. This purchase gave the station 10.25 acres. John H. Foster's warranty deed included the reservation of his "exclusive right to gather and make use of Sea weed drifting on the Beach, East side of the [property]."

The site chosen was not on the barrier beach, as at the Fire Island Light Station. The barrier beach was investigated as a possible site, but the sands were not deemed stable enough to support the lighthouse. The site chosen, on Ponquogue Point in Good Ground, was about one mile north of the beach.

Construction began in 1857. The engineers in charge of the project were Lieutenants J. C. Duane and J. St. C. Morton. Many of the materials for the lighthouse came from Connecticut. These were brought by schooner, across the Long Island Sound and Great Peconic Bay to Canoe Place. There, a team and wagon owned by Nathan Foster, brother of Edward H. Foster, took the lumber to the site. The bricks and concrete were transferred to a scow owned by another Foster brother, James R. Foster. The scow later wrecked in high winds.

A large hole, over ten feet deep, was dug for the foundation, then pine logs, 12 inches by 12 inches, were put perpendicular to each other, forming a grillwork. Concrete then brought the foundation to near ground level, where large blocks were used as a foundation for the approximately 800,000 bricks used to build the tower. As masons built the tower, pine poles were cut from local woods to create scaffolding. A central iron column inside the tower held iron steps. At the top of the brick tower, large coping stones were set as a base for the lantern. These were hoisted by hand, using a system of blocks and falls. As the first stone was being hoisted into place, nearly 150 feet above the ground, the hoisting mast splintered. Fortunately, no one was hurt.

A cast iron lantern containing a First Order lens was placed atop the coping stones. This expensive French lens was over six feet in diameter and, with a Fresnel-Arago designed four-concentric-wick lamp inside, cast the most powerful light yet seen from a Long Island lighthouse. The Great West Bay tower and the new Fire Island tower that followed it, were the only two Long Island lighthouses designed to house a First Order lens.

When completed, the brick tower was given a wash of cement, which was colored with umber to look like brick. The total cost for the new lighthouse was $47,000.

Once Lieutenant Duane had completed the tower in late 1857, Lieutenant Morton went to work on the two two-and-one-half-story dwellings. These were attached to the tower by a covered walkway. The western dwelling was for the head keeper. His two assistants resided in the eastern dwelling, with one family on each of the two floors.

To get oil for the lamp, coal for the stove, and other supplies to the top of the tower, ropes were used. These were also used for painting the tower. Sometimes, during the years that families resided on the station, the keepers' children would swing on the ropes.

Charles A. Conley was appointed as the first Keeper of the Great West Bay Light on December 7, 1857, at a rate of $500 per year. On January 1, 1858, he lit the station's oil lamp for the first time.

With the building of the Great West Bay Light, the construction of a new lighthouse at Fire Island later that year, and the modification of the Montauk Point tower in 1860, Long Island's Atlantic shore now had the aids to navigation it needed. These tall towers, with powerful lamps and lenses, provided the mariner along the South Shore with an almost constant aid to navigation. The 20–mile visibility of these powerful lights meant that, on a clear night, a Long Island lighthouse could be seen from 20 miles east of Montauk Point to 20 miles west of Fire Island. At points midway

U.S. Coast Guard photo

Tower and keepers' dwellings in an undated photograph.

between Great West Bay and its neighbors, two lights could be seen at once. The three lighthouses covered nearly 110 miles.

The addition of the Great West Bay Light, as welcome as it was, was not without its early problems. When the lighthouse was built, it was given a fixed (steady) white light. This was the same characteristic as the Montauk Point Light had shown for many years (Montauk's characteristic was changed to fixed, varied by flashes). When the *John Milton*, a ship returning from South America, came upon the steady white light on February 19, 1858, her captain, Ephraim Harding, believed the light to be that from the Montauk Point lighthouse. It was a dark, snowy, stormy night and Captain Harding had no way of knowing that another lighthouse had been built during his long voyage. The *John Milton* continued eastward and, when Captain Harding believed they were clear of the point, turned north to pass between Montauk Point and Block Island. This miscalculation, caused by a combination of bad weather and the decision to use a fixed white light at Shinnecock, cost all 33 men aboard their lives. The smashed wreckage of the ship was found along the beach of Montauk Point the following morning. Legend says that the wreckage was found because of the tolling of the *John Milton's* bell in the surf. That bell still resides in the Hamptons.

About the same time as the *John Milton's* disaster, the whaling ship *Washington* encountered the same confusion regarding the steady light at Great West Bay. Unlike Harding, Captain Henry Babcock was not fooled by the new light. Despite unrest from the weary crew eager to return to port, Babcock would not turn north after sighting the light, and later picked up the Montauk Light. His belief in his navigating skills saved his crew and cargo.

Keeper Conley was given two assistants, James M. Hallock and Norman Wines, on June 17, 1858. On May 14, 1860, Henry S. Griffin replaced Conley, who had resigned. Griffin was, in turn, replaced by Richard Wells on April 15, 1861. Wells and his wife, the former Clarissa J. Foster, had their seventh child, Rose C. Wells, on November 12, 1861.

Wells remained exactly two years, when Benjamin Franklin Hallock became the keeper of Great West Bay. Hallock, born January 11, 1804, only remained 20 months, until his death in December 1864. Isaac Sweezy replaced Hallock on December 16, 1864. Sweezy was removed September 18, 1866, and was replaced by Alonzo Foster, a Civil War veteran who served in Company F, 6th New York Cavalry.

Many repairs were made at the station in 1867, including new doors for the dwellings, new shutters, new foundations for the barn and outhouses, repairs to the well and cistern, and various other repairs. It was also noted that "the stone deck of the tower leaks, and the parapet wall is cracked horizontally in a line with the air registers, caused, it is thought, by the oscillation of the tower." The fix proposed was to "cover the deck with an iron plate, and encase the parapet with cast-iron plates which will be fastened to the parapet and lantern deck." An appropriation was requested to accomplish the repair. That summer, the deck was repointed, which stopped the leak. At the same time, a cement wash was applied to the parapet, and only a small portion of the crack, on the northwest side, returned. This changed the opinions of the engineers regarding the cause of the original crack. Rather than oscillation, shrinkage of the original cement wash was suspected, and the appropriation request was withdrawn.

The 1869 *Annual Report* indicated that the tower was doing well, and all that had been needed in the previous year was a new stove and pipe, as well as six panes of glass for the lantern, and some window glass for the keepers' quarters. The request for the lantern glass was probably due to a problem that the tower would have for many years: the crashing of birds into its lantern.

In the years when the lighthouse cast a steady white light, it took a great toll on birds. This was more pronounced during stormy nights. Wire fencing was even put up around the lantern to help protect the expensive lens. The most extreme instance was probably on September 30, 1883. A total of 160 birds were reported killed that night in a storm. Of these, 85 were reportedly ruined by the rain—the other 75 were sent to a local ornithologist for identification. These were 59 Black-Poll Warblers, four Red-Eyed Vireos, three Connecticut Warblers, two Summer Tanagers, two Gray-Cheeked Thrushes, one Veery, one Ovenbird, one Olive-Backed Thrush, one Parula Warbler, and one Yellowthroat. Many of these birds were in their Fall migration.

When Foster was removed on July 19, 1869, Isaac Sweezy was appointed again. Less than three years later, there was another change of keepers. Wesley H. Squires became the light's keeper on

February 12, 1872, at the rate of $700 per year. Squires was a native of England.

In 1885, Squires was given two new assistants. John Raynor became his First Assistant on April 15, and Samuel Squires was appointed Second Assistant on December 5. These two remained with Wesley Squires until his removal on August 18, 1888.

Wesley Squires was replaced by Charles Miller, who was dismissed on September 26, 1893. Raynor was then promoted to Keeper of the Great West Bay Light and Samuel W. Squires was appointed First Assistant Keeper. John Penny was appointed Second Assistant Keeper on October 25, 1893. Shortly thereafter, on October 27, 1893, the station's name was officially "changed by direction of the Light-House Board" from Great West Bay to Shinnecock Bay.

During Raynor's time at Shinnecock Bay, he kept cows, pigs, and a horse on the site. While at the lighthouse, his wife, Sarah Bellows, gave birth to three children, none of whom survived.

In 1898, a "telephone connection with [the] Shinnecock Bay life-saving station was established by 1 mile of submarine cable laid across Shinnecock Bay, supplemented by bare copper wire on poles." In December, the connection was lost, but the problem was found, the cables spliced, and the connection reestablished.

On December 6, 1901, the Secretary of Treasury Lyman J. Gage wrote the following to Speaker of the House of Representatives David B. Henderson:

> This Department has the honor to state, at the instance of the Light-House Board, that the present fixed light at Shinnecock Bay, New York, is at but little greater height than the masthead of a large vessel, and being in the track of vessels bound east and west the light from its low position, as seen from seaward, may easily be taken for the light of a fishing vessel or other craft, thereby causing confusion and leading to possible disaster.
>
> It is obviously desirable that incoming trans-Atlantic steamers shall run at high speed as long as possible, and it is therefore imperative that the means for fixing position after a run in thick weather shall be as definite and prompt as practicable.

The Light-House Board, at its session on November 4, 1901, considered the question of changing the characteristic of the light at Shinnecock, New York, light-station, when it decided, in view of the fact that incoming trans-Atlantic vessels now make Shinnecock and not Fire Island, after sighting Nantucket Shoals light-vessel, that there ought to be substituted a third-order lens of three flash panels, separated each from the other by intervals of 5 seconds and the group by an interval of 15 seconds, the proposed light to be electric, with a power of more than 200,000 candles. The proposed change in the characteristic of this light is urgently recommended by the leading trans-Atlantic lines as being greatly to the interests of safe navigation in the approaches to New York Harbor. It is estimated that a suitable third-order electric revolving lens with all accessories can be provided, including the necessary electric plant, engines, power house, etc., and placed in position, for a cost not to exceed $25,000.

This Department concurs with the Light-House Board in deeming it necessary to make these improvements in the light at Shinnecock Bay, New York, and recommends that an appropriation of this amount be made therefor.

This letter was included in the Board's *Annual Report* to Congress in 1902, and again in 1903 and 1904.

In 1903, an estimate of $25,000 was submitted to convert the station's light to electric and change the lens. The lighthouse's five-wick oil lamp would remain in service until 1907, when it was replaced by an incandescent oil vapor lamp. This increased the candlepower of the light from 12,188 to 45,690.

The team of Raynor, Squires, and Penny worked together 13 years, from 1893 to 1906, when Squires left. Penny was then promoted to First Assistant, and Olaf Olsson was appointed Second Assistant Keeper. Raynor remained at the station until April 16, 1910, after nearly 17 years as the keeper of the Shinnecock Bay Light. Penny left the station later that year, on September 10, and was replaced by James J. Barnes.

Charles Redfern was appointed keeper on April 16, 1910, and was followed by Jorgen Bakken (January 28, 1911), and William H. H. Lake, Jr. (April 1, 1912). In 1915, Lake assisted a boat, "with woman occupant." Lake helped get the boat off of a shoal.

Throughout history, lighthouse keepers have done many of these small, yet important, deeds.

Also in 1915, $7,332 was spent improving the illuminating apparatus at Shinnecock Bay. This included the switch from a fixed light to a flashing light. The new lens consisted of eight panels. Four of these panels contained bull's eyes and prisms, with the other four having solid brass plates. The lens lacked the upper cone-shaped set of prisms that most Fresnel lenses have, as well as the lower set of prisms. The lower weight of this lens, as compared to more conventional First Order lenses with many more glass prisms, allowed the lens to be rotated faster, at a rate of two revolutions per minute. The new rotating lens required that its clockworks mechanism be wound every four hours.

During World War I, Navy Reserve personnel were stationed at Shinnecock Bay. One of these men was Thomas Clayton Sprague. He was put on active duty and assigned to the lighthouse from May 24, 1917 until February 12, 1919. Sprague was not fond of his station. In one letter home, he complained, "I want to take a man's part in this war—not a lighthouse keeper's." His duties at the lighthouse included cooking, washing dishes, keeping "the fires going night and day," getting water from the pond (the pump was broken), "and lots of other things. The worst is getting up at six-thirty." Sprague would later become a mechanic for the Burroughs Adding Machine Company on Long Island, as well as a musician and radio entertainer. He lost his life in a car accident in Huntington in 1931.

On February 16, 1922, the town around the lighthouse had its name changed from Good Ground to Hampton Bays, a name it retains to this day. The change was probably made to take advantage of the growing commercial value of the "Hamptons" mystique.

In 1929, the government sold 1.83 acres of the station to the Southampton Beach Corporation for use as a roadway to a new bridge across Shinnecock Bay. The bridge, built not long afterward, was replaced in the 1980s with a new structure.

Just after sunrise on Saturday, August 1, 1931, Keeper George Thomas extinguished the lamp at Shinnecock Bay for the last time.

Thomas Clayton Sprague on the tower's catwalk in 1918.

Photo courtesy of Jean Ruland

This era saw the decommissioning of many of the area's lighthouses; although the first, Shinnecock Bay would not be the only one. An automated light on a metal skeleton tower replaced the old brick tower.

U.S. Coast Guard photo

Shinnecock Bay Light Station on June 25, 1928.

The station was offered for sale in June 1934, but the sale was withdrawn due to opposition from local interests who wished to have the site made into a public park. The local Board of Supervisors approved the idea on June 25, 1934, but rescinded that action on September 5, stating that it "found it would not be advisable to accept a revocable license, nor would they be justified in expending monies on leased properties." The local Congressman, Robert L. Bacon, followed up on the matter, asking that the property be transferred to the Town of Southampton. At the time, the law only allowed the transfer of federal property to non-federal entities by sealed bids.

On November 22, 1935, Third District Superintendent J. T. Yates recommended that the station be sold "by sealed bids after newspaper & poster advertisement." This did not happen, but the lighthouse reservation was declared surplus on December 23, 1935. On April 29, 1936, the station was transferred to the U. S. Department of Agriculture (USDA), at their request. The USDA wanted to establish a migratory waterfowl refuge. An executive order on January 8, 1937, established the bird refuge, but put the site under the jurisdiction of the Department of Commerce, following the opinion of the Attorney General that the site had been improperly transferred.

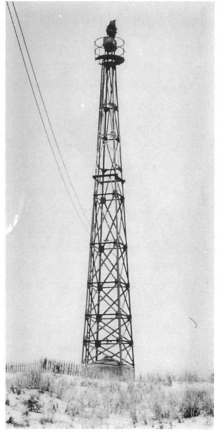

Skeleton tower that replaced Shinnecock Bay Lighthouse.

U.S. Coast Guard photo

The September 21, 1938 hurricane destroyed the 60–foot skeletal tower that had replaced the Ponquogue Light, and it created the Shinnecock Inlet. The old brick tower weathered the storm. A second skeletal tower replaced the lost one on December 16, 1939. This new tower, painted red, was on the west side of the Shinnecock Inlet. Its flashing red light sat 67 feet above water.

When the administration of America's lighthouses was transferred from the Commerce Department to the Coast Guard in 1939, jurisdiction over the Shinnecock Bay Light Station was transferred as well. By 1940, the Coast Guard was reporting that the tower was in dangerous condition. Residents in the area, however, who wanted the lighthouse preserved for its historic value, had engineers examine the building. These engineers believed that the tower was "safe and stable" and that it could be put in excellent condition for as little as $2000, but no action was taken.

In 1945, the dwellings were still in use by a private party with a special-use permit. The Coast Guard considered the possibility of using them for family housing, but upon examination concluded they were in poor condition and should be declared surplus and destroyed.

By January of 1948, the tower's fate was sealed, when a contractor for razing the tower was selected from 10 bids. The destruction of the tower had been approved July 28, 1947.

On December 23, 1948, the end finally came. Workers shored up the base of the tower with timbers, then jack hammered the bricks away on one side. The timbers were then soaked in gasoline and lit. When the fire sufficiently weakened the timbers, the majestic tower fell to the ground, making a sound that was heard for miles. The lighthouse that had once been one of the most important in the United States was reduced to a pile of bricks.

Today, the locals sometimes remember the Ponquogue Light, as they called it. Unfortunately, there is not much more to remind us of the service of this lighthouse and its keepers. The site of the old lighthouse is still an active Coast Guard station, at the base of the Ponquogue Bridge. The only remaining building from the site's lighthouse history is a 1902 brick oil house.

When the Long Island Chapter of the U.S. Lighthouse Society was formed in 2000, the lighthouse to be used on its logo was quite obvious. The logo, as seen in this book, depicts the Shinnecock Bay tower standing over an image of Long Island. Its presence on the logo, and the many items that logo adorns, reminds us of what can happen to our precious history.

If the Shinnecock Bay Lighthouse still stood today, it would be considered a historical treasure, and one of the most beautiful lighthouses of the Atlantic Coast. The story of its loss, and the part of Long Island's soul that was lost with it, illustrates, better than any other local lighthouse story, the importance of public attention and vigilance in the preservation of our historic lighthouse heritage.

Demolition of the Shinnecock Bay Tower on December 23, 1948.

U.S. Coast Guard photos

Workers jackhammer base of tower.

Timbers inside base of tower.

Fire is lit at base of tower.

Smoke billows from windows.

Tower begins to fall.

The South Shore

Wreck of the Oregon Lightship (1886)

Fire Island
(1827, 1858)

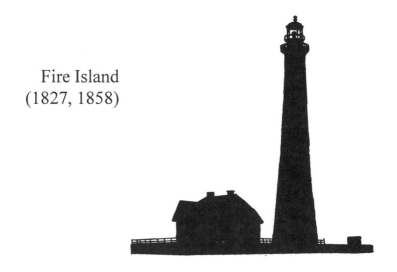

Fire Island Lightship (1896)

Coney Island
(1890)

Wreck of the Oregon Lightship

The 518-foot steamer *Oregon* was the pride of the Cunard fleet in 1886. She was three years old and had set the record for the Atlantic crossing, making the trip from Queenstown to Sandy Hook, New Jersey, in six days, ten hours, and ten minutes, an average of 18.65 knots. The iron-hulled ship could carry 1700 passengers.

The *Oregon* had been built in Scotland in 1883 for the Guion Line, which was known for its speedy, record-setting ships named after American states. The line was also known for losing money, and the Cunard Line obtained the luxurious *Oregon* in 1884.

In the dark, early hours of March 14, 1886, the *Oregon* was on her way from Liverpool to New York, with 640 passengers aboard. She was off Long Island, south of what is now Mastic Beach, when she was hit by another ship. The vessel that hit the *Oregon* is often thought to be the schooner *Charles Morse*, but the wooden sailing ship sank quickly after hitting the *Oregon* and no survivors or wreckage were ever found to confirm her identity.

The collision punched a hole in the *Oregon's* largest watertight compartment, and she began to fill with water. The passengers were all awakened, and prepared to abandon the ship. The captain, who had been sleeping when the collision occurred, was woken and he ordered distress flares to be fired. Three nearby ships arrived, and all of the *Oregon's* passengers were rescued. As is the custom, the captain stayed aboard until all of the passengers were safe. The *Oregon* sank eight hours after the collision. When she sank, bow first, 130 feet to the floor of the Atlantic, her tall stacks and masts still posed a danger to maritime traffic in the area. The masts still pierced the surface of the water.

Light Vessel *No. 20*, then serving as a relief vessel for New York, was sent to mark the site. *LV 20* had been built in 1867 in Greenpoint, New York. She was a wooden-hulled ship, 81 feet long, with two masts, propelled by sail. In 1880, *LV 20* had been rebuilt, and her lamps changed to burn kerosene.

Illustration from Harper's Weekly, circa 1886

No. 20 on station at the wreck of the Oregon. The Oregon's masts and stacks are visible to the left of the lightship.

Prior to her station marking the wreck of the *Oregon*, *LV 20* had been used as a relief vessel in the Fourth District (1867–1868), at the site of the wreck of the *Scotland* (1868–1870, 1876–1880), and as a relief vessel in New York (1870–1876, 1880–1886).

After wreckers dismantled the *Oregon's* stacks and masts, she was no longer considered a threat to navigation. The lightship was removed from its station in late 1886.

On March 2, 1889, an act for once again establishing a lightship with fog signal on the site was approved by Congress. The act was never funded.

After leaving the South Shore of Long Island, *LV 20* was assigned as a relief vessel in Connecticut (1886–1918), and was then stationed at Cross Rip, Massachusetts (1918–1922), spending her last year as an unused relief ship. *No. 20* was sold in 1923, and was reported to have been used by bootleggers for warehousing their goods. Eventually, she was burned at a July 4 celebration.

No lives were lost on the *Oregon* when she sank, but 112 years later, on July 10, 1998 the site was involved in a death. An experienced Long Island diver, on his second dive at the site that day, suffered a mishap related to his regulator valve and was later discovered near the wreck.

Although a light vessel only marked the site for less than one year, the *Oregon* has remained at the bottom of the Atlantic, off Long Island's South Shore. She continues to be one of the area's more popular shipwrecks, with divers often recovering a variety of artifacts. Over the years, most of the ship has collapsed, but the ship's engine still stands.

Fire Island

Standing guard over some of the Long Island's most popular beaches, the Fire Island Lighthouse casts its light out to mariners in the Atlantic Ocean and Great South Bay. Since 1827, a lighthouse at Fire Island has helped to guide transatlantic ships, recreational boaters, and commercial fishermen.

Throughout American history, the waters south of the Fire Island Inlet have been nearly as dangerous as they have been important. These waters have seen a great deal of commerce and immigration, as well as many shipwrecks.

U.S. Coast Guard photo

Fire Island in the early 1900s.

Before the arrival of European immigrants, the area's inhabitants used the Great South Bay and Atlantic Ocean to harvest seals, whales, fish, shellfish, and other necessities. As the American colonies became established, gained in economic strength and welcomed large numbers of European immigrants, the Atlantic waters off of Fire Island became important to the nation's growth, as well as a danger to more ships, passengers, and cargo.

The name of the island has long been the source of much conjecture. The most likely explanation appears to be one explored in the January 1973 edition of the *The Long Island Forum*. The article by Lavern A. Wittlock, Sr. was based on a 1798 map made by surveyor Samuel Wheeler in Islip. Wittlock discussed the early Dutch influence on Long Island. In the days when New York was known as New Amsterdam, many of local towns and landmarks had Dutch names. Over time, these names became Anglicized. One of the more famous examples is Breuckelen, which is now known as Brooklyn. The Dutch word for four is vier (pronounced "fear"). Wheeler's 1798 map showed the inlet as "Great Fier Island Inlet or Ship Channel," with four islands just inside the inlet, near present-day Sexton Island, marked "Fier Islands." It seems likely that the pronunciation of vier, for the four islands, caused the written interpretation. Over time, it is easy to see how Vier became Fier, and then Fire. Wheeler's map did show what we now call Fire Island, but it was labeled "East Beach." The island would later be called Great South Beach, and eventually Fire Island.

When the federal government began implementing plans to build a lighthouse on Fire Island, there was some confusion regarding who, if anyone, owned the property on the east side of the inlet. The local Superintendent of Lighthouses, Jonathan Thompson, asked New York State to cede jurisdiction over the site. This jurisdiction was granted on April 20, 1825, and Tredwell Scudder, Smith Carll, and Samuel S. Gardiner were appointed to "appraise and estimate the value" of the site. The site was valued at $50, which Thompson paid.

Thompson entered into a contract with Haviland Wicks to construct the tower and lantern at a cost of $7000. Another contract, with George W. Thompson, provided for the lamps, reflectors, "and all the necessary apparatus to make the same complete," for $1200.

Photo by the author

Base of the original Fire Island tower in 1999.

Construction started in 1826. When completed, the lighthouse was built of Connecticut River blue split stone, in the shape of an octagonal pyramid, at a cost of $9999.65, a sum 35 cents under budget. The tower, with six windows, was painted white. The 74–foot tower cast a light from 89 feet above the water. In the lantern room, the 18 lamps with 15–inch reflectors, of Winslow Lewis' design and much-maligned construction, did not cast a powerful, focused light. The lamps hung on a chandelier that rotated once every minute-and-a-half, giving the light a flashing characteristic as each lamp and reflector aligned with the observer's eye. The light was further hindered by the design of the lantern room, with small panes of glass and large astragals. In order to see the light, ships would often have to travel dangerously close to offshore sand bars. Consequently, some of these ships ran aground. In 1842, Fire Island's lantern room was refitted with 14 lamps with 21–inch reflectors, but these did not perform any better than the previous apparatus.

One of the earliest keepers of the Fire Island Light, appointed in 1835, was Felix Dominy. He had been born February 12, 1800, in East Hampton, and became a watchmaker. His father, Nathaniel, had been a windmill builder. On October 26, 1928, he married Pheobe Miller. The couple had five children: Nathaniel (born 1827), Jerusha (born 1835), Mary (born 1840), Arthur (born 1841), and Ned (born 1846).

In 1838, while George Bache was reporting on most of Long Island's lights, U.S. Navy Lieutenant William D. Porter made a trip to Fire Island. It was part of Porter's inspection of the Fourth District, which ranged from New York to Norfolk, Virginia. His report on the Fire Island light read:

> *Fire-island light-tower.*—Revolving; burns 18 lamps with spherical reflectors, placed on three parallel rows: reflectors are badly placed, and do not stand perpendicularly, but have an inclination of two or three degrees from the line of focus. The stone of which the tower is built, good; but the cement is bad, and crumbles; arch leaks. The deck outside of lantern, soapstone; inside, porous sandstone. Lantern appears to be too small for the number of lamps; I therefore recommend that the lower tier be dispensed with. Sills of windows rotten.

Porter also included an extract from Dominy's "private note-book":

> 1836, June 21, brig Rhine stranded. December 14, brig General Trotter came on shore; total loss. January 14, ship Tamarac, (English, from Liverpool,) assorted cargo, 120 passengers; cargo lost, first boat upset; passengers and crew landed in long-boat, with the assistance of people from shore. November 29, sloop Report on shore. August 21, white-washed the house; Captain Barker ten day's repairing the light-house. September 9, sloop Traffic on shore. September 24, Great Western passed.

Porter also mentioned the Fire Island Light in his summary comments, noting that "the main tower erected on Cape Henlopen, years previous to the American Revolution, is at present strong and solid, without crack or flaw in the workmanship, and still exhibits evidence of continued durability; whereas the tower at Fire-island inlet, built apparently after the model of that at Henlopen, is of modern date, has undergone several repairs, and is yet leaky." As with all of Long Island's other Pleasanton-era lights, the original Fire Island tower had not been built well.

On March 30, 1840, Keeper Dominy wrote about a shipwreck in a letter to his son, Nathaniel:

> Yesterday a brig got on shore about a mile west; on the bar – from Palermo in Italy, Capt Nicolo Haggio, bound to N.Y. loaded with wine, oranges, Madeira nuts, almonds, figs, raisins, lemons, grapes, anchovies, capers, apricots, preserve[s], cherries, etc. etc. The men eleven in number all speak Italian & one of them speaks English rather broken but we can make out to understand him so he interprets for the whole. They seem to be quite a nice set of men altogether. They have over 300 boxes of oranges, lemons, sweet-oil & pickles they went ashore on West Beach & were pick'd up by some men from Babylon. I went over to day in the fog and brot [sic] home 1 box oranges & one of lemons the crew brot [sic] on shore figs & nuts & Jerusha is in clover. It has been so foggy they have not been able to board the brig since they first left her but we are in hopes of getting on board in the morning and getting out the chronometer, sailors dunnage, and a few boxes of silks and silk velvet belonging to the Captain. They seem very clever and liberal telling us to get as many nuts, oranges, lemons, wine etc. as we want.

He also told of a little accident in the tower:

> [O]ne night I went up in the lt. house to trim the lamp & walking back wards fell down the trap door until my right foot reach'd the stairs & thought at first my leg was broken crawled up & laid down on the floor for a while & got partly over it & hobbled down. Tis about 10 days & I have got pretty much over it my knee is a little stiff it was so lame for 2 days I was obliged to use a cane & once in a while it made me fairly <u>hallow</u> <u>out</u> <u>loud</u> now I can run quite spry.

Nathaniel spent his life in East Hampton, his family's ancestral home, and worked at watch and clock making, and building boats and windmills during his 83 years.

The Dominy name would later become better known in the area near the lighthouse for innkeeping both on Fire Island and in Bay Shore. This talent was already evident during his time at the lighthouse. The local superintendent, Edward Curtis, wrote in 1843 that Dominy "entertains boarders and company at his dwelling in the Island and devotes so much of his time and care to that, and other business personal to himself, that the public charge committed to him, is not faithfully exercised; his Light House duties are made subordinate objects of attention."

Eliphalet Smith replaced Dominy as keeper on January 15, 1844. On June 26 of that year, Smith received a visit from a cousin from Illinois. Elizabeth Howell Blanchard had been born in Baiting Hollow in 1800, married Seth Blanchard in 1817, and moved to Illinois in 1820 to establish a farm, named Suffolk Grove. By 1844, Elizabeth was in poor health. She decided a trip home might help. She spent five months in New York City and on Long Island, from May to October, 1844. She kept a diary of her travels. On June 26, she wrote of a "large party" of people going to Fire Island, where they "[a]rrivd at Capt Smiths, found them finely situated. Had a fine dinner. Took a walk over to the ocean side of the beach. The sea breaking majesticaly on the shore, then receeding. We rested awhile, then proposed to go up to the top of the Light-house. It is seven stories high. Quite a curiosity to see the apparatus up there, the large silver reflectors which cost forty dollars apiece. They are splendid. Then to look abroad on the vast ocean and think of the dangers of the great deep and turn and look the other side and see a broad expanse of water calld the bay. With numerous crafts of all sizes almost and pursuing as many occupations . . .."

The next day, Blanchard noted that her cousins were "paid by the government five hundred dollars for lighting and tending the light house and they do live very finely indeed." She also made mention that Smith's daughters, Catherine and Georgiana, were "two very handsome girls" and regarded them as "splendid singers and performers on the accordion."

On the next day, June 28, Blanchard wrote of her time atop the light tower:

Took my pen and ink and assended the 7 flights of stairs and am now comfortably seated in the top of the light house on Fire Island, a grand oppty to contemplate the majesty and power of him who can say to the winds and waves, "Peace be still." The sun shines glorious and the wind blows tremendous. The surf and surge, roar and beat upon the shore. A true touch of the sublime is this view of the mighty ocean, constantly pouring and roaring and foaming its white billows against the sandy beach. None but an omnipotent arm could save a

291

frail barque of a ship from the ravages of the great deep. I do not, cannot see how tis possible for man to presume to sail out upon the wonderful expanse of water without imploring divine protection from the dangers of the sea! . . . None seem to be coasting today. A sloop has just come in through the inlet and saild on through the bay east, probably to Pachougeo or some of those towns along the coast. Bell-Port, Moriches, Fire Place, Blue Point, etc. The beach is about ¼ a mile wide and extends almost the length of the Island. The bay was formd a century ago. Some old men knew it when [it was] a forest.

I am calld to dinner and must now descend from this high situation in life. Wish I could describe the prospect from here, from this lofty and commanding view—vast, vast! Eligible and grand and awful, yet sublime to look abroad as far as the eye can possibly reach on the great ocean and think of the trying scenes witnessd and felt by millions, and recollect many circumstances that come within our knowledge is enough to make us feel our insignificence . . ..

After her visit, Blanchard wrote: "I think I would like to live on L.I.—but feel quite content with my home in Illinois." Blanchard's vacation did not bring back her health. She died two years after returning to Illinois.

Selah Strong was appointed Keeper on July 14, 1849. The following June 12, he received a visit from Captain Howland's supply ship. Howland reported that the tower had had some recent repairs, such as whitewashing, and repointing of the tower, "where the cement was

Keeper Eliphalet Smith.
U.S. Lighthouse Society photo

292

off and loose." The lantern was undergoing an upgrade at the time, with larger glass plates being installed. Repairs were also needed on the dwelling, such as fixing the well, installing a new oven, painting, and installing a new fence. The lighting apparatus was declared to be "in good order and clean."

A little over a month after Howland's visit, on July 19, 1850, the bark *Elizabeth*, on her way to New York from Italy, wrecked off of Fire Island. The captain had contracted smallpox and died during the journey, leaving a junior officer with inadequate experience to pilot the boat to New York. On the approach to New York Harbor in bad weather, the officer lost his bearings and slammed into the sand bar off Fire Island at about 3:30 AM, throwing passengers from their bunks. A wave picked up the stern of the ship and put the ship broadside to the bar. The impact was reportedly so hard that it propelled some of the cargo of marble through the ship's wooden hull.

The waves and weather quickly destroyed the lifeboats, making rescue difficult. Some of the ship's occupants floated to shore on planks, but the heavy seas prevented many from making the attempt. Lifesaving gear did make it to the scene, but the heavy winds and surf made rescue impossible. By 3:00PM, the ship was breaking up. Many of those aboard eventually jumped into the sea.

In all, 14 of the 21 people aboard made it to shore. Among those that did not was Margaret Fuller, who was America's first literary critic and female foreign correspondent. Her husband and infant child were also lost in the wreck, with only the child's body being recovered.

A great deal of looting of the *Elizabeth's* cargo occurred. Several people were eventually arrested in the thefts. Among the materials stolen were $15,000 worth of silk. One of the marble items lost was a statue of Southern statesman John Calhoun. It was recovered by divers, about 300 feet offshore, and installed in the Capitol building in Columbia, South Carolina. On February 17, 1865, the statue was destroyed by fire when Sherman's troops burned the building.

When Congress changed the administration of America's lighthouse system in 1852, the new Light-House Board focused much of its efforts on improving the important coastal lights. On Long Island, this meant improvements at Montauk Point, the construction of a lighthouse at Great West Bay, and the construction of a new lighthouse at Fire Island.

A little less than three years after the wreck of the *Elizabeth*, on April 29, 1853, Benjamin Smith became the keeper of the light at Fire Island Inlet, at a rate of pay of $500 per year. His assistant was Willett Smith, probably a relative.

As had been the case at Great West Bay, Lieutenants J. C. Duane and J. St. C. Morton were the engineers when the Fire Island Light was rebuilt. They generated much correspondence prior to, and during, the building of the lighthouse.

On August 31, 1854, Duane submitted an estimate of $10,000 to cover the costs of the materials and labor required to rebuild the Fire Island Lighthouse. This would prove to be only a fraction of the final cost.

Preparations for the rebuilding of the lighthouse began in 1857. A "wharf, store-house, and temporary barracks for the accommodation of the workmen" were built, and many of the materials were procured. It was estimated that the light could be exhibited by the middle of 1858.

On April 8, 1857, Duane wrote to the Secretary of the Light House Board, Lieutenant William B. Franklin. In this letter, he expressed his concern that brick "does not appear to me to be by any means adapted to a work of such importance and in such an exposed situation. I would therefore recommend stone to be used in this case." Duane's recommendation was not heeded.

Duane submitted an estimate for the cost of the brick tower on June 1, 1857:

800,000 Brick	$8,000.
1,200 lbs. Cement	1,500.
Stone for Foundation	2,820.
Concrete for Foundation (650 yds.)	3,250.
Stone Steps 160	1,600.
Stone for Cornice 500 ft.	500.
Post Iron	1,000.

Stone Floors	300.
Wrought Iron Ladders, Railing	200.
Work Masons 1610 days	4,000.
Work Carpenters 250 days	500.
Work Stone Cutters	375.
Work Blacksmith	300.
Work Laborers	2,500.
Freight	4,000.
Machinery Tools, etc.	1,500.
	$32,345.

The eventual construction of the lighthouse would be somewhat different, including iron steps, rather than stone, but Duane's estimate was close to the actual cost.

On April 9, 1858, Morton wrote to Franklin to report that he had found the concrete in the foundation "had a bad appearance," and, upon examination, "found the concrete, as far down as I got (2'6") quite friable and porous: the mortar could be rubbed into a powder between the fingers easily; it was in fact no stronger than hard sand." Morton was concerned that "it would be assuming a great risk to my reputation to build on a foundation that might prove unreliable," and wanted to remove the concrete in question. The next day, he received a reply, and was told to continue on with the work; his suggestion, like Duane's a year earlier, was unheeded.

On April 12, Morton sent another letter, acknowledging the directions to continue the work. He also proposed to double the number of iron reinforcing bands in the bottom ten feet of the tower. These bands, embedded in the brickwork, were to prevent the tower from "spreading or cracking."

Morton wrote, in a P.S. to an April 19 letter to Franklin, that the "concrete samples that I took from the F. I. Foundation have become much firmer, and quite hard in fact, by being allowed to set, in a warm room."

On May 27, 1858, Morton wrote a letter referring to trials of lamps for the Fire Island Lighthouse. He determined that one type of lamp, called a Moderator lamp, was sensitive to any minute particles or filaments in the oil, which was common in American lamp oil. "This is not a defect," he reported, "provided the Light Keepers were sensible and careful enough to clean the tube every day; but the generality of Keepers will not take the trouble, and it becomes a great objection to the Lamp." The Hydraulic lamp, however seemed "to be a great improvement on the Moderator, from its burning our oil without ever needing cleaning; or at most, about 4 times a year."

By July, experiments with cement washes, as a covering for the brick tower, were underway. Morton estimated that two coats, making a one-eighth-inch layer, would "render the tower impervious to water." He was experimenting with different colorings to "find one which will give an agreeable cream yellow colour."

U.S. Coast Guard photo
Undated aerial view of the station's second tower
and keepers' dwelling.

When completed, the new tower, 200 feet northeast of the old tower, was the tallest lighthouse in New York. Its shape was unique, as well. The sides of the tower curved rapidly at the bottom then the curve diminished, until the tower was nearly straight at the top. The curve used in creating this shape was a "hyperbolae." The tower's walls were built with air spaces to allow the tower to breathe.

The lens installed was a First Order flashing lens from Paris. Each of its eight sides was composed of three sections: a cone-shaped upper section of prisms, a center section with a bull's eye and prisms, and a lower section of prisms. The lens produced a flash once each minute, as the eight-sided lens rotated one-eighth of a turn per minute. Each winding of the clockworks mechanism, the weights for which were in the central iron column, allowed the lens to rotate for about four hours.

The new tower's magnificent height and powerful light allowed mariners to spot it easily, making it a great improvement over the former lighthouse. Benjamin Smith officially lit the new lamp for the first time on November 1, 1858. Morton reported that it "burned excellently."

When the new keepers' dwelling was completed, it contained accommodations for the keeper, two assistants, and their families. The keeper and his family lived on the west side of the dwelling, with a kitchen and sitting room on the first floor, and two large (20 feet by 13 feet, 6 inches) bedrooms upstairs. Each assistant had a kitchen downstairs, on the east side of the dwelling, and two bedrooms upstairs—one large, and one smaller room. On March 19, 1859, Smith was given a second assistant, S. M. Smith.

After Benjamin Smith left the lighthouse in the early 1860s, C. W. Fordham, then David L. Baldwin, replaced him. When the government decided to remove Baldwin in May 1865, they reportedly had a difficult time finding a replacement. Newspaper ads and postings in post offices had failed to produce an applicant, possibly due to concerns over whether the tall brick structure could actually survive the harsh conditions of wind, wave, and sand at the site. A local postmaster recommended Samuel E. Hulse, who owned a small fleet of boats, and was said to know the area "as well as he knew the inside of his own home." Hulse became Fire Island's keeper on May 26, 1865. He remained nearly four years. Hulse had been born in 1830 or 1831 in Patchogue, and spent much of his life in Bay Shore. He never drank, but did smoke cigars, and preferred ham and potatoes for breakfast. He lived until 1913, and is buried in Bay Shore.

In 1869, the tower was reported as being in good condition, but the illuminating apparatus needed some attention. Part of the overhaul and adjustments made was the replacement of the lamp. A variety of supplies including "[l]anterns, curtains and fixtures, new pump, tool chest and necessary tools" were provided for the station.

Hugh Walsh was appointed keeper on January 2, 1873. Ralph Munroe, a boatmaker, photographer, and South Florida pioneer, visiting the area in late Fall 1872 to early Spring 1873, wrote an account of the "one-legged" keeper, saying that he "had been appointed on political grounds rather than for fitness." Munroe wrote the following one day when the assistant keepers, John Burke and William J. Bailey, had gone to the mainland and had not returned by late in the day:

> Walsh relied on one of his assistants for all mechanical details, and on this day of their absence he had foolishly taken the lamp apart for cleaning; about half an hour before lighting up he discovered that the big glass chimney and the sheet iron one were out of alignment. This was easy to correct with the three leveling screws under the font, but losing his head, he attempted to bend the sheet-iron pipe, nearly wrecking it; then remembering that I was somewhat of a mechanic, he fairly jumped the whole of the iron stairway down the tower—180 feet—and I can see him now coming along the beach with the sand flying from his crutch, one leg and a cane. I met him part way, and hurrying back ahead of him, had the lamp connected and ready for him to light just in time to save his billet.

Seth R. Hubbard was appointed Acting Keeper of the Fire Island Light on April 24, 1874. He would not receive his permanent appointment until December 2, 1881, but his pay remained the same in both capacities, at $740 per year. Hubbard was a Civil War veteran, reportedly serving as a spy for the North. After the war, he wanted to do something nice for his mother-in-law, who had cared for his wife and two children while he was away. Using the money he was paid when he mustered out of the military, he purchased bricks and built an outdoor oven for her, so she could make bread. Many of her neighbors also brought firewood to help with the baking, creating a sort of community oven.

In November and December of 1875, Hubbard tested some new wicks in the station's First Order lamp. These wicks burned a little more oil than the old ones had the previous year (two gallons more in November, six gallons more in December). The new wicks, in Hubbard's opinion, did not give off as bright a flame.

By 1876, some repairs to the illuminating apparatus were needed. The tower required a new cement wash and recoloring. These repairs were accomplished within a year.

On July 23, 1888, Ezra S. Mott became Fire Island's keeper. Mott had been born February 9, 1845, and spent his early years as a farmer, then in local shipping, and was part owner of three vessels: the *Mary Brush*, *L. D. Girard*, and *Sloop Opera*. He and his wife, Melissa, married in Port Jefferson in 1869, had four daughters: Mary, Lucy, Evilyn, and Melissa. Before coming to Fire Island, he had worked on lightships, and at the Stratford Shoal Light.

By December, there was some concern over the fact that the lamp was consuming too much oil—19% more than the maximum allowance for November. Mott's local inspector thought that the keeper's measurements must be erroneous, so he sent Joseph Funck, a lamp expert, to Fire Island. Funck found that Mott's measurements were correct and that the lamp was, indeed, burning much more oil than expected. This was traced to two recent modifications: an increase in the lantern room draft by the installation of pipes for that purpose; and a new burner on the lamp, which had larger supply tubes. These modifications had not only increased the consumption of oil, but they had created a larger, and brighter, flame. Standard instructions for the lamp specified a flame three-and-one-half to three-and-three-quarters of an inch in height. The flame at Fire Island was a steady, solid five inches. Since the Fire Island Light was "the most important one in this district if not on the whole

Sea-Coast," Mott was instructed to "maintain the highest flame [possible] . . . without regard to the quantity of oil consumed."

In 1889, Mott's wife, Melissa, who was described as "a loving and devoted companion and a woman of value to the community," passed away. It appears that the Motts were well respected. Ezra was known for his "strict attention to duty, unfaltering purpose and honorable methods," which "gained for him the high regard of all, and . . . many warm friends."

On August 6, 1891, Commodore James A. Greer, Chairman of the Light-House Board, issued a *Notice to Mariners* stating that the color of the tower would be "changed from yellow to alternate bands

Photo by the author

1999 photo showing the tower's daymark.

of black and white, two of each color." These bands, each about 35 feet wide, make up the tower's distinctive daymark.

The 1894 *Annual Report* contained a great deal about the Fire Island Light, starting out by stating that it was "the most important light for transatlantic steamers bound for New York. It is generally the first one they make and from which they lay their course." A brief description of the current illuminating apparatus followed, then a description of the bivalve lens, also called a "lightning light on account of the brilliancy and short duration of the flash," that had been displayed at the 1893 World Columbian Exhibition in Chicago. The lens, which consisted of "two powerful range lenses, 9 feet in diameter, back to back," housed an electric "arc light . . . of very high candlepower." The Light-House Board had been so impressed by this apparatus that it purchased it for installation at Fire Island.

Work to make the switch proceeded rapidly. A coal-fired, steam-powered generator was built at the general depot on Staten Island and delivered by mid-1894. A narrow-gauge track and other needed structures followed shortly thereafter.

Just as quickly as the plan for the new light was developed and put into motion, this plan was changed. The establishment of a lightship station nine miles south of Fire Island was considered a greater aid to mariners, and the lightning lens plan was scrapped. The "entire steam and electric plant and one 4th order iron lantern," which was to house a temporary light while the change was made, was sent back to Staten Island on December 31, 1896. The huge lens was later installed at the lighthouse at Navesink, New Jersey, where it still resides, having been the subject of a recent restoration.

William F. Aichele was appointed as keeper on October 1, 1909. The Aichele family had two sons born at the lighthouse, Fritz and Hans. Fritz was born about 1912, and Hans in 1915. Fritz would later become a charter boat captain in the Shinnecock Bay area, and Hans a policeman in Southampton.

Aichele had some personnel problems while at Fire Island. A letter from his Inspector on March 26, 1912, informed him that the "difficulty between yourself and the assistant Keepers is due to your lack of enforcement of discipline at the station." On April 8, another letter stated:

> It has been noted from inspection report of Fire Island Light-Station that the two assistant keepers are unable to perform their share of work of painting tower on account of nervousness.
>
> As this work is part of keepers and assistant keepers duties, the assistant keepers should do their proportionate share of same.
>
> And you are hereby directed to have the assistant keepers do so, or else employ at their expense substitutes to perform this duty for them.

Given the height of the tower and power of the winds at Fire Island, many would understand the "nervousness" of the assistant keepers.

The tower was reinforced in 1912, when a large crack was detected in the tower. The reinforcement consisted of round iron bands and metal mesh set on top of the brickwork, which was chipped rough, with a cement coating over the entire tower.

In 1914, personnel problems once again arose. Aichele and his First Assistant Keeper, Chester B. Harper, were not getting along, and Harper had requested a transfer. A letter from Inspector Yates on May 11 told Aichele, "this office is of the opinion that the differences existing between yourself and the Asst. Keeper of the Station are due to petty and personal quarrels. You are informed that the continuance of such a condition will not be tolerated." Yates further instructed to Aichele to see that his conduct promoted "harmony and efficiency at the station at which you are employed." By September, problems with Harper led to his dismissal.

By 1916, it must have been obvious to Third District Lighthouse Service officials that Aichele would prefer a quieter station. He was offered the opportunity to take a position at the Crown Point Light, on Lake Champlain, which he eventually did.

Another assistant during Aichele's time at Fire Island was George Thomas. Thomas and Aichele were cribbage partners, and would play against the men from the nearby Western Union and Postal Telegraph towers. The winners would receive a roast beef dinner. Thomas had two daughters, Lucy and Alice. Lucy was to wear a wide-brimmed red straw hat when she played outside, so that she could be spotted from the tower at all times. The Thomas family kept chickens, and had a garden at the station.

On August 29, 1918, the Fire Island Light was struck by lightning. The bolt left a one-inch long hole in the ventilator ball, then traveled down through the watch room, and followed the call bell wire "to the hall of the dwelling and burned out the telephone wire and demolished the switch box connected with the telephone."

George Thomas rescued two aviators from a "sinking hydroplane" in the Great South Bay in 1918, and took them "to aviation camp at Bay Shore." That year, he also helped put out a fire that had destroyed "several cottages, fishing buildings, etc."

Thomas remained at Fire Island until May 30, 1919. He was then transferred to Shinnecock Bay, where he would be that tower's last keeper. In 1987, Lucy Thomas returned to Fire Island, and donated some photographs, dolls, and other artifacts from her childhood at the lighthouse.

In 1921, Keeper Frank Oberly was accused of breaking into houses on the beach. He was held in $500 bail, but a grand jury did not indict him and he was dismissed of all charges in May of that year.

As Fire Island extended west due to littoral drift, the lighthouse reservation grew in size. In 1924, the 68th Congress passed an act transferring much of this new land to New York State. The land extended from the Fire Island Lighthouse "to the western end of Fire Island, with the exception of such land as is occupied or needed by the United States Coast Guard." This land totaled about six hundred acres. The act included provisions that the land was subject to federal use "for any and all military, naval, or other governmental purposes," and that the land would revert to federal control if it was not used for public park purposes. These provisions also applied to "all additional lands that may be formed by accretions of the sea." These lands, including the additional accretions since 1924, are now known as Robert Moses State Park. The entire park, a popular place for sunbathers, kite flyers, birdwatchers, fishermen, and tourists, consists of land that did not exist when the first Fire Island Light was built.

In 1927, while Isaac Karlin was stationed at the lighthouse, the keepers' dwelling received a central heating system. A radiator was installed in each room on both floors. Two boilers were placed in the basement; one for each side of the building.

The Fire Island Light's First Order Fresnel lens was changed in 1933. The lens that had been in the tower since 1858 gave off a five-second flash once a minute. The lens from the decommissioned Shinnecock Bay Light, replaced it. The new lens, much lighter than the original because of its fewer glass prisms, could be rotated faster. This allowed for a more frequent flash, making it easier for mariners to determine their location. It was at this time that the current flash every seven-and-one-half seconds characteristic was established at Fire Island.

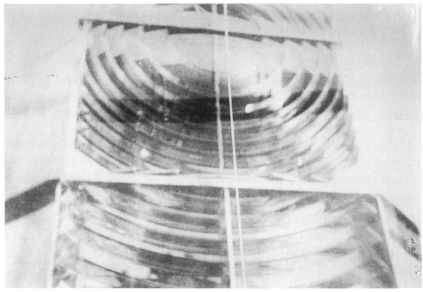

Photo courtesy of Gottfried and Marilyn Mahler

Rare photo of the lens that was moved from the
Shinnecock Bay Light to the Fire Island Light in 1933.

From 1934 to 1941, Adrien Boisvert was the light's keeper. Boisvert was 33 when he and his wife, Alice, came to Fire Island. An article in the *Sunday Island News* on January 20, 1935 referred to him as a "serious, rolly-polly lighthouse keeper," as well as a "friendly little lighthouse boss," and his wife as a "sweet, shy feminine person." Boisvert's First Assistant in 1935 was Arthur Miller, who had been at Fire Island since 1928. Miller's wife had been a munitions worker in World War I, and was missing a kneecap and half a finger, and had an eye "closed due to shell shock" to show for it. The Millers had a son, Arthur Edward, die at the age of four in 1933. They kept the casket with his ashes with them because they never knew when Miller's job would transfer them.

Boatswain Mate First Class Frank Estler spent nine years on Fire Island as a Coast Guard surfman, beginning in 1935, with two of those years at the lighthouse during World War II. Frank's accomplishments during his stay on Fire Island included the naming of the dirt road that passes by the front of the lighthouse. Frank was still stationed at the Coast Guard station in 1939. The many Coast Guardsmen stationed there often had to drive in the middle of the island, when tides or weather made the beaches impassable. The interior road was tough, though. In Frank's words, they "[v]ery often got stuck in the sand, hit many bumps, and snow drifts in the winter, over boardwalks, plus hazards made it a very tough trip." One day, Frank and other crewmembers were relaxing in the station's Recreation Room, listening to the news reports on the radio. One of the reports was about The Flying Tigers protecting the Burma Road in China. The report stated what tough duty it was to keep the road open. Frank then stood up, suggested that they name "this sand strip of a road" Burma Road. The rest of the crew agreed and the name stuck.

The infamous hurricane of September 21, 1938, pounded Fire Island, along with the rest of the northeastern U.S., washing away homes and leaving many coastal areas under water. Frank Estler remembers the hurricane. He was on duty at the top of the Coast Guard station's watch tower at 4AM when the winds unexpectedly picked up. He was relieved at 8AM, but his relief was removed from the tower by 10AM, as the winds had become too fierce.

During the hurricane, Frank used one of the two tractors at the station to move around the island. Between the Coast Guard station and the lighthouse, the island had broken through in 11 places. At one point the tractor got stuck. In getting the tractor free, Frank was exposed to poison ivy.

Estler's parents had a home in nearby Fair Harbor. The hurricane moved the whole house 200 feet. It may have been moved further, if not for a telephone pole that smashed through a window, with its wires wrapping round the house, acting as an anchor. The lighthouse stood strong through the hurricane, while many nearby structures were destroyed.

The next year, as the Coast Guard absorbed the Lighthouse Service, the Fire Island Light was electrified. From 1939 on, scores of Coast Guardsmen and their families served at this light station.

Gottfried Mahler, from Springfield Gardens, Queens, was assigned to the Fire Island Light Station on September 14, 1948, replacing Shelbert Payne. He was 23 and his wife, Marilyn, was 21. They had a one-and-a-half-year-old son, Richard. Mahler had joined the Coast Guard on July 8, 1942, inspired as a child by the clean ships and noble work of the Coast Guardsmen at the Atlantic Beach Coast Guard Station, near where Mahler and his father had often fished.

Prior to his assignment to Fire Island, Mahler served in several capacities, including as quartermaster on the buoy tender *Mangrove*. This was where Mahler developed an affinity for aids to navigation work.

Mahler's duties at the lighthouse included tending the light, maintaining generators, polishing the lamp and lens, and sometimes clearing the remains of birds that had hit the lantern glass. He took his duties seriously, yet always with an enjoyment of life.

In April of 1950, the 432–foot freighter *SS Hurricane* hit the sandbar off of Fire Island in a fog, not far from the lighthouse. The ship was so close that its horn rattled dishes in the keepers' dwelling and woke the family. The next morning, the ship could be seen from the lighthouse. It had come to rest west of the lighthouse, not far from the Coast Guard station. An unusually high tide had carried the ship

Photo courtesy of Gottfried and Marilyn Mahler

The freighter SS Hurricane ashore at Fire Island. A Dodge Power Wagon and amphibious vehicle are among the rescue apparatus assembled.

far inside the sand bar. The *Hurricane* remained stranded for 13 days, until two oceangoing tugs from the Merritt, Chapman and Scott Company pulled her off the beach.

The Mahlers possessed a sense of humor that they retain to this day. When Marilyn gave birth to a son in December of 1950, they issued the following announcement:

GOTTFRIED E. MAHLER, Quartermaster 1/c
U. S. COAST GUARD
MARILYN E. MAHLER, Housewife 1/c
CIVILIAN

Announce the launching of a new
Coast Guard Cut-Up
the

"GODFREY GORDON MAHLER"

At Mercy Hospital, Rockville Centre, L. I.
on December 1, 1950 at 0830

Displacement · 7 Pounds
Stem to Stern · · · · · · · · · · · · · · · · · · · 18 Inches
Capacity to Hold· · · · · · · · · · · · · · · · · · 8 Ounces

SPECIAL FEATURES

1. Perpetually wet decks
2. Super-Strength fog horn
3. Shock-proof after bulkhead
4. Water-tight integrity—None!
5. Steering gear strictly unreliable

Will be anchored at home port after 12 December
at Fire Island Light Station, Fire Island, N. Y.
Launching details handled by Dr. LaMariana
(Due to the present war shortage of materials,
this model was launched bare of all excess rigging.)

Results of trial run:
    Smooth sailing.
    Weathered all storms.
    Weather forecast: WET!

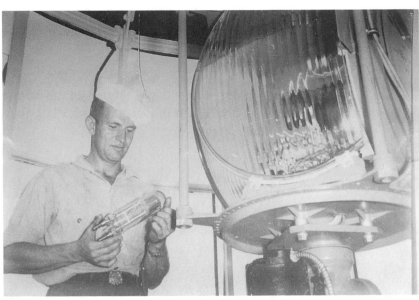

Photo courtesy of Gottfried and Marilyn Mahler

Gottfried Mahler, in the Fire Island lantern room,
holds one of the Crouse-Hinds light's bulbs.

In 1952, the First Order Fresnel lens, which had been moved from Shinnecock to Fire Island in 1933, was replaced by a new Crouse-Hinds electric light. A crew of four civil service engineers from the depot on Staten Island spent one month at the station making the change. The light was out for ten days during the switch. The new light, actually two lights stacked one on top of the other, used 1000–watt halogen bulbs. This light remained in service for over 20 years, and is now on display at the lighthouse.

The old Fresnel lens was hoisted down by hand, with blocks and tackles. Unfortunately, the lens was greatly damaged by the time it arrived at the depot on Staten Island.

Although difficult to imagine from the crowded beaches of Robert Moses State Park, during the Mahlers' time at Fire Island, indeed for most of the time there has been a lighthouse on Fire Island, the waters around the station were often busier than the land. As a result of the offshore activities, much washed up on shore. Mahler and Bob Hodges built a walkway from the boathouse on the bay to the lighthouse from "flotsam and jetsam." Rene Prud'Hommeaux and Patricia Gordon, friends of the Mahlers who were writers, had built a home in a dune from driftwood (the first floor was in the dune, the second floor overlooked the ocean).

Even odder things were brought to the beach. One day, six-year-old Richard Mahler and two-year-old Godfrey spotted a small dog struggling near the shore on the bay side of the island. They rescued him and brought him back to the lighthouse. As many young boys would, the young Mahlers wanted to keep the dog. Their decided, however, to try to find the little dachshund's owners. A call to the local Coast Guard Station revealed that the one-year-old dog, Schnappsie, had gone overboard from the 38–foot cabin cruiser *Seamaid*, owned by Lincoln Schmitt of Patchogue. The pup stayed at the lighthouse for nearly a week, until Mr. Schmitt could pick him up.

Although the Mahler boys did not get to keep Schnappsie, they were not without animal companions. Their father had made a fresh water pond, using the water from an artesian well. In this pond were goldfish, ducks (a mallard with one good wing, and a Muscovy), and white geese. Nearby were a couple of Rhode Island Red chickens from Sears and Roebuck.

On December 17, 1953, the 50th anniversary of the Wright brothers' first flight, the Fire Island Light received a visit from the Flying Santa. Mahler was in the tower servicing the lens when a plane buzzed past the tower. Mahler descended the tower's 182 steps, and went behind the tower as the plane made another pass. Just west of the light, the plane dropped a box with a parachute. The box landed near Burma Road. Inside were gifts for the Mahlers and Hodges, including a flannel shirt for Gottfried, scarves for the wives, and handmade wooden cars for the boys. The Flying Santa, Edward Rowe Snow, dropped a package later that day at Point Vincente, California, celebrating the Wright brothers' accomplishment with a coast-to-coast flight. Snow wrote about the visit, and included the thank you note from the Mahlers and Hodges, in his 1955 book, *Famous Lighthouses of America.*

Not all was fun and games at Fire Island. In May of 1954, the Mahlers witnessed a tragedy when a plane piloted by a 25–year-old Civil Air Patrol pilot crashed into the Great South Bay in view of his own wife and parents. The

Gottfried Mahler looks out from the Fire Island lantern room in 1952.

Photo courtesy of Gottfried and Marilyn Mahler

pilot later died at Southside Hospital in Bay Shore.

While at Fire Island, Marilyn Mahler had a 1931 Ford for transportation. As a civilian, she could not drive the Coast Guard vehicles at the station. The Mahlers had bought the Ford in Hicksville for $50 in 1949, towed it to Bay Shore, where it was loaded on a freight ferry and brought to Fire Island. Marilyn would drive the car along the sand and dirt roads of Fire Island. It was how she traveled to and from meetings of her knitting club, the Knitwits.

In December of 1954, Mahler was assigned to the tender *Sassafrass*, where he had served just prior to his Fire Island assignment. He would also go on to conduct hydrographic and plankton studies aboard the 255–foot cutter *Owasco*, while also serving as the ship's quartermaster, for which he would earn several citations. Mahler retired from the Coast Guard on July 1, 1962, and returned to Fire Island to work for the Village of Saltaire.

The Mahlers still live in the area, regularly attending historical society meetings, and traveling. In recent years, Gottfried has kept busy with such activities as hang-gliding at North Carolina's Outer Banks, and bodysurfing in St. Augustine, Florida, as well as speaking to groups about his life as a lighthouse keeper.

Bob Hodges was an assistant during Mahler's time at the light. Hodges had been at Fire Island since 1947, and remained until 1958, when he was transferred to Montauk Point. He retired from Montauk in the 1960s.

By the time Arnie Leiter arrived at the lighthouse, in March of 1957, Hodges was the head keeper. Leiter remembers a great deal of scraping old paint and applying new paint, both inside and outside the lighthouse. Hodges would often work in the local towns while his assistants worked at the lighthouse. When Hodges once criticized the assistants for not accomplishing enough work, Leiter made the mistake of commenting that they would have accomplished more if Hodges had been present. As in any military situation, Leiter was quickly reminded of the importance of rank. He served at Fire Island until December of 1959, and also served at the lighthouses at North Brother Island, Saugerties, and Lloyd Harbor.

For many years, Coast Guardsmen manned the radio station next to the lighthouse. One of these radio technicians, Bob "Chatt" Chapman, recalls his two tours there in the 1960s with fondness. A unique aspect of life at Fire Island at that time was the 1930 Ford, with no hood, windshield, or seat, other than that for the driver, that was used as a supplementary form of transportation (in addition to the official Coast Guard Dodge trucks). Driving the old Ford required that the driver wear a welding mask for protection from the steaming water that would come through the windshield opening. If passengers were carried, an upside-down five-gallon bucket was the seat of choice. Chapman remained in the area after his tour of duty, and is active in historic lighthouse preservation.

For the first 137 years of the Fire Island Light's existence, the station was accessible only by boat, or by foot or iceskates if the bay was frozen. On June 13, 1964, that changed when a bridge was built over the Fire Island Inlet. At the opening of the bridge, Robert Moses, describing himself as "a simple year-round South Shore boy," spoke of his love of the bays and beaches, and his relationships with "herons, sandpipers, gallinules, horseshoe and spider crabs, blowfish and skates." He also spoke of the work for which he was largely responsible—that of creating a system of parks and beaches along Long Island's South Shore. His prediction, though, that there would "[s]omeday . . . be a continuous Ocean Drive from Tottenville on Staten Island to Smith Point by way of the Narrows, Marine, Atlantic Beach and other bridges, along all the barrier beaches of Rockaway, Long Beach, Jones Beach and Fire Island" does not look likely to happen. That drive now ends at the Fire Island Lighthouse.

Nearly 150 years of lightkeeping on Fire Island ended on December 31, 1973, when the lighthouse was replaced by a strobe light on the nearby Robert Moses State Park water tower. The light, giving two flashes every ten seconds, was produced by flashtubes filled with xenon gas. At $61,000, its cost was less than that of repairing the old lighthouse. The change was "essentially one of economy." This new light only cast a light out to the ocean, leaving mariners on the Great South Bay without the benefit of the tall, powerful light they had used for so many years.

Photo courtesy of Nancy Bahnsen

Fire Island in 2003.

In 1981, the abandoned lighthouse was deemed unnecessary and unrepairable. The following year, the Fire Island Lighthouse Preservation Society was formed. As had happened elsewhere in the nation, and continues to happen today, a small group of concerned local citizens, aware of the importance of historic preservation, got together to save an important part of American history. The Society raised over one million dollars to save the light station and, on May 25, 1986, at 9PM, the Fire Island Lighthouse was relit. Unfortunately, Bob Hodges had passed away six months prior, at the age of 68.

The Society continues to work with the National Park Service, which owns the lighthouse and surrounding property, and the Coast Guard, which maintains the lighthouse's optic, to allow the Fire Island Lighthouse to serve the public. Not only does the lighthouse guide mariners in the Great South Bay and Atlantic Ocean as it had for years, it now also serves as an educational center. The keeper's quarters contain a museum exploring the history of the lighthouse and the U.S. Life-Saving Service. The boardwalks around the lighthouse and surrounding dunes allow visitors to enjoy the unique marine environment. Society volunteers and staff conduct tower tours that give visitors the opportunity to walk around the gallery—Fire Island is the only lighthouse on Long Island that allows this—while discussing local history, lighthouse history, and Life-Saving Service history.

The Fire Island lighthouse is a popular destination, with about 100,000 visitors each year. The fresh Atlantic breezes, bright sun, white sandy beaches, crashing waves, fine birdwatching, and abundant wildlife combine with a beautiful lighthouse, rich history, and friendly tour guides to make this one of the best lighthouse experiences in the nation.

The Fire Island Lightship

The waters off Fire Island have long been an important part of American maritime traffic, bringing ships into New York Harbor. They have also long been noted for being dangerous.

In her book, *Ship Ashore!*, Jeanette Edwards Rattray related a description of the sandbar along Long Island's South Shore from Everett J. Edwards, "a seafaring man who knew it well":

> The length of Long Island, from Fire Island to Montauk, a sandbar formed by the undertow runs parallel with the beach about a quarter of a mile offshore. On the bar is an average depth of about 8 feet of water; and inside it the water is 18 to 20 feet deep. Outside of the bar, the water deepens gradually until it is about ten fathoms deep (60 feet) a mile offshore.

> When the swell is heavy, the heft of the sea breaks on this bar. Vessels stranded on this coast invariably stop on the outer edge of the bar; and if of too deep a draft, they are apt to get torn to pieces there. It takes a very heavy sea to wash a ship over; but if it is once over the bar, with a good anchor offshore to prevent its going onto the beach, a large vessel is fairly safe.

Nathaniel S. Prime, in his 1845 *History of Long Island*, also spoke of the dangers of the south shore, noting how its "exceedingly uncertain and precarious" conditions caused "those awful disasters which have so often been attended with the most appalling consequences on this ill-fated shore."

Although Fire Island had become the home of New York's tallest and most powerful lighthouse in 1858, it was believed that the site's usefulness to mariners could be strengthened. The dangers posed to the many transatlantic ships caused the government to look for ways to increase safety in the area.

In the early to mid-1890s, the lighthouse was considered for a First Order bivalve lens. The light from this lens would be more powerful and it was believed that it would be more easily sighted by ships. That lens was never installed. Instead, a lightship station was established off of Fire Island. Prior to the lightship, a whistling buoy occupied the station. Unfortunately, the buoy's signal was often inaudible.

Light Vessel *No. 68* (*LV 68*) was ordered built, to be stationed off of Fire Island. An appropriation of $80,000 was made for the project. There was a delay in the building of *No. 68*, so she would not become the first lightship on the new station.

LV 58 was put on station at Fire Island in 1896. The Craig Shipbuilding Company of Toledo, Ohio, had built the steel-hulled ship in 1893, at a cost of $50,870. She was 121 feet 10 inches long, with a beam of 28 feet 6 inches and a draft of 12 feet. Her gross tonnage was 449. *No. 58*'s one cylinder steam engine used a four-bladed propeller to a speed of 7.5 knots; she was also rigged for sail. Two steels masts held the lanterns that cast fixed white light from oil lamps out to mariners from 39 feet above sea level. For fog, she was equipped with a 12-inch steam chime, with an emergency hand-rung bell. Prior to her duty off of Fire Island, *No. 58* had been stationed at Nantucket New South Shoal from 1894 to 1896. When *LV 58* left Fire Island in 1897, she became a relief vessel in Massachusetts until sinking in a storm in December 1905. While at Fire Island, the ship was tended by David H. Caulkins, Master, and Charles E. Acorn, Mate.

LV 68 took over the station in 1897. She was built at a cost of $74,750 in Bath, Maine. Her two lanterns, at a height of 57 feet, cast out fixed white light from clusters of three 100–candlepower electric lamps (these would be changed to acetylene in 1920, then back to electric in 1928) for 13 miles. *LV 68*'s composite hull (steel frame, wood bottom, and steel plate topsides) was 122 feet 10 inches long, with a beam of 28 feet 6 inches, a draft of 12 feet 6 inches, and a displacement of 590 tons. Her one-cylinder steam engine moved the ship along at 8.5 knots with a four-bladed propeller; she was also rigged for sail. *LV 68* was equipped for fog, with a 12–inch steam chime whistle and a hand operated 1000-pound bell.

On December 5, 1902, *LV 68* lost her anchor and chain in a storm. She steamed to Staten Island for replacements and was towed back the next day. Four months later, the anchor and chain were recovered. On January 14, 1904, *No. 68* once again lost her chain.

National Archives 26 LG 68-1

LV 68 on station at Fire Island.

The ship once again steamed to Staten Island, and was then towed back.

In June of 1914, *No. 68* was painted with a "new brand of red paint" as a test. The test lasted ten months, "at the end of which time the paint was found to be in excellent condition, no perceptible fading having occurred." This same paint was also tested on buoys in the Seventh and Eighth Lighthouse Districts, where "unfavorable conditions as to heat and moisture" tended to rapidly fade the red paint on buoys. The paint also held up well on the buoys.

At 5 a.m., on May 8, 1916, the steamship *SS Philadelphian* rammed *LV 68*. The lightship's "side . . . was cut and stove in to a depth of about 2 feet from a point 4 feet below the water line to the spar deck." Her crew acted quickly, and "by means of emptying tanks, shifting coal, and slinging out boats and filling them with water, were able to list the vessel so that the greater part of the damage was out of the water and the vessel could be kept free with her pumps." The *Philadelphian* towed *No. 68* to a point near the

Ambrose lightship. There, the tender *Pansy* took the lightship under tow to the Staten Island depot.

A tender was put on *No. 68's* station on the night of May 8, and a relief light vessel arrived the next day. The crew of *LV 68*, including Mate Julius Ortman, engineer Peter Hanson, firemen Walter Dure, John Anderson, and Richard Tepelman, and seamen C. Pieplow and John Lind, were commended by the Secretary of Commerce for their actions in saving *No. 68*. Ortman and Hanson had been slightly injured in the collision.

In 1918, *No. 68* was taken off station for some repairs, and temporarily replaced by *LV 78*. While *No. 78* was on station, her crew assisted the crew of the schooner *Edith M. Prior*. The schooner, "in leaking condition," was trying to get to port. *LV 78's* crew provided water, provisions, and coal. An odd rescue was also credited to *No. 68's* crew that year, as they "towed aeroplane with two occupants to ship."

On May 1, 1921, *LV 68* became one of the three first radio fog signal stations in the nation. Similar stations were established at the Ambrose lightship and the lighthouse at Sea Girt, New Jersey.

A little more than eight years after being hit by the *SS Philadelphian*, *No. 68* was involved in another collision. According to the April 1, 1924 *Lighthouse Service Bulletin*:

> At 2:45 p. m., March 30, the English steamer *Castilian* ran into Fire Island Light Vessel, striking the lightship on the port quarter and cutting a large hole in the side of the ship from the upper deck to the water line. There was a dense fog at the time of the collision, and all fog signals, steam whistle, submarine bell, and radio fog signal were in operation and had been in operation since the previous night, and continued until one and one-fourth hours after the collision, when the fog cleared up.

The report continued, with an account from *No. 68's* assistant engineer:

> About 2:45 p. m. I heard three ships, two off the port quarter and one off the stern. I went on deck looking for them and they continued blowing. I then heard a sudden rush of water coming straight toward us. I looked up and saw the steamer heading for us amidships. I then

rang the alarm bell. Somehow or other the steamer sheared off and when I stopped ringing the alarm bell she struck the light vessel on the port quarter. After she struck us she started to pass along the light vessel and as she went by I saw the name on her.

At first it seemed as though the water was rushing in faster than the ship's pumps could remove it, but the crew acted quickly. They put slings over the side and temporarily patched the hole "with planks and tarpaulins." This slowed the water enough for the pumps to keep pace.

The crew of the lightship was told to proceed toward the Staten Island general depot. The tender *Spruce* met up with *No. 68* and towed her the rest of the way, arriving at the depot at 4:30 a.m. the next morning.

The new lightship for the Five Fathom Bank, New Jersey, station, *LV 109*, was at the depot when *No. 68* was damaged. The Service decided to paint the hull red, the same as *No. 68*, and put her on the Fire Island station. She arrived on March 31, 1924.

The crew of *No. 68*, including Frank Seastedt, her commander, was commended for "rendering efficient service and showing fine seamanship and devotion to duty in standing by their ship after the collision." *No. 68* had twice been hit and damaged by ships, and both times saved by the quick thinking and bravery of her crew.

By 1927, *LV 68* was showing her age. Three lightships were scheduled for replacement that year: *No. 70* (San Francisco, California), *No. 52* (Fenwick Island, Maryland), and *No. 68*. She remained at Fire Island until 1930, when she left to be a relief ship for the Third District for the final two years of her working life. She was then auctioned off, selling for $825.

In 1930, Fire Island received another brand new lightship. This time, it was the $228,121 steel-hulled *LV 114*, which would later be known as *WAL 536*. This new lightship was built in Portland, Oregon, by the Albina Marine Works. It was "the first time that a lighthouse vessel [had] . . . been built on the west coast for service upon the Atlantic seaboard." She was 133 feet 3 inches long, displacing 630 tons with a beam of 30 feet and a draft of 13 feet 3 inches. She could average nine knots using her 350–horsepower diesel electric motor. Light was cast from two electric 375mm lanterns at a height of 57 feet. An air diaphone and hand operated bell provided the fog signal.

On July 15, 1930, Captain J. Nielsen started *LV 114* on her 5892–mile journey to New York. Nielsen took the ship to the depot at Astoria, Oregon, and remained there while she was fitted with navigational equipment. Leaving the depot on August 5, *LV 114* headed for San Francisco. According to Nielsen, this "was the most trying run of the whole trip, as we ran into dense fog about 50 miles south of Astoria, and did not see or hear anything until we sighted the San Francisco Lightship. This run was made entirely on radiocompass bearings."

At San Francisco, some heavy chain and a spare mushroom anchor were removed, "lifting the bow 2 feet" and "making the vessel steer much better." *LV 114* left San Francisco on August 14, and arrived in San Pedro on August 16, to fill up on fuel oil. On August 18, the ship headed for the Panama Canal, and arrived at Balboa, Panama, on September 2. Although the ship and its crew had encountered a two-day storm along the way, Captain Nielsen reported that *No. 114* handled it well: "at no time did she ship a sea."

Minor repairs and adjustments were made to *LV 114* by the Panama Railroad repair shop, then she left for the Panama Canal, passing through on September 4. More difficult weather, including "a southwest gale and heavy seas" tested the ship, "proving the vessel a very fine sea boat." A four-day stop was made at Charleston, South Carolina, on September 12 for provisions and minor adjustments before moving on for Portsmouth, Virginia, "under ideal conditions." After a short stop at Portsmouth, *LV 114* headed for New York, once again "under ideal conditions, making 10 knots per hour."

No. 114 arrived at the Staten Island general depot at 3:30 p.m., September 20, 1930, having made the trip from Astoria, Oregon to Staten Island, New York in 30 days, 19 hours, and 44 minutes. The long trip had impressed Captain Nielsen:

> I wish to express my admiration for this vessel for the way she handled, and her comfort and seaworthiness. At no time during the

voyage were the engines pressed to full capacity, running on the average 275 revolutions per minute. Due credit should be given the engineers in making this voyage with new machinery and without any stops at sea.

The lightship stayed at the Staten Island depot, being fitted up for duty and tested, until 4:45 a.m., on Monday, December 1. Then Arthur Bruggeman piloted her to her station, arriving five hours later. Bruggeman would finish his career on *No. 114*, retiring in 1936.

LV 114's last year on station off Fire Island was 1942. The Light List for that year gives her position as 9.4 miles 172–degrees from the Fire Island Lighthouse, in 96 feet of water. The characteristic of her light was group flashing white (flash one second, eclipse one second, flash one second, eclipse three seconds). The fog signal was a diaphone, giving a 2.5–second blast every 20 seconds. Her radio call and code flag signal was NNBK, and her radiobeacon transmitted groups of two dashes on 286 kilocycles.

From 1942 to 1945, *No. 114* was an examination vessel in Bay Shore. After the war, she was stationed at Diamond Shoal, North Carolina and, in 1947, *LV 114* became a relief vessel for offshore lightships in the First Coast Guard District. During 1956–1957, Ken Black, of Shore Village Museum fame, was her commander. *LV 114* spent 1958–1969 at Pollock Rip, Massachusetts and 1969–1971 at Portland, Maine. She was decommissioned November 5, 1971, after 41 years of service. At that time, the Coast Guard intended to use her as a floating museum, but she ended up in New Bedford, Massachusetts, with "NEW BEDFORD" painted in white on the red hull (there has never been a New Bedford lightship station). *LV 114* is now one of only 15 remaining American lightships. The City of New Bedford hopes to be able preserve *No. 114* and open her to the public, but funding for this has not yet been found. Meanwhile, a growing number of local residents have shown an interest in bringing *No. 114* back to Long Island as a floating museum.

The Fire Island Lightship Station was unmarked from 1942 to 1945. Afterward, a buoy marked the station. The site's markings, from buoy to lightships to buoy, had come full circle.

Photo by the author

LV 114 at New Bedford in 2002.

Although there were three different ships stationed at Fire Island from 1896 to 1942, they were similar in appearance while on station at Fire Island: red hulls with "FIRE ISLAND" in white. *LV 68* also had the number 68 painted on the hull. And all three exhibited lights from two masts.

Lightships, which succumbed to the same technological obsolescence as lighthouses, may not have gained the notoriety or romance of lighthouses, but they remain an important part of our lighthouse heritage. The history of the Fire Island Lightship Station also reminds us of the importance and perils of Long Island's South Shore.

Coney Island

For many, the name of Coney Island conjures images of crowds, roller coasters, beaches, and recreation. For those interested in lighthouses, it also brings to mind a special lighthouse and its last keeper.

As at Fire Island, the name of the island is the subject of much conjecture. Several possibilities have been put forth over the years, including an anglicized Dutch word for rabbits, the name of a former family, and the possible appearance of cone-shaped features on the island.

In the mid–1800s, Coney Island's sea breezes and accommodations attracted many famous people, including Herman Melville, Washington Irving, P. T. Barnum, John Calhoun, Henry Clay, and Daniel Webster. By 1846, the development of the west end of Coney Island, where the lighthouse would be built, had begun. This area attracted a different crowd and would become known as a very rough area. Gambling, drinking, and fighting were western Coney Island activities.

In the late 1860s, a New York politician named Norton established the Point Comfort Hotel on the western end of the island. The area's reputation grew even worse, as unsavory types frequented the area and lawlessness spread. It was not uncommon for bodies to wash up on the shores of Coney Island in those days.

The growing popularity of Coney Island increased the maritime traffic to and from it. Ferries from Manhattan made regular stops on the island. An aid to navigation was soon needed to help "guide steamers to the Coney Island iron piers," as well as help "guide the scows of the street-cleaning department to their dumping ground."

On March 2, 1889, Congress appropriated $25,000 for the building of a pair of range lights on two different sites at the western point of Coney Island. The contract for the metalwork of the rear tower was made in January 1890. On March 1, the contract for the foundation and erection of the rear tower, front tower, dwelling, and fog signal was signed. The $6,500 asking price for the lands for the lights was considered excessive, so the government condemned the sites and obtained them for $3,500.

The front light, designed in January of 1890, at the Tompkinsville, Staten Island depot, was a small square pyramidal wood frame structure. Its tower was 18 feet, two inches from the base to the light's focal plane. The shingled tower, eight foot, eight inches square at its base, sat upon four square concrete footings. Inside were two levels, with an iron ladder between the second level and the trap door in the lantern. The lantern was composed of six sides, with each two feet, six inches across.

The rear tower was built as a square skeletal structure with a central steel column containing 87 steps. The design was exactly the same as the Throg's Neck tower; in fact, the words "Throg's Neck" were crossed out on the plans, and "Coney Island" written above them. The height from the base of the tower to the focal plane was 61 feet, three-and-three-quarter inches. An eight-sided lantern was installed on top of the tower.

The fog bell tower was designed at the same time as the front tower, in January 1890. It, too, was about 18 feet tall, square, and made of wood. The weight for its clockworks mechanism was suspended through a hole the middle of the tower.

Like the rear tower, the keeper's dwelling was copied from another station. This time it was the Gould Island, Rhode Island station. On the plans for the Coney Island dwelling, "Gould" was crossed out and "Coney" written above it. The 27–foot by 31–foot building contained a cellar, two floors, and an attic. A shed was attached to the southeast side of the dwelling by a covered walkway, and a cistern was built behind the house. A four-foot-wide gravel path, which went all the way to the shoreline, connected the dwelling, tower, and fog bell tower.

Thomas Higgenbotham, a native of Maryland, was appointed as the first keeper at Coney Island on June 30, 1890. His pay was $580 per year. On August 1, 1890, he officially lit the lamp in the Coney Island tower for the first time.

In 1896, the front range light, situated on a site east of the rear tower, was discontinued and taken back to the Tompkinsville depot.

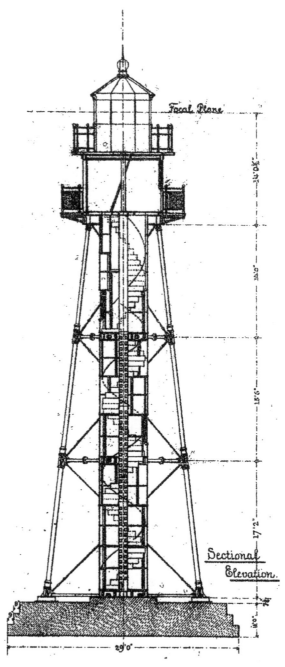

Focal Plane

Sectional
Elevation.

U.S. Lighthouse Society photo

Detail from the original Coney Island plans
showing the tower.

The plot of land on which it had stood was sold at auction on July 6, 1896.

During the Spanish-American War, there were concerns about a Spanish attack on New York. Coney Island Light was temporarily discontinued on April 28, 1898, so as not to provide navigational assistance for the possible invading navy.

In 1899, the tower was painted and various repairs were made. The characteristic of the light was also changed, on June 30, 1899, from a red flash every ten seconds to one every five seconds.

On July 2, 1910, Ernest J. Larsson was assigned to Coney Island, but was quickly replaced by Gilbert L. Rulon ten days later.

As with many lighthouses located on a point of land, the Coney Island station, on Norton's Point, suffered the effects of erosion. In 1915, a 600–foot stone wall was built to counter the forces of erosion, but storms and tides continued to batter the point.

U.S. Coast Guard photo

Undated aerial photo of Coney Island Light Station.

On April 11, 1918, a northeast storm "caused considerable damage in the third and fourth lighthouse districts." At Coney Island, "the north corner of the reservation was cut away and the fog-signal house fell into the water, but all of the apparatus was finally recovered. The sea wall recently installed at this station withstood the sea without damage." The next year, the bell was replaced and riprap added to protect it.

A right of way problem developed at the station in the early 1900s. In the 1922 *Annual Report of the Commissioner of Lighthouses*, $5,000 was requested to purchase land for a right of way. The accompanying note pointed out that when the original site was purchased, "there were no other buildings or roads on the vicinity, but since then the surrounding property has developed in such a manner as to give the lighthouse reservation no street front and no other means for egress for the occupants. A right of way is urgently needed to meet a bad situation and can only be obtained by the purchase of property priced at $5,000." The right of way was eventually obtained.

Adrien "Andy" Boisvert was assigned to Coney Island in 1941. Boisvert had begun his lighthouse service in 1926. In 1934, he was assigned to the Fire Island Light, where he and his new bride, Alice, would stay until the transfer to Coney Island. When they arrived at Coney Island, 42 soldiers were billeted at the site and the Boisverts had to live in a nearby apartment for two years. The Boisverts remained at Coney Island until July 1, 1960, when Adrien retired.

The year 1960 marked the beginning of the Coney Island lighthouse's present era. It was then that Frank Schubert was assigned to the station. Schubert, born September 13, 1915, started his career as a seaman on the tender *Tulip*, in 1938. At that time, during the Great Depression, jobs were scarce and Frank considered himself lucky to get the position.

When the Coast Guard absorbed the Bureau of Lighthouses in 1939, lighthouse service personnel were given several options: remain as a civilian, take a military rank roughly equivalent to the present position, retire (if there was enough time served), or leave the service. Frank Schubert stayed on as a civilian, and was transferred

Adrien Boisvert (Coney Island Keeper 1941-1960) in a 1930 photo.

Photo courtesy of Bernard J. Roy

to the Old Orchard Shoal Light. Schubert would comment, 35 years later, on the militarization of the lighthouse service and the ensuing change from long-time keepers to those with short tours of duty at light stations: "I expect it's hard for a man to get attached to his light under those circumstances," he said, adding that, "[t]hey also have to wear uniforms, and when you militarize the job, you kill any personal feeling you may have about it."

When World War II broke out, Schubert was drafted. Having "had enough of boats for a while," he requested that he not be assigned to the Coast Guard, Marines, or Navy. His request was granted, and he was assigned to the Army Transportation Service. His maritime background provided the skills that the Army needed for their boats, and he was assigned as a landing craft instructor at Camp Gordon Johnson. "More water, more boats, more islands," he recalled. Later, he was sent to the Pacific to serve on combat transport boats. After the war, Schubert was sent to Governor's Island, where he and two other men attended to three lights and two fog signals. During his time at Governor's Island, his wife, Marie, and three children lived on Staten Island.

Frank Schubert took the opportunity to become the keeper at Coney Island because it gave him the chance to live a more normal life. There he could reside with his wife and family. Their three

U.S. Coast Guard photo

Undated photo of Coney Island light tower.

children, Francine, Thomas, and Kenneth, could attend school nearby.

When he arrived at Coney Island in 1960, he had to tend the light and a fog bell. The bell would be turned on when he could no longer see Hoffman and Swinburne Islands. These islands were established around between 1860 and 1873 as quarantine stations for immigrants and transatlantic passengers, but were later abandoned.

In 1989, the tower's Fourth Order Fresnel lens was removed. An FA-251 optic took its place. This would later be changed to the current VRB-25 optic.

As was common with lighthouse keepers, Schubert was a man of many talents. In addition to tending the light and a family, Frank kept himself busy with many hobbies: golfing, bowling, cooking, woodworking, and marquetry, among others. He and his dog, Blazer, kept watch at Coney Island until December 11, 2003, when Frank passed away at the age of 88. Schubert's passing spelled the end of civilian lightkeepers in the United States.

The Coney Island Light has seen many fads and changes come and go. The rise and fall of the more famous and flamboyant attractions on Coney Island offer a stark contrast to the subtle, relatively unknown lighthouse on the west end of the island. Although attractions such as Steeplechase Park, the Cyclone, Luna Park, Dreamland, and the Elephant Hotel (which was actually shaped like an elephant), no longer offer their unique attractions, the nearly 115–year old lighthouse at Norton's Point continues to steadfastly serve, honoring the now-extinct American tradition of civilian lightkeeping.

Minor Aids to Navigation on Long Island

Lighthouses and lightships are not the only means by which the navigational needs of mariners have been addressed. Pier lights, breakwater lights, and a variety of other minor aids to navigation

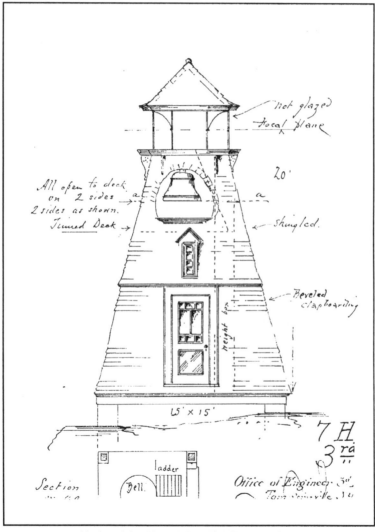

National Archives Microfilm Record Group 26, Red #3
Engineer David Porter Heap's 1888 sketch for the
proposed Hell Gate Light.

have been established over the years. Although the scope of this book does not include all of our area's aids to navigation, some of them are worth mentioning because of their location, history, or importance to the community.

Hell Gate (Hallett's Point)

One of the most dangerous spots in the East River, Hell Gate (also known as Hurl Gate), has long been known for its tricky currents, eddies, and submerged rocks. One of these rocks, called Pot Rock, caused many wrecks. In 1851, a large part of Pot Rock was blasted away, easing the eddies and the danger from the rock itself. Portions of Way's Reef and the Frying Pan were also blasted, making the area safer. It was still dangerous and laws were passed regarding the size and pilotage of vessels passing through the site.

In 1882, $20,000 was appropriated to establish an experimental electric light at Hallett's Point, Astoria, on the east bank of Hell Gate. The 255-foot tower was built in 1883, and lit on October 20, 1884. The electric light proved unreliable and there were even complaints that it was too bright and too tall. The experiment ended in late 1886. The keepers were discharged, and the tower and machinery dismantled and sold for scrap.

As with many of Long Island's major lighthouse projects of that era, David Porter Heap was the engineer in charge of the building of the new Hell Gate Light. In October 1888, Heap submitted a sketch of a proposed light and fog bell structure. This structure, designed to house a small oil light and fog bell in a wooden tower, was completed in early 1889. As was the case with many early wooden minor aids, the Hallett's Point Light was eventually changed to a skeleton tower with a small tank house.

Whitestone Point

In 1889, a small tower nearly identical to the wooden tower at Hell Gate was established at Whitestone Point, near what is now the south side of the Whitestone Bridge. David Porter Heap recommended the establishment of the station in January 1889, had arranged for a lease for the site by March, and had completed the station by the end of October. The station consisted of a small light and fog bell. In 1932, the tower was rebuilt as a black skeleton tower and white tank house on a black concrete base. The 200mm electric light showed a fixed green characteristic 48 feet above the water, and the bell sounded two strokes every 20 seconds

Hell Gate & Lighthouse,
Astoria, L. I.

Postcard from the author's collection
The Hell Gate Light in the early 1900s.

National Archives 26 DS 73-1

Glen Cove Breakwater Light.

Glen Cove Breakwater

A light had been recommended for the entrance to Hempstead Harbor as early as 1880. By 1894, petitions and studies had been assembled for the establishment of a light in the area.

A "fixed white post lantern light" was established on the Glen Cove breakwater in early 1900. The light sat atop a black post with a white top, and was first tended by Eugene S. Bailey. On August 20, 1901, the light's characteristic was changed to fixed red. An oil house was built at the station in 1904. Samuel Pardue took over the responsibility for the light in 1905. Sometime after 1910, the light was rebuilt as black skeleton tower and white tank house on a black concrete base, and it appeared this way into at least the 1940s. In 1942, the 200mm acetylene light flashed white every two seconds.

Port Jefferson Breakwater

In 1838, George Bache gave a brief account of the need for a "buoy on the extremity of the bare spit, at the mouth of the harbor of Drowned Meadows [sic]." He also noted that the "harbor could, at a small expense, be made one of the very best on Long-island sound. It is at a point where a good harbor is much needed."

In the mid-1890s, petitions were submitted to Congress to establish a light and fog signal at the entrance to the harbor at Port Jefferson (as Drowned Meadow had been renamed). The Old Field Light, located a couple of miles west of the harbor, was considered too far away to be helpful in bad weather.

In 1896, two lights were established at the entrance to Port Jefferson Harbor (the East Breakwater light also included a fog signal). Gilbert Rulon was appointed as keeper of these lights on August 5, 1896, at a salary of $480 per year. He was replaced by former Stratford Shoal keeper Herman Burke in 1901. Both of these lights have been rebuilt several times, and still serve the local maritime community.

Greenport Breakwater

A light was established on the end of the breakwater entering Greenport Harbor around 1898. James D. Hallock was appointed "Laborer" at $10 per month to tend it. Hallock was followed by Fred G. Bushnell. George Conklin gained the appointment on June 1, 1904 for $15 per month. The light was rebuilt in 1908, and again in 1921. By the 1940s, the 200mm electric light, casting a red flash every two seconds from 27 feet above the water, sat atop a red skeleton tower, with a white tank house and red concrete base.

Patchogue Breakwater

The Patchogue Breakwater Light was established January 10, 1901, at the mouth of the Patchogue River. This was prompted by the submission to Congress of several petitions in May 1900. When first lit, the light had a fixed white characteristic. This was changed on December 30, 1901, to a fixed red light. The tower was rebuilt in 1926. By 1942, it was a black skeleton tower and white tank house on a black concrete base, with a 200mm electric light held 25 feet above the water. The light flashed green every three seconds. In the early 1900s, a "Laborer" was paid $10 per month to maintain the light. Among those who tended this light were George Jones (appointed December 1900), Jonathan Ciccia, and George Odell, Jr.

Jones Inlet

Two lights were established at Jones Inlet in 1939—one on the west side of the channel, and one on the south side of the channel. These two 150mm electric lights worked in conjunction with several lighted buoys. The west light flashed green every 2.5 seconds, from a black cylindrical structure atop a pipe tripod. The south light flashed red every 2.5 seconds from a red conical structure on a pipe tripod. Both lights were 12 feet above the water.

Sheepshead Bay

Two lights were established at Sheepshead Bay, on the north side of the east end of Coney Island, in 1910. These lights marked a dredged channel used by "small craft and launches." On August 31, 1910, Archie Steinhaus was appointed "Laborer in charge" to tend them for $17 per month. A new light was built, apparently replacing the two earlier lights, in 1934. It was a 200mm electric light, flashing red every two seconds, on "Creosoted Y.P. [Yellow Pine] piles," with the focal plane of the light 16 feet above high water level.

Other Minor Aids to Navigation

Many more minor aids were built around Long Island (some of them privately built and maintained), including sites at Flushing Bay, Northport East and West Breakwaters, Rockaway Point, East Rockaway Inlet, Randall Bay, Fire Island Inlet, Sag Harbor, and Mount Sinai Breakwater, among others. Although not as glamorous as "real" lighthouses, the lights listed above, and many more, have helped make Long Island's waters safer and have been an important part of our maritime history.

The Future of Long Island's Lighthouses

The coming years will pose great challenges for the preservation of Long Island's lighthouse heritage. Few of these challenges will be successfully overcome without the informed support and involvement of the community.

Erosion is a well-known danger to lighthouses. The necessary location of lighthouses near the shore makes erosion an inherent and ever-present concern for preservation. On Long Island, the erosion struggles at Montauk Point are well known. Other local stations have seen erosion problems, as noted elsewhere in this book. Erosion control can be difficult and expensive, but the knowledge and technology involved are evolving.

Environmental challenges abound at many light stations. Endangered species, eroding dunes, and fragile ecosystems all require attention. Cooperative efforts among historic preservation groups, environmental groups, and government agencies will be required to ensure that the best interests of all are addressed.

Vandalism is an ever-present problem with almost any building that is not constantly monitored. Historic lighthouses are certainly not an exception. Long Beach Bar was burned by vandals; Horton Point was vandalized during its dormant years; Cedar Island has been badly damaged, and continues to suffer at the hands of vandals. Providing adequate security for our historic lighthouses will always be a concern.

A concern that has grown along with the popularity of lighthouses is the wear caused by visitation. Although tourism provides funds and raises awareness, thereby helping to preserve historic lighthouses, the damage done by thousands, tens of thousands, or even hundreds of thousands of visitors at a light station is a matter that has drawn more attention within the preservation community of late. This damage is caused by walking along floors, walkways, and stairs, by opening and closing doors and windows, by touching walls and artifacts, and by other activities that cause vibration, friction, and physical wear. Although generally very sturdy structures, lighthouses do wear down from use. Tour guides, volunteers, and visitors will need to be more aware of their impact on lighthouses, and make ever-greater efforts to tread lightly and with respect.

The biggest challenges will be posed by the transfer of the maintenance of many of our lighthouses from the Coast Guard to other entities. Although the National Historic Lighthouse Preservation Act's support of nonprofit organization involvement appears very positive on the surface, the lack of proper oversight of nonprofit organizations poses a threat. It is easy to create a nonprofit and claim it is for the benefit of a certain cause, even when the goals and actions of those involved may not be beneficial to the community. Many stories about rogue nonprofits appear in the newspapers each year. A cover story in the October 14, 2003 *New York Times*, about nonprofit credit counseling services, included this comment from a Federal Trade Commission official: "Consumers need to know not to read too much into not-for-profit status—that's no guarantee that someone is legit." Much damage has been done, and will continue to be done, to irreplaceable historic properties and artifacts as questionable nonprofits operate without proper oversight. The lack of government funds and personnel to police the action of nonprofits leaves our historic lighthouses at risk. The responsibility for monitoring the activities of nonprofit groups must be borne by the general public—the "consumers" of historic preservation and education—if we are to minimize the damage done by groups with questionable agendas and operating procedures.

As the U.S. Coast Guard seeks to lease, license, or transfer more lighthouses, ever-greater fundraising efforts will be needed. In areas with many with historic lights, this will be more of a problem, as finding an adequate number of fundraising volunteers is already difficult. Local nonprofit groups will find themselves in greater competition with each other for funds and volunteers, and this will inevitably cause competition-based problems, rather than encouraging resource-sharing; the necessary fundraising events will overlap more and the competition will decrease returns on these events.

At some point, one inevitably has to wonder how our nation, during the period in which our lighthouses were built, managed to carefully craft beautiful structures exhibiting amazing craftsmanship, and maintain them with labor-intensive practices, while in our superpower, high-tax, high-technology present, we cannot afford to maintain these important parts of who we are. One obvious response to that question is that lighthouses no longer play a life-or-death role, thus decreasing their priority. But their importance as sources of community cohesion and pride, resources for much-needed recreation in a high-stress society, and gateways to a greater understanding of who we are, where we came from, and how we arrived at our current social, economic, and political states makes them far from being obsolete or irrelevant.

By becoming more educated about historic resources and the issues that surround them, and sharing that knowledge, we can all make a difference. That may seem like a great deal to ask, as we all try to balance our jobs, family life, and other commitments, but it is the only way the ensure the safety of our heritage. Activism and involvement are an American hallmark, going back as least as far as the Boston Tea Party. If each of us makes an effort to learn a little more, as the readers of this book will have done, and share that knowledge in daily conversations, letters to newspapers and elected officials, posts on online message boards, and other simple efforts, the results will benefit us all.

The future of Long Island's historic lighthouses is up to us. The words and actions of the American public will determine their fates. We can choose to maintain them as monuments to a unique and distinguished heritage, turn them into cheap attractions, or allow them to be damaged or even lost. But just as their history tells about the society in which they were built and manned, the history we make by our decisions regarding the future of our historic lighthouses will tell much about who we are.

Lighthouse Societies, Historical Societies, and Museums

Lighthouse Societies:

East End Seaport Museum & Maritime Foundation (Long Beach Bar Lighthouse)
PO Box 624, Greenport NY 11944
Phone: (631) 477-2100
Email: eseaport@aol.com
Website: http://www.eastendseaport.org

Fire Island Lighthouse Preservation Society
4640 Captree Island, Captree Island NY 11702
Phone: (631) 661-4876
Fax: (631) 321-7033
Email: programs@fireislandlighthouse.com
Website: http://www.fireislandlighthouse.com

Huntington Lighthouse Preservation Society
PO Box 2454, Halesite NY 11743
Phone: (631) 421-1238
Fax: (631) 423-0965
Website: http://www.longislandlighthouses.com/savehuntingtons
lighthouse/index.htm

Long Island Chapter, United States Lighthouse Society
PO Box 744, Patchogue NY 11772-0744
Phone: (631) 207-4331
Email: email@lilighthousesociety.org
Website: http://www.lilighthousesociety.org

Montauk Historical Society (Montauk Point Lighthouse)
Montauk Highway, Montauk NY 11954
Phone: (631) 668-2544
Fax: (631) 668-2546
Email: keeper@montauklighthouse.com
Website: http://www.montauklighthouse.com

National Lighthouse Museum
One Lighthouse Plaza, Staten Island NY 10301
Phone: (718) 556-1681
Fax: (718) 556-1684
Email: info@lighthousemuseum.org
Website: http://www.lighthousemuseum.org

Southold Historical Society (Horton Point Lighthouse)
PO Box 1, 54325 Main Road
Southold NY 11971-0001
Phone: (631) 765-5500
Email: sohissoc@optonline.net
Website: http://www.longislandlighthouses.com/hortonpoint/

Additional Historical Societies and Museums on Long Island:

Amityville Historical Society—Lauder Museum
PO Box 764, 170 Broadway
Amityville NY 11701
Phone: (631) 598-1486
Fax: (631) 598-7399
Email: amityvillehistoricalsociety@juno.com

Bridge Hampton Historical Society
PO Box 977, 2368 Montauk Highway
Bridgehampton NY 11932
Phone: (631) 537-1088
Fax: (631) 537-4225
Email: bhhs@hamptons.com
Website: http://www.hamptons.com/bhhs

Co. K 67th N.Y. Historical Association, 1st Regiment Long Island Volunteers
PO Box 371, Manorville NY 11949
Phone: (631) 929-4773
Website:http://www.geocities.com/heartland/farm/8963/index.html

East Islip Historical Society
PO Box 389, Great River NY 11739
Phone: (631) 650-5285
Fax: (631) 277-0898
Email: eihs@eastislip.org

Farmingville Historical Society
PO Box 311, Farmingville NY 11738

Greater Patchogue Historical Society
PO Box 102
Patchogue NY 11772-0102

Historical Society of Islip Hamlet
PO Box 601, Islip NY 11751
Email: info@isliphistory.org
Website: http://www.isliphistory.org

Lake Ronkonkoma Historical Society
PO Box 2716, 328 Hawkins Avenue
Lake Ronkonkoma NY 11779
Phone: (631) 467-3152

Long Island Maritime Museum
PO Box 184
86 West Avenue
West Sayville NY 11796
Phone: (631) HISTORY
Fax: (631) 854-4979
Email: limaritimemuseum@aol.com
Website: http://www.limaritime.org

Miller Place–Mount Sinai Historical Society
PO Box 651, Miller Place NY 11764
Website: http://www.millerplacemountsinaihistoricalsociety.org

Society for the Preservation of Long Island Antiquities (SPLIA)
PO Box 148, 161 Main Street
Cold Spring Harbor NY 11724
Phone: (631) 692-4664
Fax: (631) 692-5265
Email: splia@aol.com
Website: http://www.splia.org

Southampton Historical Museum
17 Meeting House Lane, Southampton NY 11969
Phone: (631) 283-2494
Fax: (631) 283-4540
Email: hismusdir@hamptons.com
Website: http://www.southamptonhistoricalmuseum.com

Springs Historical Society
PO Box 1860, East Hampton NY 11937
Website: http://www.springslibrary.org

Valley Stream Historical Society
PO Box 501, Valley Stream NY 11582
Phone: (516) 872-4159
Email: vshistorical@earthlink.net
Website: http://www.nassaulibrary.org/valleyst/vshist.html

Suggested Reading

If you'd like to learn more about Long Island, lighthouses, and related topics, but don't want to read everything in the references and bibliography, I suggest these books. Most are in print, but some are historic.

The World's Lighthouses from Ancient Times to 1820.
   By D. Alan Stevenson. Mineola (NY): Dover Publications. 2002. ISBN: 0-486-41824-3. Ask a group of lighthouse researchers what their favorite lighthouse book is, and most of them will probably say it is this one.

Journeys on Old Long Island: Travelers' Accounts, Contemporary Descriptions, and Residents' Reminiscences: 1744–1893.
   By Natalie A. Naylor. Interlaken (NY): Empire State Books. 2002. ISBN: 1-55787-161-2. This book is a must-read for anyone with an interest in, or love of, of Long Island.

Florida's Territorial Lighthouses: 1821-1845.
   By Thomas W. Taylor. Allandale (FL): Thomas W. Taylor. 1995. ISBN: 1-885853-05-X. This hard-to-find book, by one of America's best lighthouse researchers, is one of my favorite lighthouse books.

Lighthouses of New York: Greater New York Harbor, Hudson River & Long Island.
   By Jim Crowley. Saugerties (NY): Hope Farm Press. 2000. ISBN: 0-910746-32-X.

America's Lighthouses: An Illustrated History.
   By Francis Ross Holland, Jr. New York: Dover Publications. 1988. ISBN: 048625576X

Women Who Kept the Lights: An Illustrated History of Female Lighthouse Keepers.
   By Mary Louise Clifford and J. Candace Clifford. Alexandria (VA): Cypress Communications. Second Edition. 2000. ISBN: 0-9636412-4-7.

Anatomy of the Lighthouse.
   By Michael J. Rhein. New York: Barnes and Noble Books. 2000. ISBN: 0-7607-2321-4.

Caleb West, Master Diver

By Francis Hopkinson Smith. Boston (MA): Houghton, Mifflin and Company. 1898. Copies of this book may be found through antique book dealers, online auctions, or in the collection of the Long Island Chapter of the U.S. Lighthouse Society.

Captain Thomas A. Scott Master Diver.

By Francis Hopkinson Smith. Boston (MA): American Unitarian Association. 1908. A full transcription is online at: http://www.lilighthousesociety.org/historicalcollection/masterdiver/default.htm

Instructions to Light-Keepers: A Photo reproduction of the 1902 Edition of Instructions to Light-Keepers and Masters of Light-House Vessels.

Allen Park (MI): Great Lakes Lighthouse Keepers Association. 1989. ISBN: 0940767015. A nice reproduction of one of the more detailed editions of this government document.

Wrecks and Rescues on Long Island: The Story of the U.S. Life Saving Service.

By Van R. Field. Center Moriches (NY): Van R. Field. 1997. ISBN: 0-9660224-0-8.

Lighthouses of the Mid-Atlantic Coast.

Text by Elinor DeWire. Photos by Paul Eric Johnson. Stillwater (MN): Voyageur Press. 2002. ISBN: 0-89658-570-0.

North Atlantic Lighthouses.

Photos by Jean Guichard. Text by Ken Trethewey. Paris (France): Flammarion. 2002. ISBN: 2080105639. Guichard is probably the world's most famous lighthouse photographer, and this book shows why.

Guardians of the Lights.

By Elinor DeWire. Sarasota (FL): Pineapple Press. 1995. ISBN: 1-56164-077-8.

The Lighthouse Almanac: A Compendium of Science, History, & Fascinating Lore about our Favorite Seamarks.

By Elinor DeWire. Norwich (CT): Sentinel Publications. 2000. ISBN: 0-9657313-2-4.

Members of the Long Island Chapter of the U.S. Lighthouse Society receive both of the following periodicals as benefits of membership:

The Long Island Light Keeper.

The bimonthly newsletter of the Long Island Chapter of the U.S. Lighthouse Society. ISSN: 1546-3761. Contains history and travel articles, preservation news, and more.

The Keeper's Log.

The quarterly magazine of the U.S. Lighthouse Society. ISSN: 0883-0061. High-quality research, writing, and production make this the standard for American lighthouse periodicals.

Bibliography

A Breakwater for Gardiner's Island Light. *East Hampton Star*. March 9, 1894.

A Horrible Accident. Unknown publication. 1919.

Adamson, Hans Christian. *Keepers of the Lights*. New York: Greenburg. 1955.

Allen, Everett S. *A Wind to Shake the World: The Story of the 1938 Hurricane*. Boston (MA): Little, Brown and Company. 1976.

Allen, Warren. Personal Communication. 2002, 2003.

Ambro, David. Judgment Near for Eaton's Neck Station: Town Board, Yacht Club Leaders Lobby Coast Guard During D.C. Trip. *The Observer*. June 11, 1998.

Ambro, David. New Life for Huntington Light: Restoration Group's Meeting a First at Historic Structure. *The Observer*. July 16, 1998.

Ambro, David. One of a Kind: Last Known Keeper Tells Tale of Old Days. *The Observer*. July 16, 1998.

American Coast Pilot. New York: Edmund and George W. Blunt. 1804.

American Coast Pilot. New York: Edmund and George W. Blunt. 1827.

American Coast Pilot. New York: Edmund and George W. Blunt. 1927.

An act to vest in the United States of America the Exclusive Jurisdiction in and over a piece of land in the Town of Islip in the County of Suffolk and for other purposes. April 20, 1885.

Anderson, John F. Letter to Third District Inspector. November 10, 1911.

Anderson, John F. Letter to Third District Inspector. May 9, 1912.

Annual Report of the Light-house Board to the Secretary of the Treasury. Washington (DC): Government Printing Office. 1853, 1855, 1856, 1857, 1858, 1866, 1867, 1868, 1869, 1871, 1872, 1873, 1874, 1875, 1876, 1877, 1878, 1879, 1880, 1881, 1882, 1883, 1885, 1886, 1888, 1889, 1890, 1891, 1893, 1894, 1895, 1896, 1897, 1898, 1899, 1900, 1902, 1903, 1904, 1905, 1907, 1908, 1910, 1915, 1918, 1922.

Assistant Keeper and Machinst Drowned Near Orient Point Light. *The Suffolk Times*. May 30, 1924.

Atlantic Coast Pilot. Washington (DC): Government Printing Office. 1878.

Bachand, Robert G. *Northeast Lights: Lighthouses and Lightships, Rhode Island to Cape May, New Jersey*. Norwalk (CT): Sea Sports Publications. 1989.

Bache, Hartman and Totten, Joseph G. Letter to the Light-House Board. July 6, 1863. National Archives Letter Book No. 138, page 25.

Baker, John. Letter to the Light-House Board. October 12, 1861. National Archives Letter Book No. 127, page 228.

Bang, Henry R. *The Story of... The Fire Island Light*. 1981.

Bear, Joy. The Lighthouse Keeper's Granddaughter: Plum Island, 1840–1844. *The Long Island Forum*. August 1984.

Benfield, Cliff. Plum Island Lighthouse Clockworks and Lens Assessment. *Seaport Journal*. Spring 2003.

Benham, Inspector. Letter to the Light-House Board. June 11, 1886. National Archives Letter Book No. 648, page 774.

Benham, Inspector. Letter to the Light-House Board. September 21, 1886. National Archives Letter Book No. 682, page 590.

Benham, Inspector. Letter to the Light-House Board. August 22, 1887. National Archives Letter Book No. 726, page 276.

Birth Announcement of Godfrey Gordon Mahler. December 1, 1950.

Bleyer, Bill. Lighthouse's Future Weighed. *Newsday*. July 9, 1996.

Bleyer, Bill. Montauk Point Lighthouse: A Beacon for Tourists, Too. *Newsday.* May 22, 1987.

Bleyer, Bill. Plum Island Lantern on Loan to East End Group. *Newsday.* April 24, 1994.

Bleyer, Bill. Work of Preservationists Shines: Aglow Again, Fire Island Lighthouse Marks Anniversary of its Restoration. *Newsday.* May 21, 1996.

Blossom, Beth. Eaton's Neck Lighthouse: Long Island's Second Beacon of Light. Unknown publication. Undated.

Blossom, Beth. Sands Point Lighthouse. *The Dolphin.* Fall 1994.

Boivert, Keeper of the Light. *Sunday Island News.* January 20, 1935.

Boy Charmed by Lighthouse Travels 3,000 Miles. Unknown publication. Undated.

Brennan, Kevin. Personal Communication. 2003.

Brown, Inspector. Letter to the Light-House Board. June 5, 1884. National Archives Letter Book No. 588, page 646.

Brown, Inspector. Letter to the Light-House Board. July 9, 1884. National Archives Letter Book No. 617, page 46.

Brown, William. Letter to Thornton A. Jenkins and E. L. F. Hardcastle, Secretaries of the Light-House Board. November 22, 1853.

Bullington, Neal. Searching for Missing Lightkeepers. *The Fire Island Tide.* May 31, 1985.

Burning of the *S.S. Lexington* Off Eaton's Neck, 1840. Unknown publication. Undated.

Cagney, W. Oakley. "Execution Rock" Terrified Sailors. Unknown publication. July 25, 1971.

Cagney, W. Oakley. Lighthouse Guided Pilots of Long Island Sound. *Long Island Press.* April 18, 1971.

Cairns, Barbara. Personal Communication. 2003.

Captain Arthur Jensen Dies, Keeper of Eatons Neck Light Thirty Years; Rites on Friday. *Northport Observer.* September 1947.

Carpenter, Judy. Personal Communication. 1999.

Carr, Edward A. T. For 200 Years, Eaton's Neck Light Has Warned Away Unwary Vessels. *The Observer.* June 11, 1998.

Case, Inspector. Letter to the Light-House Board. February 27, 1857. National Archives Letter Book No. 50, page 355.

Chapel, William Oliver. Letter to Barbara Cairns. January 2, 1976.

Chapin, Vivian Jensen. Personal Communication. December 1, 2000.

Church of Jesus Christ of Latter-day Saints. 1880 Census. http://www.FamilySearch.org.

Cirillo, Paul F. Letter to Chief of the Disposal Branch. December 21, 1959.

Clifford, J. Candace and Clifford, Mary Louise. *Nineteenth Century Lights: Historic Images of American Lighthouses.* Alexandria (VA): Cypress Communications. 2000.

Clifford, Mary Louise and Clifford, J. Candace. *Women Who Kept the Lights: An Illustrated History of Female Lighthouse Keepers.* Alexandria (VA): Cypress Communications. Second Edition. 2000.

Coney Island Light Station. http://www.coneyislandlightstation.com.

Connecticut Gazette and Commercial Intelligencer. October 15, 1800. Reprinted in *Capsule Histories of Some Local Islands and Light Houses in the Eastern Part of L.I. Sound,* by Benjamin F Rathbun. Niantic (CT): Presley Printing. 9th printing. 1999.

Contract between Geroge W. Thompson and Jonathan Thompson, Collector of the Port and District of New York. September 13, 1824.

Corbin, Thomas W. *The Romance of Lighthouses and Lifeboats: An Interesting Account of the Life-Saving Apparatus and Appliances Used in Guarding Against the Dangers of the Sea.* Philadelphia (PA): J. B. Lippincott Company. 1926.

Corwin, Tho. *Letter from the Secretary of the Treasury transmitting the report of the general superintendent of the Light-house Establishment* (Document 14). Washington (DC): Government Printing Office. December 20, 1850.

Covert, James W. Letter to the Light-House Board. November 25, 1893. National Archives Letter Book No. 1027, page 658.

Daly, Don. Personal Communication. August 12, 2003.

Davis, Azariah. *Life at the Old Field Lighthouse, 1869–1874.* From the Diary of Azariah Davis.

Dean Kamen. *Current Biography.* November 2002. Volume 63, Number 11.

Deed from Lighthouse Service, Department of Commerce, to Alva E. Belmont. November 21, 1923.

Deed from the United States to the State of New York by the 68th Congress. June 26, 1924.

DePalma, Anthony. As a Guide for Ships, the Last of a Breed. *New York Times.* April 13, 1991.

Description and Plans of Lights for Lighthouses According to the Catadioptric System of Augustin Fresnel, and the Holophotal System and Other Improvements. Birmingham: Chance Brothers and Company. 1855.

Devil Blamed By Indians for Rocks in L.I. Sound. Unknown publication. January 26, 1923.

Diamond, Stuart. Flames Gut Old Landmark at Cedar Point. *Newsday.* June 7, 1974.

Dominy, Felix. Letter to Nathaniel Dominy. March 30, 1840.

Duane, J. C. Form 36: Description of Light-House Tower, Buildings and Premises: Race Rock. March 1880.

Duane, J. C. Letter to Liet. W. B. Franklin. April 8, 1857.

Duane, J. C. Letter to T N Jenkins. August 31, 1854.

Duane, J. C. Letter to the Light-house Board. April 4, 1857. National Archives Letter Book No. 51, page 54.

Duane, J. C. Letter to U.S. Navy Rear Admiral John Rodgers. March 17, 1881.

Dumas, Edward. Mystery of the Fire Island Light Ship No. 68. *The Fire Island Tide.* June 26, 1987.

Dutton, Engineer. Letter to the Light-house Board. July 24, 1855. National Archives Letter Book No. 29, page 605.

Ebbitts, Robert (obituary). *The Suffolk Times.* June 18, 1926.

Efforts to Save Old Lighthouse Are Followed Up. Unknown publication. August 1940.

Engineering Committee. Letter to the Light-House Board. January 5, 1894. National Archives Letter Book No. 1032, page 44.

Engineers Raze Shinnecock Lighthouse by Fire. *New York Herald Tribune.* December 23, 1948.

Erosion Project for Lighthouse Nears Completion. *New York Times.* March 8, 1998.

Erwin, W. S. Letter to Procurement Division, Public Works Branch. December 23, 1935.

Estler, Frank. How Fire Island's Burma Road Got Its Name. *The Long Island Light Keeper.* May/June 2003. Volume 3, Issue 3.

Events at Long Beach Bar Light. *Brooklyn Daily Times.* November 25, 1905.

Ferguson, Charles B. *Twenty-seven Views of Race Rock Lighthouse in the Four Seasons.* Shelter Island (NY): North Hill Press. 2000.

Field, Van R. *Wrecks and Rescues on Long Island: The Story of the U.S. Life Saving Service.* Center Moriches (NY): Van R. Field. 1997.

Fire Island's Famous Beacon. *The Long Island Forum.* November 1957. Volume XX, Number 11.

Flint, Willard. A History of U.S. Lightships. Http://www.uscg.mil/hq/g-cp/history/h_lightships.html.

For the Safety of Ships: A Lighthouse to be Built at Nortons Point. *Brooklyn Daily Eagle.* June 15, 1890.

Forward, W. *Letter from the Secretary of the Treasury transmitting a Report from I. W. P. Lewis, civil engineer, upon the condition of the light-houses, beacons, buoys, and navigation* (Document 183). Washington (DC): Government Printing Office. February 25, 1843.

Gardiner's Island Light. *Sag Harbor Express.* January 11, 1894.

Gardiner's Island Light. *The Watchman.* May 24, 1894.

Griffin, Isabelle McGlone. My Childhood at Lloyds Beach Lighthouse. *Huntington Preservation Society Newsletter.* Undated.

Griffing, Eugene S. Passing of a Lighthouse. *The Long Island Forum.* April 1956.

Haberstroh, Joe. Coast Guard Station to Stay Afloat: $10M Alloted for Repairs in Eaton's Neck. *Newsday.* February 26, 1999.

Haberstroh, Joe. Saving a Light That's Going Out: On Off-Limits Plum Island, Historic Beacon is Crumbling. *Newsday.* June 8, 1997.

Hamilton, Harlan. Latimer Reef Light (1884): Fisher's Island Sound, CT. *Long Island Boating World.* November/December 2000.

Hamilton, Harlan. *Lights and Legends: A Historical Guide to Lighthouses of Long Island Sound, Fishers Island Sound and Block Island Sound.* Stamford (CT): Wescott Cove Publishing Company. 1987.

Hamilton, Harlan. North Dumpling Light (1849): Fisher's Island Sound, NY. *Long Island Boating World.* October 2000.

Hamilton, Harlan. Race Rock Light (1878) off Fishers Island, NY. *Long Island Boating World.* September 2000.

Hamilton, Harlan. Stepping Stones Light (1877): Western Long Island Sound, NY. *Long Island Boating World.* March 1999.

Havemeyer, Harry W. *Along the Great South Bay: From Oakdale to Babylon, the Story of a Summer Spa, 1840–1940.* Mattituck (NY): Amereon House. 1996.

Haze Gray and Underway: Naval History and Photography. *Wilderness.* http://www.hazegray.org/danfs/steamers/wilderns.htm.

Heap, David Porter. Letter to the Light-House Board. July 22, 1892. National Archives Letter Book No. 959, page 78.

Heap, David Porter. Letter to the Light-House Board. December 29, 1893. National Archives Letter Book No. 1010, page 792.

Heap, David Porter. Letter to the Light-House Board. February 9, 1894. National Archives Letter Book No. 1011, page 160.

Heap, David Porter. Letter to the Light-House Board. March 12, 1894. National Archives Letter Book No. 1011, page 286.

Heap, David Porter. Letter to the Light-House Board. March 27, 1894. National Archives Letter Book No. 1011, page 354.

Heap, David Porter. Letter to the Light-House Board. June 28, 1897. National Archives Letter Book No. 1139, page 806.

Heap, David Porter. Letter to the Light-House Board. January 23, 1899. National Archives Letter Book No. 1252, page 134.

Hefner, Robert J. Montauk Point Lighthouse: A History of New York's First Seamark. *Long Island Historical Journal.* Volume 3, Number 2.

Hendrey, Elisa. Old Field Lighthouse. *The Landpaper.* September/October 1988.

Henry, Joseph. *A Summary of Researches in Sound: 1865-1877, from Smithsonian Report 1878.* Washington (DC): Government Printing Office. 1879.

Holland, Francis Ross Jr. *America's Lighthouses: An Illustrated History.* New York: Dover Publications. 1988.

Humeston, Rev. Dr. Edward J. Untitled article. *The Long Islander.* November 20, 1947.

Illustrated Coast Pilot with Sailing Directions. Boston (MA): N. L. Stebbins. 1896.

Invitation, Bid and Acceptance for Sale of Surplus Real Property Facilities. New York: General Services Administration. Disposal Number 2PS-184.

Instructions to Light-Keepers: A Photoreproduction of the 1902 Edition of Instructions to Light-Keepers and Masters of Light-House Vessels. Allen Park (MI): Great Lakes Lighthouse Keepers Association. 1989.

Kassner, Robert George. Noah Mason and Sands Point Lighthouse. *The Long Island Forum.* January 1982.

Keeler, Bob. Lighthouse Gets a Quick Fix-Up. *Newsday.* July 20, 1974.

Keepers of the Light. *The Fire Island Tide.* June 13, 1986.

Killed While Snipe Hunting. Unknown publication. July 1903.

Knowles, Howard N. *A Lighthouse of Stone: A History of the Eaton's Neck Lighthouse, Northport, New York* (reprint). Northport (NY): Northport Historical Society.

L'Hommedieu, Ezra. Letter. November 19, 1792.

Lighthouse Keeper Freed. *Babylon Leader.* May 13, 1921.

Long Beach Light Destroyed by Fire on July Fourth. Unknown publication. Undated.

Long Island News. *Sag Harbor Corrector.* June 16, 1860.

Mahler, Gottfried. Personal Communication. 2003.

Mahler, Marilyn. Personal Communication. 2003.

Marquis, Violet. Personal Communication. 2003.

Martin, Douglas. Step Right Up! See a Boardwalk! It's Coney Island! *New York Times.* February 16, 1986.

Mather, Andrew. Letter to George M. Bache. August 25, 1838.

McAdam, Roger Williams. *Salts of the Sound: An Informal History of Steamboat Days and the Famous Skippers who Sailed Long Island Sound.* New York: Stephen Daye Press. 1957.

Melville, David. *An Expose of Facts, Respectfully Submitted to the Government and Citizens of the United States, Relating to the Conduct of Winslow Lewis, of Boston, Superintendant for Lighting the United States' Light Houses.* Providence (RI): Miller & Hutchens. 1819.

Memorandum to the Regional Director. New York: General Services Administration, Real Property Disposal Division. December 9, 1955.

Menzel, Diane. Lighthouse: A Sands Point Legend. *Port Washington News.* July 25, 1991.

Meyn, Kenneth D. A Lighthouse with a Legend. *New York Times.* Undated.

Miller, Josiah P. Gardiner's Island Light Besieged by Wind and Wave (letter). *East Hampton Star.* April 29, 1893 (published May 5, 1893).

Miller, William. Letter to Secretary of Treasury, Oliver Wolcott, Jr. July 5, 1798.

Mintz, Phil. Fire Island's Beamin' Beacon. *Newsday.* May 26, 1986.

Moeller, Henry W. *Shattering an American Myth: Unfurling the History of the Stars and Stripes.* Mattituck (NY): Amereon House. 1995.

Montauk and Plover Shooting. *Sag Harbor Corrector.* 1868.

Montauk Point Bicentennial, 1796–1996. Montauk (NY): Montauk Historical Society. 1996.

Morris, Charles. Letter to Stephen Pleasanton. November 1, 1837.

Morris, Tom. Pup Overboard for 19 Hours Wins Fight with Inlet Tide. Unknown publication. Undated.

Morton, J. St. C. Letter to Capt. W. B. Franklin. April 9, 1858.

Morton, J. St. C. Letter to Capt. W. B. Franklin. April 12, 1858.

Morton, J. St. C. Letter to Capt. W. B. Franklin. April 19, 1858.

Morton, J. St. C. Letter to Capt. W. B. Franklin. May 27, 1858.

Morton, J. St. C. Letter to Capt. W. B. Franklin. July 12, 1858.

Morton, J. St. C. Letter to Capt. W. B. Franklin. November 4, 1858.

Moses, Robert. Remarks of Robert Moses at the Opening of Robert Moses State Park and the Fire Island Inlet Bridge. June 13, 1964.

Mrs. Pearl White (obituary). *The Suffolk Times.* May 17, 1929.

Muller, Robert G. Francis Hopkinson Smith: Engineer, Artist, Author. *The Long Island Light Keeper.* January/February 2003. Volume 3, Issue 1.

Munroe, Ralph Middleton and Gilpin, Vincent. *The Commodore's Story.* Miami (FL): Historical Association of Southern Florida. 1985.

Murphy, Jim. *Blizzard: The Storm that Changed America.* New York: Scholastic Incorporated. 2000.

Navy and Marine Living History Association, Inc. The Assault on Fort Fisher, January 15, 1865. http://www.navyandmarine.org/ondeck/1862fortfisher.htm.

Naylor, Natalie A. *Journeys on Old Long Island: Travelers' Accounts, Contemporary Descriptions, and Residents' Reminiscences: 1744–1893.* Interlaken (NY): Empire State Books. 2002.

Notice from Collector's Office. *Sag Harbor Corrector.* February 18, 1837.

Office of the Light-house Board. *Notice to Mariners.* August 6, 1891. Number 82 of 1891. Reprinted in *The Keepers Log.* Summer 2000. Volume XVI, Number 4.

Old Horton's Pt. Light Extinguished for First Time in 90 Years. *The Suffolk Times.* July 21, 1933.

Orient Pt. Lighthouse to be Razed. *The Suffolk Times.* 1970.

Pelletreau, William S. *A History of Long Island: From its Earliest Settlement to the Present Time.* Volume II. New York (NY): Lewis Publishing Company. 1903.

Penny, Anne P. Venerable Shinnecock Lighthouse. *The Long Island Forum.* February 1943.

Prime, Nathaniel S. *A History of Long Island: From its First Settlement by Europeans to the Year 1845.* New York: R. Carter. 1845.

Purchase of Winslow Lewis. Washington City: R. C. Weightman. 1812.

Rathbun, Benjamin F. *Capsule Histories of Some Local Islands and Light Houses in the Eastern Part of L. I. Sound.* Niantic (CT): Presley Printing. Ninth Printing. 1999.

Rattray, Jeanette Edwards. *Ship Ashore! A Record of Maritime Disasters off Montauk and Eastern Long Island, 1640–1955.* Southampton (NY): Yankee Peddler Book Company. 1955.

Rattray, Jeanette Edwards. *The Perils of the Port of New York: Maritime Disasters from Sandy Hook to Execution Rocks.* New York: Dodd, Mead and Company. 1973.

Records of the United States Coast Guard. Microfilm, Record Group 26, Red 3. Washington (DC): National Archives.

Records of the United States Coast Guard. Microfilm, Record Group 26, Red 5. Washington (DC): National Archives.

Records of the United States Coast Guard. Microfilm, Record Group 26, Red 6. Washington (DC): National Archives.

Registers of Lighthouse Keepers. Microfilm, Record Group 26, M1373, Rolls 1 and 2. Washington (DC): National Archives.

Reid, Giorgina. *How to Hold Up a Bank.* South Brunswick (NJ): A. S. Barnes. 1969.

Roach, Marion. The Last Crew at a "Utopia." *New York Times.* December 4, 1977.

Robert Hodges Ex-Light Keeper (obituary). *Newsday.* December 22, 1985.

Roy, Bernard J. Letter to Robert G. Muller. August 9, 2001.

Ruff, Joshua. Beacons For All: A History of Long Island Lighthouses. *Long Island Historical Journal.* Volume 11, Number 2.

Sands Point Light Burned 113 Years. *Port Washington News.* May 22, 1952.

Sangenito, Eve. Diary Offers Glimpse of Life in Old Field Lighthouse. *The Village Times.* August 15, 1996.

Saunders, John. They Came to Milton. Http://awt.ancestry.com/cgi-bin/igm.cgi?op=GET&db=:2675948&id=I549520464.

Schley, W. D. Letter to the Light-House Board. April 28, 1892. National Archives Letter Book No. 919, page 746.

Schley, W. D. Letter to the Light-House Board. March 2, 1894. National Archives Letter Book No. 992, page 392.

Secretary of the Treasury. Letter to the Light-House Board. September 28, 1886. National Archives Letter Book No. 709, page 1158.

Secretary of the Treasury. Letter to the Light-House Board. March 7, 1894. National Archives Letter Book No. 1024, page 424.

Sen, Indrani. Enduring Beacon of Old Ways, Hard Work. *Newsday.* October 21, 2002.

Shapiro, Pat. Personal Communication. January 24, 2003.

Shepard, Inspector. Letter to the Light-House Board. November 18, 1899. National Archives Letter Book No. 1227, page 754.

Shiel, John B. Dr. Samuel Latham Mitchell. *The Long Island Forum.* October 1977. Volume XL, Number 10.

Shubrick, W. B. *Report from the Secretary of the Treasury.* October 31, 1873.

Smith, Francis Hopkinson. *Caleb Smith, Master Diver.* Boston (MA): Houghton, Mifflin and Company. 1898.

Smith, Francis Hopkinson. *Captain Thomas A. Scott Master Diver.* Boston (MA): American Unitarian Association. 1908.

Snow, Edward Rowe. *Famous Lighthouses of America.* New York: Dodd, Mead and Company. 1955.

Snow, Edward Rowe. *Famous New England Lighthouses.* Boston (MA): Yankee Publishing Company. 1945.

Snow, Inspector. Letter to the Light-House Board. September 4, 1896. National Archives Letter Book No. 1120, page 490.

Snow, Inspector. Letter to the Light-House Board. November 24, 1897. National Archives Letter Book No. 1167, page 418.

Sprague, Thomas Clayton. Letter. January 19, 1918.

Sprague, Thomas Clayton. Letter. January 1, 1919.

Squires, Edward L. Hampton Bays Resident Tells of Building Shinnecock Light. Unknown publication. Undated.

Stanton, Jeffrey. Coney Island—Early Years. 1997. Http://naid.sppsr.Ucla.edu/coneyisland/articles/earlyhistory.htm.

Starace, Carl A. *Historic Long Island.* Unknown publication. Undated.

State of New York. An Act of the Legislature of New York Granting Jurisdiction to the United States Over Light House Sites. January 24, 1855.

State of New York. Title Papers of Cedar Island. August 20, 1838.

State of New York. Title Papers of Latimer's Reef. March 27, 1883.

Statement of Appropriations, &c. from March 4, 1789 to June 30, 1882. 1886.

Stevenson, D Alan. *The World's Lighthouses from Ancient Times to 1820.* Mineola (NY): Dover Publications. 2002.

Stonington News. *Westerly Sun.* December 22, 1898. Reprinted in *Capsule Histories of Some Local Islands and Light Houses in the Eastern Part of L.I. Sound,* by Benjamin F Rathbun. Niantic (CT): Presley Printing. Ninth Printing. 1999.

Strong, Inspector. Letter to the Light-House Board. September 19, 1871. National Archives Letter Book No. 300, page 378.

Strong, Inspector. Letter to the Light-House Board. March 10, 1873. National Archives Letter Book No. 321, page 158.

Superintendent of Lights. Letter to the Light-House Board. July 4, 1861. National Archives Letter Book No. 130, page 650.

Tag, Thomas A. *American Made Fresnel Lenses.* Dayton (OH): Thomas A. Tag. 1999.

Tag, Thomas A. *David Porter Heap: The Great Improver.* Dayton (OH): Thomas A. Tag. 1999.

Tag, Thomas A. *Early American Lighthouse Illumination.* Dayton (OH): Thomas A. Tag. 1998.

Tag, Thomas A. *The Doty Dilemma.* Dayton (OH): Thomas A. Tag. 1999.

The Opposing Forces at Fort Fisher. Battles and Leaders of the Civil War. Available at: eHistory.http://www.ehistory.com/Uscw/library/books/ battles/vol4/ 662.cfm.

Third District Inspector. Letter to Vice Admiral Stephen C. Bowan. December 8, 1883.

Third District Inspector. Letter to William F. Aichele. March 26, 1912.

Third District Inspector. Letter to William F. Aichele. April 8, 1912.

Third District Inspector. Letter to William F. Aichele. March 13, 1916.

Thompson, Benjamin F. *History of Long Island from its Discovery and Settlement to the Present Time*, Volume 1. New York: Robert H. Dodd. Third Edition. 1918.

Tillinghast, Albert J. Letter to the Light-house Board. April 10, 1862. National Archives Letter Book No. 127, page 380.

Tuliano, Tony. My Story: Life at the Plum Island Lighthouse in 1977. *The Long Island Light Keeper.* May/June 2003. Volume 3, Number 3.

Tuma, Debbie. Celebrating Two Hundred "Light" Years. *The Independent*. May 29, 1996.

Twomey, Douglas. Fire Island Map of 1798. *The Fire Island Tide*. August 7, 1992.

Untitled. *New York World*. March 11, 1894.

Untitled. *Sag Harbor Corrector*. August 28, 1826.

Untitled. *Sunday Island News*. January 20, 1935.

U.S. Coast Guard. *Light List, Atlantic and Gulf Coasts of the US*. Washington (DC): Government Printing Office. 1942.

U.S. Coast Guard. *Light List, Atlantic and Gulf Coasts of the US*. Washington (DC): Government Printing Office. 1946.

U.S. Coast Guard. *Light List, Atlantic and Gulf Coasts of the US*. Washington (DC): Government Printing Office. 1984.

U.S. Coast Guard. Press Release No. 178-73. December 21, 1973.

U.S. Coast Guard. Press Release to City Editor of *New London Day*. April 9, 1958.

U.S. Coast Guard. Vessel Designation: LV 12 (II). Http://www.uscg.mil/hq/g-cp/history/WEBLIGHTSHIPS/LV12_2.html.

U.S. Coast Guard. Vessel Designation: LV 17. Http://www.uscg.mil/hq/g-cp/history/WEBLIGHTSHIPS/LV17.html.

U.S. Coast Guard. Vessel Designation: LV 25. Http://www.uscg.mil/hq/g-cp/history/WEBLIGHTSHIPS/LV25.html.

U.S. Coast Guard. Vessel Designation: LV 58. Http://www.uscg.mil/hq/g-cp/history/WEBLIGHTSHIPS/LV58.html.

U.S. Coast Guard. Vessel Designation: LV 68. Http://www.uscg.mil/hq/g-cp/history/WEBLIGHTSHIPS/LV68.html.

U.S. Coast Guard. Vessel Designation: LV 114/WAL 536. Http://www.uscg.mil/hq/g-cp/history/WEBLIGHTSHIPS/LV114.html.

U.S. Department of Commerce. *Instructions to Light Keepers of the United States Lighthouse Service*. Washington (DC): Government Printing Office. 1911.

U.S. Department of Commerce. *Lighthouse Service Bulletin*. June 1916. Number 54.

U.S. Department of Commerce. *Lighthouse Service Bulletin*. May 1, 1918. Volume II, Number 5.

U.S. Department of Commerce. *Lighthouse Service Bulletin*. October 1, 1918. Volume II, Number 10.

U.S. Department of Commerce. *Lighthouse Service Bulletin*. December 1, 1921. Volume II, Number 48.

U.S. Department of Commerce. *Lighthouse Service Bulletin*. April 1, 1924. Volume III, Number 4.

U.S. Department of Commerce. *Lighthouse Service Bulletin*. April 1, 1926. Volume III, Number 28.

U.S. Department of Commerce. *Lighthouse Service Bulletin*. February 1, 1930. Volume IV, Number 2.

U.S. Department of Commerce. *Lighthouse Service Bulletin*. October 1, 1930. Volume IV, Number 10.

U.S. Department of Commerce. *Lighthouse Service Bulletin*. August 1, 1932. Volume IV, Number 32.

U.S. Department of Commerce. *Lighthouse Service Bulletin*. March 1, 1934. Volume IV, Number 51.

U.S. Department of Commerce. *Lighthouse Service Bulletin*. April 1, 1934. Volume IV, Number 52.

U.S. Department of Commerce. *Lighthouse Service Bulletin.* February 1936. Volume V, Number 2.

U.S. Department of Commerce. *Report of the Commissioner of Lighthouses.* Washington (DC): Government Printing Office. September 15, 1915.

U. S. Department of Commerce. *Report of the Commissioner of Lighthouses.* Washington (DC): Government Printing Office. September 15, 1917.

U. S. Department of Commerce. Revocable License for Use of Portion of Horton Point Light Station Reservation. October 24, 1933.

U. S. Department of Commerce. *Survey of Public Property.* November 22, 1935.

U.S. Department of Commerce. *US Coast Pilot 1904, Part IV.* Washington (DC): Government Printing Office. 1904.

U.S. Department of Commerce. *US Coast Pilot 1918.* Washington (DC): Government Printing Office. 1918.

U.S. Department of Commerce. *US Coast Pilot 1940, Section B.* Washington (DC): Government Printing Office. Fourth Edition. 1940.

U.S. Department of Commerce. *US Coast Pilot 1950.* Washington (DC): Government Printing Office. Fifth Edition. 1950.

U.S. Department of Commerce. *US Coast Pilot 1960.* Washington (DC): Government Printing Office. Sixth Edition. 1960.

U.S. Department of Commerce. *US Coast Pilot 1984.* Washington (DC): Government Printing Office. 1984.

U.S. Department of Commerce. *US Coast Pilot 1987.* Washington (DC): Government Printing Office. 1987.

U.S. Department of Commerce. *US Coast Pilot 2001, Volume 2.* Annapolis (MD): Lighthouse Press. 2001.

U.S. Department of Treasury. *Description of Light-house Tower, Buildings and Premises at Eaton's Neck.* March 1880.

U.S. Department of Treasury. *Report of the Lighthouse Board* (Document Number 23). January 15, 1853.

U.S. Department of Treasury. *Report of the Lighthouse Board* (Document Number 3). November 11, 1853.

U.S. Department of Treasury. *Report of the Lighthouse Board* (Document Number 37). October 31, 1854.

U.S. Department of Treasury. *Report of the Lighthouse Board* (Document Number 54). October 31, 1855.

U.S. Light-house Board. *Instructions to Light-keepers.* Washington (DC): Government Printing Office. July 1881.

U.S. Light-house Board. *List of Lights and Fog Signals of the Atlantic and Gulf Coasts of the United States* [corrected to March 1, 1907]. 1907.

U.S. Lighthouse Establishment. Form 31: Keepers' Receipt for Property on Taking Charge. October 1, 1903.

U.S. Lighthouse Service. Description of Lloyd's Harbor Light Station. December 29, 1912.

U.S. Sells Lighthouse to Lawyer for $2,002. Unknown publication. 1937.

Van Wyck, Frederick. *Recollections of an Old New Yorker.* New York: Liveright. 1932.

Voyce, Mary. History of Eaton's Neck Light. *The Long Island Forum.* June 1958. Volume XIX, Number 6.

Warranty Deed from John H and Mary Jane Foster to the United States of America. June 22, 1855.

Weeks, George Lewis Jr. *Some of the Town of Islip's Early History.* Bay Shore (NY): Consolidated Press. 1955.

Weiss, George. *The Lighthouse Service: Its History, Activities and Organization.* Baltimore (MD): Johns Hopkins University Press. 1926.

Weston, Martin. Lighthouse to Beam Again. *Newsday.* December 17, 1984.

Wetmore, Nelson. Personal Communication. September 7, 2003.

Wetmore, Nelson. Personal Communication. September 8, 2003.

Whitford, Ed. Personal Communication. 2003.

Wike, S. Letter to Treasury Department. February 15, 1896.

William Janse (obituary). *The Suffolk Times.* June 19, 1925.

Wood, Jean. Childhood Memories of the Fire Island Lighthouse. *The Fire Island Tide.* September 4, 1987.

Woodbury, Levi. *Letter from the Secretary of the Treasury Transmitting A Report of the Fifth Auditor, in Relation to the Execution of the Act of 7th July last, for Building Light-houses, Light-boats, &c* (Document Number 24). Washington (DC): Government Printing Office. December 13, 1838.

Wreckage. *Newsday.* May 17, 1954.

Yates, Inspector. Letter to William F. Aichele. May 11, 1914.

Glossary

Appropriation – An act of legislation authorizing the expenditure of a designated amount of public funds for a specific purpose.

Argand lamp – A lamp using a circular hollow wick and glass chimney. Patented in 1784 by Swiss chemist and inventor Aime Argand (1750-1803). Winslow Lewis' lamps were based on Argand's design.

Automated lighthouse – A lighthouse that has been modified with technological advances so that it no longer requires the services of a full-time keeper.

Bell tower – A tower on which a fog bell is hung. The elevation afforded by the tower allows the bell to be heard further.

Bivalve lens – A type of Fresnel lens that consisted of two bull's-eye style lenses, one mounted on each side of the lamp. Also known as a clamshell lens, because of its appearance, or a lightning lens, because of its powerful flash. Montauk Point's 1903 bivalve lens now resides in its museum.

Brig - A sailing ship with two masts, both of them square-rigged.

Buoy – A floating minor aid to navigation, moored to the seabed. Some have been designed with lights, sirens, gongs, or bells to make them easier to locate at night or in bad weather.

Butt – A large barrel, of approximately 126 gallons volume, used to hold oil.

Caisson base – A watertight foundation that extends beneath the water line.

Characteristic – The identifying features of a light, such as its color and flashing sequence.

Cistern – A tank for storing rainwater. These were often built into the cellars of keepers' quarters.

Clockworks – The mechanism used to operate machinery, such as a rotating lens or a fog bell. Early versions were wound by hand.

Daymark – The size, shape, and markings that identify a lighthouse in the daytime.

Diaphone – A fog signal that makes a two-tone sound, as in the well-known "BEEEE-OOOOH" sound.

Flotsam and Jetsam - Objects found floating or washed ashore.

Fresnel lens – A type of lens developed in the 1820s by French physicist Augustin Jean Fresnel. Its power and efficiency allowed for the use of one lamp in place of many, thereby decreasing the consumption of lamp oil. These lenses came into general use in the United States after 1852. Seven sizes, or "orders," were commonly used (First, Second, Third, Third-and-One-Half, Fourth, Fifth and Sixth). The only active Fresnel lens on Long Island is at Eaton's Neck. Others are on display at Fire Island, Montauk Point, Horton Point, and the East End Seaport Museum.

Illuminating apparatus – The means by which light is produced and sent out from a lighthouse. These could include oil lamps and reflectors; an oil lamp and Fresnel lens; a modern electric light; and others.

Incandescent Oil Vapor (IOV) lamp – A type of lamp that used pressurized and vaporized oil burned in a mantle. These powerful lamps were the last oil-fueled lighthouse lamps.

Lantern – The glass-enclosed part of the lighthouse, where the illuminating apparatus is mounted.

Lard oil – A form of animal-based oil used as a lamp fuel in the mid- to late 1800s. It was cheaper than whale oil, but produced acrid fumes and often congealed in cold weather.

Lewis, Winslow (1770–1850) – The man whose lamp and reflector designs were used in American lighthouses from the early to mid 1800s. The origins and construction of his lamps and reflectors were the subject of much criticism.

Light vessel – A ship with one or more masts, on top of which one or more lights is mounted. Also known as lightships, these vessels were anchored at offshore locations where a lighthouse was needed but could not be built. Light vessels generally also included a fog signal. There are no longer any lightships on active duty in the U.S.

Mineral Oil – Kerosene; A thin distilled oil used for American lighthouse illumination in the late 1800s and early 1900s.

Oil house – An auxiliary building used to store oil. These were built at American lighthouses with the introduction of mineral oil, which was much more volatile than previous lamp fuels. On Long Island, most oil houses were built between 1902 and 1904, and were made of brick.

Order – The size of a Fresnel lens. A First Order lens was the largest; a Sixth Order was the smallest.

Pleasanton, Stephen (1777–1855) –Superintendent of Lighthouse for the U.S. from 1820 to 1852, as Fifth Auditor of the Treasury. As a clerk in Washington, D.C. in 1814, Pleasanton saved the Declaration of Independence and other important early American documents by taking them away from the city before it was burned by the British.

Radiobeacon – An aid to navigation that consists of a radio transmitter sending out distinctive signals.

Range lights – A pair of separate lights used in conjunction with each other for navigation. Generally used to indicate a channel.

Reflector – A highly polished parabolic metal surface placed around a lamp to direct the lamp's rays in a particular direction. These were used in the U.S. in the early- to mid 1800s.

Riprap – Large, irregularly shaped rocks piled loosely to protect the foundation of a lighthouse.

Schooner - A sailing vessel with at least two masts, fore-and-aft rigged.

Screwpile – A type of lighthouse foundation that used multiple iron piles screwed into the seabed and braced together. These foundations were rare in northern waters because of their susceptibility to ice floes.

Shoal – A shallow area in a body of water.

Siren - A fog signal that used compressed air or steam through a rotating perforated disk to create a loud sound.

Skeleton tower – A tower made of exposed metal tubing.

Sloop – A single-masted, fore-and-aft rigged sailing vessel.

Soapstone – A soft rock, composed mostly of mineral talc.

Spider lamp – An early form of oil lamp that used multiple wicks from a single source of oil. In some designs, the wicks looked like the legs of spiders.

Trumpet – A fog signal consisting of a long metal tube, flared at the end, through which air is forced to create a loud sound.

Whale oil – The fuel used to power Long Island's lights until the mid 1800s. The rapid rise of its price led to its replacement with cheaper oils, mostly lard oil.

Whitewash - A mixture of lime and water, sometimes with additives, used to whiten lighthouse towers, walls, fences, or other structures.

Wick, concentric – A series of two to five hollow wicks, set one inside the other. This created a brighter flame.

Wick, hollow – A wick that formed a tube. Its invention improved the power from an oil lamp by allowing air to flow inside the flame, as well as outside of it.

Index

369

374

The Long Island Chapter of the United States Lighthouse Society

The U.S. Lighthouse Society's Long Island, New York chapter is an all-volunteer organization that was formed in the Summer of 2000. The Chapter's mission is *"To Preserve and Promote the Lighthouse Heritage of Long Island."* This mission is accomplished through an array of preservation and education activities.

The Chapter preserves Long Island's lighthouse heritage through research, building and maintaining archives, collecting and preserving artifacts, assisting other preservation groups, nominating local lighthouses for inclusion on the National Register of Historic Places, and raising funds for preservation projects. The Chapter also has a stewardship agreement with the Suffolk County Parks Department to preserve the Cedar Island Lighthouse. The Chapter and Parks Department have made great strides towards the site's restoration, with work beginning in 2003.

The Chapter educates the public about Long Island's lighthouse heritage through a bimonthly newsletter (*The Long Island Light Keeper*), a web site (www.LILighthouseSociety.org), lectures, appearances at fairs and festivals, and publications, such as this book. A four-day lighthouse history course, taught by this book's author, lighthouse keepers, and others, is open to the public. The course includes written materials, trips to lighthouses, and more.

Various tours, cruises, and the annual Suffolk County Lighthouse Day celebration help the Chapter raise funds and awareness, benefiting both the preservation and education aspects of its mission.

The Chapter works with individuals, businesses, other nonprofit groups, government agencies, and others to accomplish its mission. All of this work is accomplished by volunteers, and new volunteers are always welcomed.

Become a member and help the Long Island Chapter of the United States Lighthouse Society
Preserve and Promote the Lighthouse Heritage of Long Island

Membership dues cover membership in the U.S Lighthouse Society and the Long Island Chapter. Membership benefits include the U.S Lighthouse Society's quarterly magazine, *The Keeper's Log*, and quarterly bulletin, plus the Long Island Chapter's bimonthly newsletter, *The Long Island Light Keeper*. Members also get discounts at our chapter events (including the Gold Coast cruise, Beacons of the Night cruise, and the lighthouse history course) and the opportunity to help preserve and promote Long Island's lighthouse heritage.

Annual membership is from October 1 to September 30. Memberships are $35 for a individual ($30 for a senior over 65) or $50 for a family.

You may join, using the form on the following page, via our web site, www.LILighthouseSociety.org using PayPal, or by sending your a check with your name and mailing address (telephone number and email address are optional but helpful), to the address below.

Volunteers are always needed. If you have experience or special interests, please let us know. Some of the areas where you might help include:

- Events including planning, historic narration, welcoming and registration, merchandise sales and raffles.
- Fundraising including corporate relations, grant writing, raffle sales.
- Communications: newsletter writing, web site development, media relations, press releases.
- Office assistance: file maintenance, research, database creation and maintenance, phone/letter/e-mail responding
- Education: classroom lecturer, educational materials development
- Leadership positions including coordinators or assistants

Long Island Chapter, US Lighthouse Society
PO Box 744
Patchogue, NY 11772-0744
631-207-4331
email@LILighthouseSociety.org

Membership Application
Long Island Chapter of the
United States Lighthouse Society

Name_____

Street Address_____

City, State, Zip _____

Telephone (optional)_____

Email (optional, but helpful)_____

Membership Level (please check):
  ☐ Individual: $35   ☐ Family: $50   ☐ Senior: $30

If you are interested in volunteering, please check areas of experience and/or interest:

Events: ☐ Planning   ☐ Welcoming/Processing of Attendees
        ☐ Historic Narration   ☐ Merchandise/Raffle Sales

Fundraising: ☐ Corporate Relations   ☐ Grant Writing ☐ Raffle Sales

Communications: ☐ Newsletter Writing   ☐ Web Site
  ☐ Media Relations and Press Releases

Office: ☐ File Maintenance   ☐ Database Creation and Maintenance
        ☐ Phone/Letter/E-mail Responding   ☐ Research

Education: ☐Classroom Lecturer   ☐ Educational Materials Development

Other (Please specify): _____

Are you interested in a leadership position, such as a coordinator or assistant coordinator? ☐Yes ☐ No

Long Island Chapter, US Lighthouse Society
PO Box 744
Patchogue, NY 11772-0744
631-207-4331
email@LILighthouseSociety.org